Rough Justice

Robert Parker is ....
lives with his fam.... .... south London,
where the Richardsons were based. He has a science
degree and was for five years a reporter on *The
Times*. He also worked on the *Observer* for eighteen
months, writing about the Countryman inquiry
into London police corruption, before leaving to
complete this book.

Rough Justice

Robert Parker

Fontana Paperbacks

First published in Great Britain by
Fontana Paperbacks 1981

Copyright © Robert Parker 1981

Set in 10 on 11 point Plantin by
Fleetlines Ltd, Southend-on-Sea, Essex

Made and printed in Great Britain by
The Anchor Press, Tiptree, Essex

Contents

Acknowledgements

It is impossible in a book of this kind to acknowledge properly the extensive help I have been given. Many of those who came to talk freely to me do not want their names mentioned. But they know who they are and I thank them warmly for all the information they provided, and for the many fascinating hours I spent in their company. I would also like to thank various members and friends of the Richardson family, even though many of them will not like this book. In particular I owe a great deal to Roy Hall and Eva Brindle. I am additionally indebted to Gordon Winter, with whom I spent one of the most extraordinary weeks of my life. My former colleague Paul Lashmar also gave much valuable help and advice. Most important of all, I would like to thank Val Deacon who, for insufficient reward, and without the slightest murmur of complaint, tirelessly transcribed scores of tape-recorded interviews and typed the manuscript. This book would not have been possible without her unvarying support and encouragement.

For kind permission to quote extracts from articles, thanks are due to these newspapers: *Bedfordshire Times, Daily Express, Daily Mail, Daily Telegraph, Evening Standard, News of the World, Rand Daily Mail, Sunday People, Sunday Telegraph* and *The Times*. For permission to reproduce those photographs not owned by the Richardson family, I am grateful to Associated Newspapers Group Ltd (no. 7), Wendy Kochman (no. 13), S. & G. Press Agency Ltd (nos. 10 and 11), and Gordon Winter (no. 15).

Preface

The events described in this book took place fifteen years
ago and more. Today, virtually all the main characters have
settled down to basically decent and respectable lives.
Charlie himself is about to finish his swingeing prison
sentence and looking forward to the time when he can try
and start life anew. Eddie, having been released in 1976, has
already established a good business and has a family of
whom he is justifiably proud. Middle age and calmer times
have also overtaken most of the others portrayed here,
including Roy Hall, Tommy Clark and even Jack Duval.
For them, and most of the others, this story has become a
matter of faded memories — memories which they would be
happy to forget forever.

August 1981

Introduction: Flight of Fancy

At precisely 10.41pm on 23 May 1980, Charles William Richardson drew the curtains of his little room in Spring Hill Open Prison in Oxfordshire. The former London gang leader was agitated. His plan to escape and get his first taste of freedom in fourteen years was running twenty-five minutes behind schedule. He should have slipped out of his room at 10.15. But a group of fellow prisoners in the next hut had decided to chuck buckets of water over two mates. Unlike Richardson, they had nothing to lose: they were soon to be released. . . .

By the time the night watch in the relaxed country prison had doused down the commotion, Richardson was on the point of abandoning his escape attempt. But a signal from a friend came through indicating that the coast was all clear. He locked his door behind him and made his way almost recklessly to the sports ground, still lit up with powerful arc lights. He angrily muttered not the first curse of the evening. He went around the edge of the sports ground, over a wire fence and dropped into a field. It was pitch black. He felt an intense but short-lived burst of relief. But there was no time to savour that. He quickly looked for the light of the Fox pub, a mile away. In a letter and map previously smuggled out of Spring Hill he had arranged for an old friend to wait in the pub car park. The order was not to wait a second after 10.45pm.

Richardson, forty-six but still powerful and fit, set off across the rough field at full pace towards the solitary and distant light. He crashed blindly into a large bramble bush, not even feeling the grazes. He forced his way through an opening and charged across the next field. Twenty-five yards from the track that led to the Fox, he saw a car drive past, lighting up the lane. He knew it was his car. He crouched down behind the hedge in the hope that the car would come back, just for a final check. He knew his friend would be concerned. It was a forlorn hope, and he waited in vain. All was not lost, however. Richardson had arranged with his south London friend to come back the next night if the first attempt failed.

But what to do now? All kinds of thoughts flashed through his mind. He knew that he would not yet have been missed: anticipating his escape, Richardson had, two months before, initiated a pattern of behaviour that resulted, as planned, in the night watchmen stopping their checks on him every two to three hours. This had been simply achieved by his having furious arguments with them every time he was disturbed during the night. They had decided to leave 'old Charlie Boy' alone. After all, he had done fourteen, and would probably soon be going home. . . .

Having escaped, the last thing he wanted to do was to break back into prison. But he had no choice. Ironically, it was even harder getting back than escaping from it. All the lights had been turned off, and there was nothing to aim for through the black night. Eventually he found the sports ground and then the hedge that led to the prison and his hut.

The next night there were no hi-jinks in the neighbouring hut. One of Richardson's friends inside made sure of that. Richardson again packed his briefcase with his various papers and photographs and left a note for the prison chief, amending the one left the night before because he didn't want to get the date wrong. This time it was easier. He slipped along the same route – avoiding the bramble bush – arriving near the Fox in plenty of time. His friend was there sitting in his car in the pub car park. Richardson checked that the coast was clear, then strolled casually across to the car.

It was his first taste of freedom since 7am on 30 July 1966 – the day England won the World Cup. That day he had been in bed when a team of detectives had burst into his Camberwell house and carted him off to West End Central police station. But that was an age ago.

He changed into the suit, shirt and shoes that his friend had brought for him. Then he sat back into the seat as the car made towards London. He opened a can of beer and lit a cigar. As the car sped through the dark Oxfordshire countryside, he felt euphoric.

He and his pal could not stop laughing. Once in London, Richardson was dazed by the sight of the traffic and the people as they drove down the Earls Court Road. It had changed so much since he last saw it.

'Do you want to have a drive round Piccadilly?' his friend asked, rightly guessing that that would amaze him even more.

'Why not!' said Charlie, relishing the sense of freedom that making even such a simple decision gave him.

An hour later he arrived at a flat in Southwark Park Road in his native Camberwell in south London. A member of his family was there and a bottle of scotch and dry ginger was produced. Charlie was never a big drinker but he spent a convivial few hours talking excitedly. Plans were made to obtain an Irish passport and a driving licence, the kind of transaction which in his heyday had never been a problem. Only hours after his escape, he also talked about the matters that had preoccupied him most during fourteen miserable years in prison — his case and the circumstances of his conviction, the twenty-five-year sentence and the certain fortune that it prevented him from making.

He had been refused parole every year for the last seven years. Each time had made him more determined to try and show that he had been 'fitted up' — falsely imprisoned — for his notorious crimes. He thought about it so much, he actually came to believe it in the end. The last parole refusal had been the most bitter blow of all. He had been transferred to Spring Hill Open Prison fourteen months earlier from Maidstone where he had made great headway. He had got on well with the governor there, had obtained Open University qualifications, and had started and run an active prison newspaper. He was told, he says, that if he behaved himself in Spring Hill for twelve months he would be released on a conditional licence. He was even measured up for a discharge suit. When his parole application – the fourth in a row with the backing of the local prison authorities – was refused by the Home Office, Richardson felt flattened. He had already served more time than most murderers, and he had never been convicted of murder.

'When I was called up to the Governors and told that the Parole Board had once again refused me, I was absolutely sick,' he later wrote. 'Particularly knowing how upset my mother, my children and the rest of my family would be. On my last knock back at Maidstone Prison, my mother and daughters cried on the visit. My eldest daughter, who was breast feeding her baby, lost her milk over it.

'I realised that if I was not to become a robot and vegetable, and a liability on my family when I had completed my sentence, I needed a break from the deprivation of prison environment. I had miraculously survived prison so far without it destroying me – but I was at my limit, I never had the strength of mind to stand up to a further three years. It was escape or go under!

'In the prison, souls and minds are vulnerable things, and so easily destroyed, sensibilities become blunted, despair holds court and it is so easy to give up and become a vegetable. So many times have I seen it happen to others, that I fear it, and it has been a constant struggle, a psychological struggle, to survive prison.

'The British penal system, they tell us, has advanced a long way from the physical barbarity of hanging, drawing and quartering. But has it? – the mental suspension is still with us, the drawing of the emotions, the quartering of the personality. How have we advanced in this country? To survive a sentence of fourteen years, is possible physically; but to survive emotionally, is almost impossible. Some partially survive, few, very few, survive with their emotions intact and their sensibilities unblunted ... there comes a time in the course of a sentence when psychologically a man has had enough; when that time passes, the man begins to die in his soul, and what is a man without a soul? A zombie. I knew I was at that critical stage and I had to leave Spring Hill or go under.'

It was in such language that Richardson wrote a few days later to *The Times* and *Guardian* newspapers. The fact that they and the rest of Fleet Street gave such prominence to his escape and letter was itself an acknowledgement of the notoriety that Richardson and his gang achieved during their ten-week trial at the Old Bailey in 1967.

Even before the trial started, it had been universally dubbed 'the torture case', partly due to sensational articles in the *People* and *News of the World*. Their stories included allegations of frightened men all over London, of bloody gang warfare and horrendous beatings and tortures of victims. Most of the information for their stories came from men who were victims, and who were later to become prosecution witnesses. Extraordinary security procedures were devised to restrict the prisoners and to protect the members of the jury and the prosecution witnesses. Even special phones were installed on the judge's orders in the jurors' houses – in case the 999 system was too slow.

After sentencing Richardson to twenty-five years for a series of brutal beatings and tortures, Justice Lawton told him: 'I have come to the conclusion that no known penal system will cure you but time. The only thing that will cure you is the passing of the years.'

Eddie, Charlie's younger brother by two years, was sentenced to ten years. Three other members of the gang were sentenced to similar periods. All had denied in the strongest terms every charge against them.

It was as if every evil in society at that time had been cleaned up in one fell swoop. The Richardson gang seemed to have become synonymous with all the ills in the world.

At the time of Richardson's escape I had been writing for the *Observer* on the vexed question of corruption among London detectives. It was virtually impossible to print anything like the truth. Several senior provincial police officers had told me things which were so shocking that if the information had not come from them, I could not have believed it. When Richardson took his 'walk', one of my police friends wryly observed that 'there's a man who probably knows more about corruption than almost anybody else around', even though he had been away for fourteen years.

It was mainly as a result of this that a couple of weeks later I found myself on a plane to Alicante in Spain to meet Richardson. The trip had been organised by a colleague who had become acquainted with the Richardson family and who was trying to persuade Richardson, for £4000, to let a newspaper cover his surrender to the authorities.

Richardson, smaller than I expected, met us at the airport. He had with him his 'minder' (the equivalent of an underworld valet), a nice man called Dave who had a kind face and a big laugh. In a battered Fiat Ritmo, Richardson drove us to his hotel in Benidorm, an hour along the coast. He was a little uneasy: welcoming but cautious. He had no reason to trust journalists. Nothing had ever been printed about him that he liked.

He told us in the car that he had spent a week in hiding in London after arriving at the flat in Southwark Park Road. He had emerged with a beard and went to Waterloo Station to get some passport photographs. 'The station really blew my mind – I thought everybody was looking at me. It took me months to get this feeling removed from my mind, before I could relax.' Richardson had planned to catch a plane to France from Manchester, but the day before, he received a message that one of his daughters was in a Jersey hospital, having miscarried. He went to see her, and there also bumped into a life-long friend and his family. They virtually took over the bar of the hotel, and Richardson had his first real home-coming.

When his daughter was better, Richardson caught the boat to St Malo, then the train to Paris. 'Paris is a magic city for me, music in the air, so many happy memories.' He spent a few weeks here, visiting Maxims among other restaurants, and doing all the usual tourist things. From there he had flown to Nice, staying in the Hotel Negressco where in 1965 he spent five days with a South African girlfriend who had played a major part in his life. After five days' freedom in Nice, he had gone down to Majorca in Spain, where another old girlfriend came to see him. One day, he bought the *Sunday Times* and saw his photograph on the front page. He bought all four of the shop's copies but, realising there would be other newsagents on the island, decided to go on to mainland Spain.

It was listening to this account of his escape that we arrived in Benidorm, bulging with people on a baking August evening.

As soon as we sat down on the balcony of his hotel, he started to talk again. He had so much to say, he couldn't get it out fast enough. He was virtually impossible to interrupt or to lead in any particular direction. He soon revealed his persuasive, forceful personality: he was among the most single-minded men I have ever met. There was one message which, above all, he wanted to get over: fourteen years ago he had been 'fitted up'; all the evidence against him was either outright lies or grossly exaggerated. He claimed that many of the police who convicted him were bent, that the prosecution witnesses were let off their own offences on the condition that they made up evidence against him. The judge, he said, had been grossly unfair; the defence barristers had been too frightened to do their job properly; and the whole of his case involved a myth carefully constructed by the police and the press.

Richardson spoke with unvarying force and conviction. I felt that some of what he was saying must contain elements of truth — especially in view of some of the recent information I had acquired about police corruption (the disgraceful nature of some of the London police in the 1960s is now generally acknowledged).

On that first night in Benidorm, the idea of a book about his case was born. I told Charlie, in the firmest terms I could, that there was no point in his lying to me. If he was not going to tell me the truth, then I might as well catch the next plane home. After all this time, lying would only be counter-productive: the truth would sooner or later become apparent. It was the truth, and the truth alone, that I intended to write, I told him. Thus began a long series of tape-recorded interviews which formed the starting-point of this book.

Richardson started admitting deeds which he had adamantly denied in court. He *had* attacked this man – *but* it was just a question of a 'couple of right-handers'. There was no torture or anything like that. And anyway, the man was an out-and-out villain, and in the underworld code deserved everything he got – because he had 'taken a right liberty'. Such and such a place *had* been robbed – *but* only to save friends who had been put in a difficult position because of other people's actions. The notion that he was running a massive network of fraud was complete nonsense, he said. It was the prosecution witnesses who had been doing that; they simply blamed it all on the Richardsons.

Back in London I started trying to check up on Richardson's claims. The family gave me access to a huge mass of papers, court documents and letters. I contacted, with the help of members and friends of the Richardson family, some of the prosecution witnesses. In a somewhat cautious and even reluctant manner, a couple of these witnesses started admitting that they had lied in the court case. They said they had had to because of police pressure. They had been threatened with long sentences themselves if they did not agree to say such and such a thing. Their reluctance and hesitation I put down to an understandable worry about possible perjury proceedings. . . .

For a few weeks I thought Richardson might indeed have been fitted up – despite what everybody who knew about the case outside the family and friends was telling me. The position is now very different. From all my research I have no doubt that the Richardsons did commit the majority of the crimes for which they were convicted. Several other aspects of Charlie's extraordinary life have also now come to light.

It was not long after my research had begun that I realised many of the people I was seeing had obviously already been talked to by the Richardsons. So I resolved that in future I would contact everybody independently. And it was in this way that, towards the end of 1980, I met one of the more important characters in this story. At first he told me what he somehow knew the Richardsons would have expected him to tell, even though he had not seen them for years. But then at our third interview, when he had grown to trust me, he said: 'Look, if you really want to know the truth, let me tell you.' And off he went, after assurances that I would keep his secret.

Since then, other people have talked frankly to me, sometimes only after detailed assurances had been given. The majority of them had no motive for talking harshly against the Richardsons. On the contrary, most of them felt, like many other people, that Charlie had spent more than enough time in prison – even though they did mind the things he had got up to in the 1950s and 1960s.

As the true picture of Charlie and his past began to emerge, so too did the problem of what I should do about it. I didn't know whether to abandon the book, or to have it out with the Richardsons. I decided to carry on regardless and fulfil my promise to Charlie to write the truth. In discovering the huge gulf between the truth and Charlie's perception of it, I came face to face with the key to Charlie's personality. . . . There must also, inevitably, be an irreconcilable divide between the way I, with my middle-class background and coming from the outside twenty years later, assess events, and the way the Richardsons evaluate their own lives.

At the time of this dilemma, I had become friendly with Charlie's brother Eddie, who was released from prison in 1976 and now runs a successful scrap business in south London. I had also forged links with Roy Hall and other former members of the gang and their associates. I have enjoyed the many evenings I spent in their company. And I do not blame them for trying to hoodwink me in order to help a man who in their view should have been released from prison a long time ago.

I also during the course of my research got to know and respect Charlie's children, in particular Carole, his eldest daughter, and Charlie-Boy, his eldest son. Having already had many bad experiences with reporters, they were naturally suspicious of me at first. It is ironical that just as I began gaining their trust, I also started to discover some of the more shocking aspects of the Richardson story. I regret any pain or embarrassment that the book may cause them.

I feel similarly towards other relatives of men who are involved in the story, in particular Eva Brindle, the sister of 'Mad' Frank Fraser — one of the most important members of the gang and the only member besides Richardson still detained at Her Majesty's pleasure. No person could have tried harder than Eva to help her brother and clear his name.

The Richardson story is an extraordinary one. Out of a violent and criminal childhood, Charlie rose to a position where, at the age of thirty-two, he was turning down million-pound deals with some of the world's biggest companies. He ran an empire of fraud and other crime. Yet through massive mining rights which he acquired in South Africa, he came within striking distance of becoming a City tycoon. He flirted with the Conservative Party and yet behind the scenes organised the sadistic and brutal torture sessions for which he is best known. And, most surprisingly of all, Charlie ended up working for the forerunner of BOSS, the dreaded Bureau of State Security in South Africa. He arranged a series of break-ins at highly sensitive organisations in London, and fell in love with a beautiful South African spy. He was a party to helping South Africa get quantities of arms, and there is even the suggestion that he organised the bugging of Harold Wilson's private telephone at Number 10, Downing Street.

1. Blueprint

Life was tough from the start for Charlie, the eldest son of Charles and Eileen Richardson. His first memory dates from when he was about five. His mother had given him a large toy speedboat which he loved and carried everywhere, but which always seemed to get him into trouble for one reason or another. He and his younger brother, Eddie, were visiting Westcliff-on-Sea with their parents. Charlie's dad had cursed him for the bother that the boat had caused in the car going down there. As they were about to leave for home, his dad suggested that Charlie push the boat out to sea: it would sail home by itself, he said, and then they could collect it from Tower Bridge when they got back to London. That way the boat could cause no trouble on the journey home. Suspicious of this theory though he was, little Charlie trusted his father enough to launch the battered old toy. When the tide kept pushing the boat back on the sand, Charlie's father came up with an even more original idea: why not bury the boat in the sand? The tide would uncover it, and then the boat would sail back.

Charlie learnt his first bitter lesson of life that day.

Charles Richardson senior had been quite a catch for Eileen. Tall, gaunt, and with a wicked twinkle in his eye, he took a pride in his appearance, was full of sparkle and life, and had been a great success with the girls. He was mainly brought up by his grandparents, who had a successful horse business in Mitcham. He became a prize fighter and still boasts today that he was thirty-two before he took up smoking and drinking. Neither, he says, did he get into trouble with 'the law' until he was nineteen. He joined the Norfolk Regiment and served in India, doing quite well until he knocked out his sergeant during an argument and had to desert. Cunningly, he escaped from India by signing on to a ship. He was to remain in the Merchant Navy for the next twenty-five years, winning eight ribbons for his bravery with the Atlantic Convoys during the Second World War. By the time he left the sea in 1956 to join Charlie's thriving scrap business, he had become Second Engineer. He had also, he brags, been in every whorehouse in the world.

Charlie's mother was born in Camberwell. Her own mother had left Dublin at the age of six weeks and had come to live in Camberwell where eventually she ran the newsagent's shop in Wyndham Road. She did not go back to Ireland till she was eighty. Eileen was close to her mother and often helped her out in the shop which today she owns and runs herself.

Charlie was born on 18 January 1934, in a room above a grocer's shop in Hampton Road, Twickenham. The family moved shortly afterwards to a flat in Wren Road, Camberwell (just near the police station), where, two years later, on 29 February 1936, Eddie Richardson arrived in the world. Another brother, Alan, was to be born four years later, and a few years after this came a sister. Charlie and Eddie were looked after by their grandparents for much of the time: their mother worked just round the corner as a 'nippy' at the Lyons Teashop; their father was often absent and sometimes in trouble.

Charlie remembers going with his mother to visit his father in prison. His mother knocked on what seemed huge green gates. They were taken by a man in uniform to see his father who was behind a glass cubicle. The young Charlie was at a loss to understand why his mother and father were not allowed to sit together. All he had gathered was that people couldn't get in or out of the building without a key. On their next visit, Charlie produced a key which he had taken from their flat. 'I've got a key, you can come home now,' he said. He remembers the tears in his father's eyes.

When he was five, Charlie started at Comber Grove Infants' School. Eddie, aged three, used to follow him to school where he was allowed to stay with Charlie during lessons. 'When Charlie started school he wanted Eddie to go with him,' his mother recalls. 'He kept moaning, so Charlie took him in and they liked him and they kept him in and it was fine. They were always together. They used to do all the cupboards out and that. They were very well liked and trustworthy.' Every afternoon, the children lay down and rested for half an hour. All except for Charlie. He would go round each child making sure they were tucked up properly under their blankets. He was most protective of the others, which the teacher thought quite touching.

The boys saw their father less and less. His homecomings were very special occasions. He would produce exotic gifts: monkeys, plants, marvellous specimens of onions and bananas. All were put on display at the grandparents' shop for the customers to admire. When the fire bombs started dropping on London at the start of the war, the Richardsons moved to the flat above the shop, which was quite a part of the local scene. Charlie found the air raids an exciting business. The entire family slept under a large kitchen table. When the bombing stopped, Charlie would rush out with his grandfather to help put out the fires, much to his mother's alarm.

As the air raids became worse, Eileen decided that the boys should be evacuated. She told them it would be marvellous living in the country on a farm with all the cows and ponies. The boys, along with many others, gathered in a group outside Camberwell Town Hall, all carrying their bags and labels. The sense of excitement and adventure was to be short-lived, although one consolation for Charlie and Eddie was that, unlike some of the other brothers and sisters who were dropped off on the way down to the West Country, they were not split up.

The regime in the large old house in Dorset was very strict. The couple running it didn't take easily to unruly cockney lads, and used the cane at the slightest excuse, according to Charlie. The boys were not well fed and soon developed scabies and other dietary problems; food parcels which Eileen Richardson and the other mothers sent down were never received.

After their first night, a group of the lads set off to explore beyond the large lawn at the back of the house. Out of nowhere came a dozen white geese, heads cocked and hissing, and wings outstretched. The scruffy little town boys fled, quite terrified. But they soon learned that if they themselves chased the geese, it was the birds that were scared.

Charlie made friends with a boy who slept next to him in the packed little dormitory. Through the holes in the lathe and plaster wall, they could see where a bird was nesting. Charlie suggested that if they put a chicken's egg in the nest it would hatch out. They stole an egg from the roosts outside – something they were expressly forbidden to do – and planted it in the nest in the dormitory wall. That evening when they returned from the village school, their secret had been discovered. All the boys were sent to bed early. Charlie's friend, whose bed was closest to the hole in the wall, was summoned into the bathroom. The others listened to his screaming as he was beaten and then made to get into the bath. His head was repeatedly ducked under the water. The boys in the dormitory all hid under their bed clothes.

Next day, Charlie decided to do something that he would do many times again in his life – escape. He, Eddie and another boy set off determined to reach London. After what felt like three miles but was probably less, they were stopped by the local bobbie. They were collected from the local station, taken back to the house and beaten. Every night for the next week they had to go to bed without tea as soon as they came home.

Twice each Sunday the boys were sent to church, which they quite enjoyed. The vicar was a kindly man who took an interest in the evacuees. The great attraction of the service was the local robin which invariably flew in just as the vicar climbed into the pulpit. The vicar would invent all kinds of stories about the robin, much to the delight of the boys. One day Charlie was floating a matchbox in the water trough in the churchyard when the robin appeared. Charlie felt a compulsion to pick up a stone and throw it at the friendly little bird. He never intended that the stone should kill it. He was terrified and sorry, and buried the bird in the graveyard, marking the spot with a little wooden cross.

Exploring the local countryside one day, the boys came across a barn full of onions. Charlie knew how scarce they were and decided that he would take some for his mother who was coming down that weekend. He thought it would be a bit like his father bringing home presents on his leaves. But he was caught by the farmer and returned to the home, then questioned by the farmer and three men 'as if I had done a bank robbery'.

When his mother came down and found out about her boys' not getting the food parcels, she agreed to their pleas to take them home. Charlie, however, had to stay to go into hospital because he had developed scabies. But little Eddie returned that day to Camberwell. A few days later Charlie's father came home on leave. When he heard what had happened he went down to Dorset, barged into the hospital where his son was lying, picked him up across his shoulder and walked out.

By the time Charlie got back to London the war was just about over. Entire families who had been the shop's customers had been wiped out. Half Wyndham Road had been flattened. He restarted at Comber Grove school where he seemed to do nothing but fight. Charlie and his friends organised themselves into a gang and fought other local gangs. As Charlie now says, it was as if they were mimicking the grown-ups and playing at war. There were some very tough encounters between the gangs of ten-year-old boys.

There was one gang in particular with which Charlie's mob had some bloody battles. All its members lived in flats across the main road running between Vauxhall and Camberwell Green. Pitched battles took place, the boys armed with milk bottles, stones, belts and fists. When the local policeman arrived, the boys would turn on him, hoping that he would chase them through all the wrecked and damaged buildings they had come to know so well. They would taunt the copper with names, and songs like: 'No wonder, no wonder the coppers get so fat; they go down the alleys and eat all the fat; and what they can't eat they put in their hats

25

and can't say cock-a-doodle-doo.'

Charlie and his mates, like many other similar gangs in the area, were virtually running wild on the bomb-damaged streets of post-war London. There was minimum control from his parents: his mother was now manageress of the Lyons Teashop at Camberwell Green; when his father did come home on leave, it was only to sleep. He was out womanising and drinking for most of his waking hours.

The boys looked constantly for excitement. They started to wear jerseys with belts tied tightly round their waists. Not only did this look good, but belts could be whipped off in an instant when they were raided by another gang. Bombed-out buildings around their homes became gang headquarters. There was one favourite building, on the Walworth Road. It had been the Haycock Press building, and the boys called it the Thousand Doors. They all took a pride in knowing every route through its maze of corridors. From the windows which overlooked a bus stop, Charlie and his friends would drop stones on the queueing people in the hope that they would be chased through the corridors – which they often were. But they were never caught. They thought it was a great laugh.

When he was eleven, Charlie started at the Avenue Secondary Modern School. He was not much impressed by the headmaster's attempts to discipline and control him and some of the other street urchins. Charlie was already becoming impossible to handle. He simply played truant for weeks on end, getting people to write letters to the headmaster saying that he was ill. His mother didn't know half of what was going on: at home he was always quiet and polite.

He and his mates, sometimes with Eddie tagging along, engaged in some quite daring raids. The road between Camberwell and Vauxhall was one of the main routes into Covent Garden market for the fruit and vegetable lorries coming from Kent. It is also one of the longest stretches of straight road in London. Charlie would wait at the lights just above Camberwell Green and jump up on the waiting lorry. He would help himself to its contents as the vehicle made its way into London. Then he would jump off at another set of lights, and get a lift back using the same technique with lorries going the other way. (If lorries were scarce, he and his mates would climb on the back of a tram, usually managing to stay on despite the conductor's attempts to dislodge them.) They became quite good at spotting the lorries in the distance. Charlie discovered that if they jumped up and down on the traffic-light rubbers at the junction with Wyndham Road, they could actually turn the lights to red and thus not miss a possible raid. One of Charlie's mates at this time, Brian Mottram, remembered it well: 'It marked Charlie out, even at this age, as an organiser. We all looked up to him.'

It was as a result of raiding lorries that Charlie had the first of his innumerable encounters with the police. As usual, Charlie and two friends were playing truant from school: raiding lorries was much more exciting than boring old lessons. They had just jumped off a lorry at the Elephant having stolen some books, and were going through the normal procedure of dashing round the corner and immediately looking completely nonchalant. This time Charlie ran straight into the arms of 'the law'. His two mates scarpered. The policeman put his hand down the front of Charlie's jersey and drew out a book. Charlie refused to say where he had got it from. As he was marched to the police station, he made a run for it, only to be brought down with a rugby tackle. The policeman didn't see the funny side of the matter. He lifted Charlie by his shirt collar and virtually carried him choking to the police station. He got cuffed several times round his head and finally gave his name and address. But he wouldn't say where the book came from. The police used a technique with which Charlie was to become very familiar. Another cop came into the room: 'Now look, lad, what's all this about? Don't worry about him ... he gets a bit like that sometimes ... here have a cup of tea ... don't you want to go home? Think of all the worry you are causing your poor old mum. . . .'

His mother was indeed terribly upset. She couldn't believe what the police told her. Charlie, who loved his mother very much, felt sorry. But he didn't feel that way at Tower

27

Bridge Juvenile Court a few days later. The room where he waited for his case to be heard was full of other boys who talked to each other about their exploits. Charlie was impressed. Some of the boys were The Elite: they had already been to approved schools. Real tough guys, Charlie thought to himself. He had never felt more important in his life. It was some sort of confirmation to him of what he was beginning to feel, that he was a rebel, different from the other boys he knew. Not for him the dull routine of school and all that. He wanted to go his own way, do the things he pleased.

Charlie was put on probation for two years. His school reports, which were appalling, had been read out at court. He was told by the magistrate that if he didn't keep out of trouble and start going to school, he would be sent away to an approved school.

It wasn't so much because of this that Charlie really did make an effort to improve, it was more the effect that the incident had had on his mother. She already knew enough about prisons through her husband. Now it seemed to her that Charlie might be going the same way. She couldn't understand it. Charlie seemed such a quiet nice boy, always helping with little chores, never stealing anything from home. . . . A neighbour in Cameron House, where the Richardsons were now living in Wyndham Road, remembers the incident with the stolen book: 'He was always a quiet polite boy. He seemed very nice to me at the time, not nearly as bad as some of the other lads around. He would always say, "Good morning, Mr Baron, sir".' Charlie, it seems, was already developing the ability to mislead completely even those close to him about what he was really doing, or what was going on in his mind.

Charlie was nagged so much by his mother and grandmother that he did seriously try and keep out of trouble. His grandfather was now working for Smiths, putting gold leaf lettering and inscriptions on books, so Charlie helped out in the shop at weekends and did try, but it was no good. The friends his mother had banned him from seeing were there at school which was as dull and pointless as ever. His mother, when not working, was tied up with Alan, who was now five years old. His grandmother looked after Eddie and Charlie, preparing their meals in between serving customers in the shop.

Soon people started coming into the shop and reporting on Charlie's activities: 'Mrs Allen,' they would say to Charlie's grandmother, 'did you know that your Charlie has been doing so and so?' They were normally silly things that he had done for a dare, such as hanging on to the rails at the top of the block of flats in which he lived and skirting the outside of the building. His grandmother, having heard what he was up to, would come rushing up the stairs and through the door that led to the roof. She would gently persuade him to come back on the roof, clip him round the ear and, when his mother came home, report what had happened. More nagging followed.

He started doing the paper round for the shop, delivering papers morning and evening, and once on Sunday. He got two shillings a week, plus what he could make on tips. At first, he hated the Sunday morning delivery because that was when he had to collect the money, and customers would dispute the amount they owed. He quickly got fed up with this, and started keeping the most detailed records of who had had what and when they had last paid and exactly how much. Charlie was not to be fooled. Everyone soon came to realise that they couldn't fiddle anything from Charlie or his gran's shop. It was hard work for Charlie, for not very much money, but he didn't seem to mind. He was part of the shop, and had some fun with his gran, who somehow managed to put up with the trouble that Charlie and Eddie were so often in. She had nicknames for all the customers and used to tease them behind their backs to Charlie. He adopted this practice of using nicknames from then on.

He supplemented his two bob a week by scavenging the bombed buildings for metal and large areas of lead which he and two friends would sell. They couldn't deal with scrap merchants because they were too young, but Charlie knew a man who took it off them for half the sum they could have earned from the scrapyards. It was easy money with which to finance his now frequent expeditions to amusement arcades and snooker halls. And he began to see the potential for making money in scrap. He thought at the time that he would not mind having his own scrapyard one day – there seemed to be so much scope for fiddling and thieving.

Any thoughts that Charlie had had about keeping out of trouble were now being abandoned. And Eddie, too, who had been much under the influence of Charlie, now had his first rub up against the police. He had been out collecting conkers in Champion Hill, one of the better parts of Camberwell, with a friend who is today a millionaire and chairman of a public company. On the front seat of one of a row of parked cars, Eddie saw a torch. The car door was not locked and the torch joined their bag of conkers. But someone had seen them and by the time they reached the end of the road the police had arrived. The boys were cocky and cheeky and were slapped around the face a few times, then taken to Camberwell police station where, Eddie says, they were beaten. In the end they both admitted stealing the torch. It didn't help them when Eddie's father, who was home on leave, turned up at the station and exploded with rage when he heard that the police had beaten his boy.

Eddie was to have countless incidents like this. And, simultaneously, Charlie was getting deeper and deeper into trouble.

Charlie loved the life of the amusement arcade but he was thoroughly fascinated by the funfairs that often took place locally. This wasn't just because he enjoyed the atmosphere and fun, but also because he saw so many opportunities for thieving. One of the treats of the funfairs was the plentiful supply of toffee apples – illegal at the time because sweets and sugar were then still rationed – which were sold by people called spivs. Charlie noticed that every time a policeman was sighted by the spivs or their look-outs, they would quickly hide themselves and their toffee apples. One night Charlie decided he would take a whole case of toffee apples. He hid under the caravan immediately behind a spiv who was selling his wares. It was obvious that he would hide his case under the caravan if a copper was sighted. Charlie had arranged with his mates to shout a warning to the spiv. The apples went under the caravan and Charlie went off with the lot. They had a feast that night, and pulled the trick on several more occasions. The best time was when a pony and cart drew up alongside the fair bearing eight cases. The man took a case inside to his partner; Charlie and his friends drove off with the rest.

Charlie gave his group other treats as well: a free night at the cinema was one of the favourites. He would carefully undo the emergency exit from outside, using a piece of wire, and he and Eddie and his friends would slip in the back of the cinema. Sometimes they got caught on the way in and were tossed out. But if they reached their seats without being apprehended, they were normally all right: should anybody have the nerve to ask to see their tickets, Charlie would stand up and shout as loud as he could. The rest of the audience would complain angrily and the poor attendant would leave Charlie and his friends alone for fear of causing any more disturbance.

Charlie and Eddie had become very good fighters. Eddie, in particular, seemed to have no fear; they could both take on bigger boys easily. Charlie's money derived from thieving, coupled with his hardness and toughness as a fighter, established him clearly at the top of his particular pecking order. Even if he showed occasional signs of fear, he had the others to back him up. Those who went with him could expect all sorts of excitement, plenty of treats and, above all, the security of knowing that if there was a fight Charlie would be on your side. By the age of fourteen Charlie, it seems, understood perfectly the significance and role of violence in his world: it was the only way to dominate and control.

In an attempt to get Charlie off the streets, and to channel some of his aggression and energy, his uncle started taking him for boxing lessons at the local Lynn Boxing Club. He had several amateur fights and did pretty well, even boxing for his school in the National Schoolboy Championships. Eddie, whose lifelong passion for boxing dates from this time, used to go with Charlie. 'I remember the first fight he had,' says Eddie. 'He was boxing a guy who was about a foot bigger than him and a stone heavier. Charlie knocked him out in two punches, spark out.' Charlie was later to attract the attention of several good coaches, such as Teddy Butler, who were keen to turn Charlie into a professional. But he didn't bother; he had more pressing things on his mind.

Charlie thought he was Jack the Lad. He says himself that he had an over-inflated ego. He started mixing with older boys and showing an interest in girls. He was very proud of some new teddy boy clothes which he was able to buy. Sporting a drape coat down to his knees and a greased-back Boston haircut, he went dancing in West End dance palaces, rollerskating in the various London rinks, anywhere, in fact, where he might meet girls. But girls thought him rather strange; some even said they found him creepy. It was Eddie whom the girls were later to find more attractive. One of the gang who went with Charlie and the others on these outings remembers his lack of success:

'He is not a bloody good-looking fellow, is he? We were all quite big people for our age and we looked older than we were. But Charlie looked younger and I remember he always looked a little bit scruffy because he used to wear his dad's shirts tucked in at the back, and the suits always used to be that little bit too long for him. We used to spend twenty quid for a suit and look the business, but Charlie, I don't know where he used to get his suits from, but he never looked just right. He was always a little bit shy with the girls; he didn't have the gift of the gab. He used to go to a little ballroom place, up Brixton Road, just past St Mark's Church, where there used to be a dance studio and he went there to learn to dance. He just couldn't dance. He had two left feet.'

But Charlie didn't let this awkwardness cramp his style. On one of his increasingly rare visits to school, he took one of the girls behind a building and tried to grope her. He was caught by the teacher who took him upstairs for a caning – six strokes on one hand, six on the other and six on the backside. He took the strokes on the hand. But then he turned on the teacher with fury. He was smarting more from loss of dignity than with the pain. 'I ain't taking any more of that,' he shouted, grabbing the cane and laying into the shocked teacher with it. He ran off leaving the man lying on the floor.

Around this time, the school leaving age was put up to fifteen. That didn't please Charlie at all – which was a great pity, because when Charlie did go to school, he showed clearly that he had above-average intelligence. He was much more interested in the excitement outside the classroom. Some of Charlie's friends were now going into thieving in a big way, instead of just for fun. Charlie was deciding that this was where his own future lay. His horizons were defined by big-time villainy, not academic achievement. And soon he was to be in trouble again.

He had just finished stripping all the lead from the roof of the old post office at Camberwell Green, and had stored it carefully. On his way to borrow a horse and cart from the man who was going to buy the lead, he bumped into a friend of his, two years his senior, who was also a lead thief. He told Charlie that he knew a man who would pay a better price, and who had a van as well. They decided to join forces. An hour later they and the new man were back at the post office loading up the van. There was a screech of brakes, the police jumped out of their car. Charlie disappeared up to the roof – from which he managed to escape.

When Charlie got home later that night, his mother was waiting for him. The police had been round. Charlie denied any knowledge of the lead. His mother took him to the police station where he was shown a statement written by his newly found partner, naming Charlie. Still he denied it point blank. He was charged and appeared at Lambeth Juvenile Court. Again he denied it.

Charlie was furious that his friend had 'put him in it'. He already had an understanding of the Underworld Code. You never, ever, report anything to the police, and if you get caught you never inform on anybody else. Charlie experienced for the first time the phenomenon of people 'grassing' – criminals informing the police in the hope of getting more lenient treatment themselves – a device which Charlie was later to exploit for his own benefit.

In court Charlie listened amazed as the police spoke highly of the friend, saying that he had been led on. A Catholic priest was also produced to say what a nice good young man was Charlie's friend. He got a conditional discharge. Charlie, on the other hand, was ordered to be detained in a remand home for two weeks while reports were prepared on him. The police had had enough of young Charlie. They already knew him for what he was, and they were going to get him this time. It was a sharp experience for Charlie who had already begun to consider himself more or less invincible.

He was taken to the home, Stamford House in Shepherds Bush, in a coach that had bars across the windows. Charlie didn't like the home. He was made to wear short trousers, couldn't smoke, had to make and remake his bed until it was immaculate, and was continually shouted at by the masters who were quite big enough to look after themselves. When his broken-hearted mother came to see him, Charlie promised her he would never get into trouble again.

The reports that were produced two weeks later could have been worse. He was lectured by the magistrate and ordered to report once a week to the probation officer. But this seemed to do more harm than good. His probation officer was one of several based in rooms above a bank in Clapham North. Every Tuesday night Charlie met a new class of embryonic criminal. These boys, many of them older and more experienced than he, exchanged notes about their various enterprises and planned new ones. When Charlie visited his probation officer, he rattled off all the right answers. Yes, he wasn't staying out too late, he was going to school and he was keeping out of trouble. Charlie and the boys felt contempt for the officers who were so easy to mislead and hoodwink. He and his new-found friends didn't merely talk about stealing; they went out and committed a whole series of burglaries, smash-and-grab raids and car thefts. Their meeting place became a cafe up at Kennington Oval, which was run by an uncle of Charlie.

Charlie's poor mother was going spare, suspecting the worst. She went on and on at him. Charlie, with what appeared to be consummate ease, invented all sorts of excuses and stories, which his mother seemed ready to accept. She couldn't understand why he always seemed to have so much money. He explained it away by saying he had helped out his uncle at the cafe.

At fourteen Charlie had learned how to drive a car. When he and his gang stole a 'motor' of their choice, they would career it round south London, picking up girls and taking them for drives. The burglaries became a little more sophisticated. Charlie and friends made skeleton keys with which they opened many a lock. They would go out every night breaking into warehouses, shops and factories, taking what they could carry and selling it to the father of one of the gang. He didn't pay them much for the goods, but it was the excitement as much as the money they were after.

Inevitably, two of Charlie's friends were stopped by the police one night in a car they had stolen. It was lucky for Charlie that he wasn't with them. They were sent to approved school for three years; but two weeks after the case they escaped. The father who had been buying the stolen goods found them a room over a shop in Stockwell. They called on Charlie and proudly told him what had happened. Charlie was very impressed. His mates could now come and go as they pleased; could even have girls to stay with them in their secret den; could go out on their burglaries and come back to celebrate without worrying about parents. He always had to be home by 10pm, and then he would be nagged by his increasingly concerned mother.

The life of his friends made Charlie hate school even more. Luckily, the school was trying out a new system of education in which the boys could choose the subjects they wanted to study. Because no one master knew where any particular boy was, Charlie could go missing all day without his absence being noticed. To give the impression of attendance, he would persuade various friends to do his work for him, by treating them with the spoils of the thieving he had done instead of geography or maths. At night, disobeying the orders to be in by 10pm, Charlie would go out into the West End to spend his ill-gotten gains. He rarely bothered with buses or even taxis to get himself back. He would simply steal a car and leave it near his home. If you were out for the night with Charlie, there never seemed to be any problem about transport. But still the girls he drove home didn't seem to want to do much more than kiss him goodnight.

Charlie so envied the life of his older friends in their secret hideout that he secretly wished he himself could be sent to an approved school so that he could escape and join up with them. One morning, his wish was almost granted. He and a friend were on their way to the bustling East Street market – known locally as East Lane – when Charlie decided that he would steal a car to impress the girls. These days he always carried a bunch of car keys and skeleton keys: getting into a car was a doddle for him. Near the market they saw a parked car full of parcels. Two birds with one stone, thought Charlie. Just as he was about to get in, a policeman spotted him. Charlie and friend set off into the market which, as always, was completely packed out. The copper was easily lost and Charlie and his friend went to a cafe.

Half an hour later, the police, including a plain clothes detective, descended on the cafe. Charlie and his friend were arrested. Both denied any intention of stealing the car, despite the fact that Charlie's keys had been found on him. So they got a good hiding. The boys' parents were sent for. His friend's father went berserk when he saw that his son had been beaten. By the time the police had calmed him down, Charlie had noticed that they were on first-name terms.

When the boys appeared before the court six days later, the detective said that Charlie was the one who had got into the car, and that his friend was about thirty yards away. It sounded just like the deal that had been done over the stolen lead from Camberwell Green post office. Charlie was determined never to get caught in the same way again.

Charlie, as before, pleaded not guilty. The magistrate, as

36

a matter of routine, asked him if he wanted to ask any questions. It was unheard of for a boy of fourteen with Charlie's background to take up the offer. But Charlie wasn't like most of the other boys. He asked the plain clothes detective, who had appeared only at the cafe, where the uniformed officer had been when, as he claimed, he had seen the attempt to steal the car. He managed to get the detective to admit that he hadn't actually seen them attempting to break into the vehicle. Charlie told the court what he had told his distressed mother: he and his friend had only been looking into the car because it was just like his grandfather's. When the uniformed officer had shouted at them, they just ran away. If they had been guilty, they wouldn't have gone to the cafe, would they?

The case was dismissed. His friend's father was amazed: Charlie, on his own, had got them both off. Charlie thought he was the cat's whiskers.

His villainy carried on unabated. He sold *Sporting Reviews* with his uncle on Sundays at East Lane, then would go with him into Petticoat Lane to sell their remaining copies. As they made their way down the market, they would deftly help themselves to prawns, shoes and whatever else they could lay their hands on. Charlie thought it was marvellous. He admired his uncle so much: he was a real 'wide boy', dressed very smartly, knew all the villains, and was always having a laugh.

Charlie was still seeing his two friends in the Stockwell den. They had stolen a car and had driven to the skating rink at Brixton. There Charlie met a girl and offered to take her home to Lewisham. They had just dropped her off and were coming back through New Cross when a police car pulled up alongside, its bells clattering. Stunned for a second, Charlie put his foot down hard. He went screeching off towards the Old Kent Road, skidding and swerving, mounting pavements, charging down side-streets and jumping red lights. Charlie weaved the car in and out of trams and other cars while passers-by looked on astonished. The chase continued right up the Old Kent Road – about three miles long – and back again, the police car trying unsuccessfully to ram Charlie off the road. It ended when Charlie, coming back into New Cross, took a corner too fast. He swerved off the road and crashed into a wall.

Both boys, although dazed by the crash, took off on foot. Charlie was brought down a couple of side-streets away by one of the extra police who had been called in. He fought like hell but the copper just pinned him to the ground until help arrived. It was all the burly sergeant could do to hang on to him.

The boys were taken to Deptford police station. When the policemen who had chased them arrived, white and shaken, they gave Charlie and his friend a good hiding. Yet again, Charlie's poor old mum had to come down and bail him out. As usual, Charlie denied it all to her as he had done to the police.

Three days later, Charlie appeared in the increasingly familiar Lambeth Juvenile Court. The four policemen involved in the chase asked Charlie before the case started if he was going to admit the charge.

'What else?' he replied. With that, three of the police left the court, thinking it was going to be a straightforward prosecution.

But Charlie Boy, as he was now being called by all his friends, pleaded not guilty. The sole policeman left to give evidence described the car chase and the capture on foot a couple of streets away from where the car crashed. Then Charlie got in the box. He described how he met a girl at the Brixton skating rink and brought her back home on the bus. He gave the number of the bus, the cost of the ticket (which he guessed), and the address of the girl, Rita. 'I was just walking back from her house when a policeman jumped on me,' he told the magistrate with a mixture of indignation and surprise. 'I kept telling them at the police station that I wasn't nothing to do with it but they wouldn't believe me.'

Charlie Boy was acquiring the knack of dealing with the police and the courts. He was developing a nice little line in alibis, a skill assisted in its development by the excuses he was constantly having to give his mother.

The three magistrates seemed to think that Charlie might

have been wrongly arrested. They remanded him on bail for a further week, to give him time to produce the girl as a witness. He did not want to do this, not only because she knew nothing of the car chase in a stolen car, but also because Charlie had told her he was older than he was. Instead, he persuaded three friends to say that he had been at the skating rink with them and had left with the girl to take her home on the bus.

Their performance in court a week later was a fine one. Charlie told the magistrates that he could not find the girl – as indeed the police had been unable to do. He said he must have got the wrong street, or the wrong number; he had only met her just that one time. The two men magistrates appeared to believe all this. But the woman magistrate was not certain. She asked the police to make greater efforts to find the girl.

A week later, Charlie, hiding his face in his hands with shame, heard the girl give evidence. His sentence was three years at an approved school.

The only aspect that worried Charlie about the sentence was the despair of his mother. Already he was scheming and planning, though. He would escape from approved school and join his friends who were still on the run, successfully leading a life of increasingly serious crime five months after their own escape.

Charlie didn't even wait until he got to the school to escape. While walking to the van that was to take him to the school, Charlie bolted. He charged past three policemen, straight across the main Brixton Road near the town hall – causing a couple of cars to swerve violently – and rushed into Woolworths, followed by a policeman blowing his whistle. The rugby tackle did the trick again, scattering merchandise as well as shoppers. It didn't bother Charlie. He would simply escape from the school.

A day later he was being addressed by the headmaster of the Ardale Approved School in Essex along with eight other new boys. He couldn't believe his luck: the school was easy to escape from. But there was no point, the headmaster told them. 'You'll only be brought back and punished further.'

'Like hell,' thought Charlie.

The boys were given overalls for the weekdays and a pair of grey flannels and blazer for weekends. There were four houses each with about fifty boys. Charlie was put in a dormitory with boys mostly from London, aged between fourteen and eighteen. Charlie thought he'd sit tight for a few days and see how the ground lay. That night – his first – his bed collapsed as he was getting into it. The other boys had fixed it in the way traditional for all newcomers. All the other boys burst out laughing. Charlie didn't seem to see the funny side of things: he had been used to dishing out such treatment, not receiving it. He swore violently. Then the boys told him that the next morning he would have to go and see the housemaster and be measured up for a saddle.

'A saddle?' said Charlie.

'Yes, for when we go riding with the Hunt, you know,' said the leader of the boys, putting on a poor imitation of a posh voice.

Many boys before Charlie had been fooled, and actually gone to see the housemaster next morning. Not Charlie.

'Yeah, pull the other one, will you,' he muttered, without the flicker of a smile on his face.

The lights were put out in the dormitory. Charlie lay on his back, thinking that he wasn't exactly pleased by his reception. Suddenly he was smashed in the face by an avalanche of pillows. He flew out of bed with fists flying, soon scattering all the boys apart from the one who seemed to have most to say, the dormitory bully. Although younger than the bully, Charlie set about the boy. Just as Charlie was beginning to get the upper hand, the housemaster arrived and broke up the brawl. Charlie was in trouble already – he hadn't been there ten hours. He had also established himself in that space of time as the dominant boy in the dormitory – even though he was one of the younger.

Charlie and the former bully soon became friends. Charlie told him that he was going to escape and tried to persuade his new friend to come with him. He refused. He was just about coming to the end of his sentence and the school had fixed him up in the Merchant Navy which he was keen to join. He wouldn't go with Charlie, but he would give him whatever help he could. Unlike Charlie, and many of his other young contemporaries, he had seen the light and wanted to halt the life of crime he had been drifting into. In Charlie's case, the die was already cast. It was as if at sixteen there was nothing else he could be other than the man he eventually became.

But his friend told him the best way to go. One morning in the early hours, Charlie put on the flannels and blazer and woke his friend. They tied their sheets together so that Charlie could lower himself out of the window. They wished each other the best of luck and Charlie scurried off into the night while the friend pulled the sheets in through the window.

Charlie walked through fields to the road that led to Upminster. Every time he heard a car or saw its distant headlamps he hid at the side of the road. He found the tube station, and waited until it got light and the first train was due to set off. Having no money on him, he sneaked over the barrier at the side of the station and climbed on to the tube, which ran all the way to Stockwell, only a few yards from where his two friends were shacked up. He sat back in the seat, asked somebody for a light for the fag-end he had picked up outside the station, took a drag and thought about how they would all be talking about him back at the school when his escape was discovered. It made him feel good.

He knew Stockwell station well and used the emergency stairs to get out without showing his ticket. He walked around the corner to his friends' place, put his hand through the letter box, pulled out the string attached to the key and let himself in. His friends were still asleep. They were as pleased to see him as he had been to see them when they had escaped.

More than at any other stage of his life, Charlie Boy now felt he had arrived. He had served a good apprenticeship. What lay before him was a life of crime, with him as a tough guy, but also the guy with the brains and the cunning.

He told his friends about the escape, and how he nearly

41

got out of the charge in court. He appeared rather more matter-of-fact than he really was. They decided to go round to his mother's house when she had gone out to work so that he could get his prized teddy boy suit and drape coats. First of all they went round to have breakfast at Charlie's uncle's cafe. The uncle told Charlie to keep away from the cafe and any other known haunts of his. The police would soon be round.

That night they stole a car. Charlie drove. He loved the feeling of being behind the wheel. He was a good driver and cars fascinated him; it was so exciting to drive fast. They drove down to a camera shop in Croydon and smashed the window, clearing as much out as possible. They took the loot back to the flat and then dumped the car. Next day they sold the cameras through outlets which had been established in the previous months.

In the next few weeks they made hundreds of pounds like this. But it was not always as easy as that first camera raid. One night Charlie was driving his friends across London Bridge towards Fenchurch Street when a policeman stood out to stop his car. Charlie slowed to a crawl, but then put his foot hard down. He hit the policeman who went spinning up in the air. Suddenly the car jolted to a halt. The bridge was being repaired and the car had dropped into a hole. Charlie managed to drive the car out. They dumped the car in the Borough and returned to the hideout. Next day, they bought the papers. There was no report of any policeman being injured by a hit-and-run car.

Within a week, the three of them were inspecting a jeweller's in Kensington. They had parked their stolen car in a nearby street and were trying to pinpoint the best place to force the window. 'Right, you're nicked!' was all they heard before being arrested as suspected persons by a plain clothes detective. The police had seen them get out of the car, which they knew to be stolen, and followed them to the jeweller's. It was the usual routine back at the police station. All three denied everything. The police gave them tea and cigarettes; when that failed they hit them and threatened them with dozens of other crimes, some of which they had actually committed.

Charlie found himself back at Ardale, where his reception from the headmaster was very different from the first genial meeting. He decided to flog Charlie in the gym in front of the whole school. Charlie Boy didn't relish this idea at all. He was taken to the dormitory to change into his pyjamas and told to report when he was ready. The boy who had no fear in fights when he was dealing out the punishment felt unusually frightened.

He walked down the stairs and out of the building in broad daylight. He ran across several fields and hid in a clump of thick bushes, remaining there until it got dark. The search parties of boys led by masters missed him so Charlie then made his way towards Upminster station, where again he climbed across the barrier and took the tube to Stockwell. His uncle gave him a meal at his cafe and told Charlie that his father was home on leave. 'Perhaps you ought to go away to sea with him. It would be better than the life you are living now,' he told Charlie.

Charlie met his father at 6pm that day, which was Christmas Eve. He agreed that he should go away to sea. But that night, the police arrived at his home and dragged Charlie out of bed. There was a terrible commotion and the neighbours thought it awful that Charlie should be treated in such a way the night before Christmas. He was taken back to the Ardale school, where he was unable to settle down. He was moved to another school in Lincolnshire. This time he seemed to get on better with the headmaster, who took an interest in him. He finished off his sentence without much further ado.

2. Iron in the Soul

When Charlie eventually was released, on a bright spring morning, from approved school in Lincolnshire, he was sixteen. It seemed as if his period away had hardly changed him at all, despite the efforts of the last headmaster. By the time he came out, he was a perfectly formed embryo gangster. He was tough and would use violence when necessary; he had learnt about thieving and fiddling; he knew where to get rid of stolen goods; he understood the importance of alibis; and was already practised in dealing with the courts. He had seen several examples of police corruption at work, although at this stage had not himself paid the police any money. He was also getting to know pretty well who was who in the south London underworld. Some of his friends were later to become the Great Train Robbers. He had no intention of leaving his south London sub-culture or of changing his spots. Already intimate with the workings of the scrap metal business as a result of his post-war pilfering, he thought he would try and set up his own scrapyard.

But his mother was pressing him to settle down and get a steady job. The only real regret that Charlie ever seemed to have about his behaviour was the distress it caused his mother. And when she told Charlie that she was kicking his father out, her arguments won the day. Richardson senior had, on his recent home leaves, been spending most of his time with another local woman. Eileen Richardson had been patient but the new relationship didn't peter out as previous ones had. She felt he was a no-good waster anyway and decided that she had had enough. Charlie found himself increasingly in the position of the man of the house. His grandfather was getting on. His mother was very tied up with her job, the shop and the younger children.

While Charlie had been away Eddie had not been too bad. There had been some trouble, but nothing quite like Charlie had had. Eddie didn't care much for the academic side of school, but he excelled at sport. He was captain of the school cricket and football teams, and was doing very well at boxing. But being naturally strong, and because of his closeness to Charlie during his early years, he had learnt to fight. His experiences at school were no different from Charlie's: fighting was virtually the school's unofficial sport. Eddie seemed to fear no one, and nobody seemed able to knock him down. He was just about the toughest boy at school. Alan, now ten, showed signs of being a gentler boy than the other two, although his mother saw aspects of Charlie in him. Charlie had always been the get-up-and-go type; Eddie was always more placid, tending to be led by Charlie.

Charlie's first attempts at employment were short-lived and disastrous. He just could not work for anybody else. He had grown accustomed to doing exactly what he wanted. And he found totally unacceptable the discipline of *having* to get up to be at work at a certain time. It wasn't that he was lazy – he could be extremely hard-working when he put his mind to it, as when he had done the paper round two years before – but he couldn't tolerate anybody telling him what to do. He simply walked out of a couple of jobs after only a few days.

Between them, Charlie and his mother hit on an excellent idea. Charlie could sell the ice-cream that she made. As local ice-cream went, Mrs Richardson's was known to be among the best. Charlie's selling would increase the amount she could produce and, most important of all, would keep Charlie off the streets and out of trouble. It was an ideal solution. Charlie could work on his own, when he liked and how he liked. He was the first to realise that the harder he worked, the more he earned, and the closer came the possibility of his own scrapyard.

Throughout the hot months of that 1950 summer, business boomed. Charlie, complete with ice-cream bike and boundless energy, worked all the local parks and recreation centres. He found Clapham Common a particularly good place and soon learnt the best times and the best locations. He added toffee apples and other goods to his display for people to buy. All the money he made after paying his mother, he saved. He boosted his earnings by again selling the *Sporting Review*, and by occasional totting for local scrap merchants. His natural understanding of buying and selling was being developed.

It was a good few months for Charlie's mother. The family seemed to be going on very nicely. Charlie was occupied and happy; Eddie was more or less keeping out of trouble, thanks to his growing interest and involvement in amateur boxing. But Eileen was worried about the approach of winter when the ice-cream selling would come to an end. Charlie wasn't the slightest bit concerned, though. He had lots of ideas: he would get hold of a pony and cart and start totting for scrap with his mate Len. He had really taken to the way he had been able to work on his own, and the potential for making money on scrap, as he well knew, was much greater than selling ice-cream. He couldn't understand how some of the other boys he had known seemed content to work long hours cooped up inside factories for only a few pounds a week.

That winter Charlie worked hard at his totting. Camberwell was traditionally a scrap area, and the damage to buildings from the war still provided a good supply of material. Inevitably, quite a lot of the scrap he collected was stolen. When he bought material, he drove a hard bargain, always happy to con a mug who had no idea of his old metal's value. He got to know some of the scrap dealers, and started doing little deals with them. He worked hard long hours, keeping a close check on all the money that came in and was paid out. He even took up boxing again, this time being encouraged to turn professional. He was not only strong and tough, he was a clever boxer. He seemed able to find his opponents' weak spots very quickly, and to be able to predict their next move. To get on in the south London boxing clubs of this time, aspiring fighters needed more than just guts, or 'bottle' as it is called. They needed, like Charlie, to have a few brains as well.

A business acumen was evolving. Had it not combined over the next sixteen years with Charlie's already well-developed criminal tendencies, he would be a rich man, probably a millionaire, today. Everything was run very tightly, and the increasing amounts of money that Charlie made were saved. By the turn of the year he had enough money to buy a second-hand lorry – which he nicknamed the Flying Bedstead – and the £5 driving licence to go with it. He was legal at last. He broke off with his mate Len, who had worked with him throughout the winter, and joined forces with his Uncle Jim. As well as collecting scrap metal, Charlie and Jim started touring farms in the Home Counties collecting old sacks, which were in short supply at the time. Even this limited form of travel seemed to broaden Charlie's mind. He met farmers and all kinds of people who lived in a different world from the one he knew. He was particularly fascinated by the business techniques of some of the bigger sack and waste-paper merchants to whom he sold his goods. He started picking their brains, asking them about procedures. Soon he bought a large old furniture van in which he and Uncle Jim would go away for three or four days at a time, to all parts of England, loading up their van with sacks.

At the end of each day, Charlie would do his sums. He would work out exactly how much had been spent – ten bob for petrol, two bob for lunch, so much for cigarettes, so much for the purchase of goods. Everything was accounted for to the nearest farthing. The total was then deducted from what they had sold the goods for, and split evenly, after enough money had been put aside for the next day's purchases.

Much of his work was strictly legal. Only occasionally would he knowingly buy stolen material, at a much reduced price, and when the opportunity arose he would steal material himself in much the same way as many a totter does today.

Charlie became better acquainted with some of his

47

regular customers and buyers. There was one in particular, a slightly rakish upper-class man who ran a waste-paper business in south London. The man rather took to Charlie. 'He was a survivor, a bit of a toughie, and he always wanted to ask things,' he recalled. 'He worked very hard and seemed determined to get on.'

Another person also remembers Charlie during this period: 'He was always trying to suck your brains out. He wanted to know everything, what was the price of this, and what was the market for that. He seemed a nice kind of lad to me, always wanting to chat, wanting to know what you thought about such and such.'

Charlie started to feel his lack of the education which he had so determinedly rejected. He was needing now to write letters to potential customers. He realised that getting on with people could help business deals. He felt lacking in many areas of knowledge mastered by some of the people he was meeting. So he started reading books, all kinds of books. He read about Churchill and Napoleon, about other parts of the world. He bought encyclopedias, general knowledge books and teach yourself books. Every time he passed a book shop, he would dive into it, always coming out with a handful of books. There was still the brawling and crime, but increasingly Charlie spent nights at home with his mother, reading and scheming. A new world was beginning to open up for him, a world of which he had not been even dimly aware during his years in the gutters of Camberwell.

His lifestyle was beginning to be in marked contrast with that of Eddie who, now fifteen, had left school and taken up a course as a trainee draughtsman. Woodwork and technical drawing had been Eddie's only good subjects at school. So draughtsmanship seemed like a good idea at the time. He had no inclination to move in the direction of Charlie. Rather, he was beginning to assert independence from the brother who had been so dominant. While Charlie spent the evenings reading, Eddie was developing into a socialiser, 'one of the lads', doing far better with the girls than Charlie ever had. Sometimes there were some heated arguments and Charlie would lash out at his younger brother.

Charlie had been working with Uncle Jim for about a year when he pulled off his first really big deal. During their travels round the country, Charlie came across a couple of aeroplanes at an airport for sale as scrap. With them were a couple of hangars full of spares. The price was a good one, as Charlie knew, but he couldn't meet it. So he advertised in a newspaper for a businessman prepared to put up the money. As Charlie now explains the resulting partnership: 'There was all kinds of trouble with it. He kind of lost his money really.' Charlie and Uncle Jim set to work cutting up the planes and clearing out the spares. They worked hard for a month and made a lot of money. In fact, they made so much money that Charlie and his uncle started to argue about who was getting what. There were also rows about the kind of work they were doing. Neither was exactly a patient man and the quarrels grew so bad that the two men fell out. Charlie didn't worry too much. He was making so much out of the aircraft deal that it didn't matter about his uncle. But it mattered to the businessman who, when he realized that Charlie had no intention of paying him back the money, let alone his 50 per cent of the profits, went berserk.

When two men from the Fraud Squad turned up at Charlie's home, it was his first visit from the police for quite some time. It frightened the life out of him. They weren't like the police he had encountered in his previous villainy. They wore bowler hats, carried briefcases, and told him he was in trouble. They would be coming back again. There was a senior officer and a man called 'Bert'.

Charlie shot round to his uncle, thinking that he would know how to deal with the problem. But Uncle Jim was still angry with Charlie. 'Tell them to stuff themselves,' was all the advice that Charlie got.

Next day the police came back with even more paperwork. His mother was there this time, worried that Charlie was back to his old ways.

'Look,' said Charlie, 'I can't really say anything until I have seen a solicitor.'

The senior officer dipped into his case and brought out an even fatter file. 'It doesn't look at all good, son,' he said, flicking through the file, '. . . not at all good.'

Both detectives then got up to go. Charlie's mother tried to hang on to the file and asked what it said. Meanwhile Charlie managed to get a quiet word the other side of the room with 'Bert'. He pulled out a bundle of money, £150 in old notes.

'I hope you don't mind, I would like you to buy your wife something.'

The atmosphere changed in an instant. The file went back into the briefcase and the two policemen sat down with Charlie while his mother made a cup of tea.

'Ah, don't worry,' said the senior officer, referring to the partner whom Charlie had conned out of his money. 'He's a bastard anyway. The trouble he's caused us, you wouldn't believe it.'

The only thing Charlie couldn't believe was how friendly his two former inquisitors had now become. They had a long chat about various things. Clearly there was plenty of scope for further meetings when there was a spot of bother.

'I'll tell you what,' said Charlie. 'Would you frighten the shit out of my Uncle Jim? He was a right sod over this, and I really got the needle with him.'

Charlie watched from a concealed position just outside his uncle's house as the two cops banged on his door. They went inside and really put the pressure on. His uncle was beginning to crack up when Charlie knocked on the door. They couldn't keep up the pretence any more and all burst out laughing. Uncle Jim couldn't understand what on earth was going on. He was almost in tears. He had really thought he was going to take the blame for the aircraft fraud.

'Another five minutes and we'd have had a signed confession out of him,' quipped 'Bert'.

It was Charlie's first direct encounter with corruption. There were to be hundreds more occasions when he bought himself out of trouble. 'Bunging the law' was to become an institutionalised part of his world. Charlie was the first to understand the significance of this meeting. It meant that he could steal scrap, or buy material thieved by somebody else, with new impunity. There was only a small chance of getting caught anyway. If that did happen, well then, a few quid would sort it out.

Charlie carried on with his hard work. Eddie, meanwhile, had been expelled from college as a disruptive influence in the draughtsmanship classes. He'd been bored with it anyway, and got a job with the London Stone Company, cleaning the fronts of buildings. By using an older friend's cards, he got a man's wages even though he was only sixteen. This lasted only a few weeks and eventually, through a friend, he found work as a porter at Waterloo Station. He'd also started going out with Maureen, a local beauty, whom he was later to marry.

Eddie and Charlie had always been close but frequently had huge rows. Eddie had always backed off at the threat of violence from Charlie, but it was at this time that the two brothers were to have their last physical fight. Eddie, with money he had saved from his job at the station, where the tips from the American servicemen around at the time were generous, had gone to the local tailor to get himself a coat made. Eddie was away when the tailor brought it round, so Mrs Richardson decided to open the box and lay it out neatly on the bed for him. But Charlie came home before Eddie that night. When he saw the coat on his brother's bed he tried it on. He liked it so much that he decided to wear it himself for a date with a girl called Margaret. When Charlie got back, Eddie was raging. He had come home to find an empty box, and he wanted to go out that night himself. The row quickly developed into a fight. Eddie didn't back away this time and gave Charlie as good at least as he got. The fight half-destroyed the furniture in the room and was only brought to an end when their mother managed to get in between them. By the time she had cooled things down she was covered in their blood.

Charlie had just turned nineteen when his mother heard from a customer in the shop that a building and yard a quarter of a mile away at 33a, Addington Square was up for sale. It was a funny little two-storey structure, stuck on to the end of a terrace of dilapidated three-storey houses. But it

51

was ideal for Charlie, and much better than the tiny rented yard in Peckford Place, Brixton, from which he had been working. With the money he had saved, Charlie bought the freehold. Now there would be no stopping him. He took any kind of scrap at all – metal, paper, cardboard and sacks. He did much less totting himself, buying in instead what other people brought him. He paid good prices, and advanced money to totters to go out and buy. If anybody tried to con Charlie, they got a good hiding. He employed a couple of local lads, and Eddie worked for him part-time. It wasn't so much that Eddie was desperate for the money – his job at Waterloo Station was proving quite profitable – but he was honour-bound to help out with the family firm. Anyway, Charlie wanted him to help, and when Charlie wanted something he usually got his way.

Through a combination of hard work, thrift and an abundant supply of stolen metal, the Addington Square yard quickly became successful. Soon Charlie needed more help to run it. He persuaded his mother to give up her job at the Lyons Teashop down at the Green. She didn't particularly want to, but Charlie said that he needed somebody to do all the books. Eddie, too, was persuaded to join the firm full-time. The way business was going, he could see the sense of it. He would be able to make a good living, and it would have the added attraction of being the family firm just around the corner.

The police started taking an interest in the yard. They sometimes used to hang around outside, much to Charlie's annoyance, because their presence discouraged totters from coming round. Charlie realized that the police probably wanted money, but he didn't pay them because he had no reason – he hadn't been caught with any stolen metal. Then one day he was charged with receiving £5-worth of stolen scaffolding. He made all the usual excuses: he didn't know it was stolen; he just bought it from someone who came into the yard; it was one of the risks of the scrap business; how could he help it?

He was put on probation for two years and he learned another lesson: with some of the police, paying money when you are actually caught is not enough; you also have to pay them to keep out of your hair.

But this incident was to have an impact far greater than just a couple of years' probation. In the course of the case it was revealed that Charlie had not signed up for his National Service, as he should have done the year before when he was eighteen. It was all he needed. He had just got under way with his new yard, and was now going to have to spend some two years away playing toy soldiers.

3. Army Rebel

A few days after the court case, Charlie was on his way to Lee Park where he had been ordered for a National Service medical. In the next few weeks Charlie was to demonstrate how anti-authority he had become. He couldn't understand why he should get called up for two years. It was as if he was being sent away to approved school again – and this time, for once, he hadn't done anything wrong. As well as giving up the yard, it would mean not seeing his girlfriend, Margaret. She wasn't particularly attractive but she and Charlie seemed to get on pretty well, even though his mother thought she wasn't good enough for him.

He was called in front of various doctors. He pretended that he had trouble with his eyes and that he was deaf in one ear. One doctor shouted at him, true army fashion: 'Take your trousers off!'

Charlie pointedly and slowly undid his buttons and just left his trousers to drop to his ankles.

'Take them off,' the doctor screamed.

'Who do you think you are fucking well shouting at?' yelled back Charlie, losing his temper.

The argument was stopped but everybody else looked on in astonishment. The others had accepted all the shouting. But not Charlie; it was as if something in him snapped when he was bawled at like this.

The last doctor asked him if he had ever been in hospital or had any diseases. Charlie thought this was his chance to fail the medical. He told the doctor that he had been in a car accident and that he suffered dizzy spells and intense headaches. The doctors were not the slightest bit impressed and Charlie passed his medical with flying colours. But he became obsessed with the car accident excuse. By the time his orders came to report to Blenheim Barracks at Aldershot, he was determined to try it out again in the hope that he could get a discharge. His mother and Margaret had told him not to be upset. They, together with Eddie, could keep the yard going. There would be leave at weekends, and he could join the army boxing team. But Charlie was not consoled.

The station at Aldershot was full of soldiers when Charlie stepped out of the train. As the bus to the barracks drove through the town it all looked like one big prison. As he walked to the reception centre, a troop of soldiers was being marched past, with the sergeant shouting his head off at them. A sense of violent resentment started to swell up inside Charlie. Inside the barracks, all the new recruits were being processed. 'Name! Date of Birth! Employment!' They were all shouted at. Charlie was being treated like an imbecile, he felt. He could take it no more by the time he got to the desk where he was required to sign the Official Secrets Act.

'Once you have signed this, you must never tell anyone what you have seen in the army,' the officer told the recruits. 'If you do, you will be taken away and shot,' he added with a grin.

Charlie was handed a pen. 'I am not going to sign it,' he said aggressively.

The officer looked amazed. 'How dare you. You sign it here right now.'

'Ah go to hell. It's a lot of bollocks and red tape. You can stuff it up your arse!'

'Would you give away information to the Russians?' demanded the officer.

'Fucking right, I would, given half a chance.'

A crowd gathered.

'Don't be silly, you don't mean that,' said the officer, completely taken aback by this unprecedented outburst.

Charlie, his face twisted with contempt and hatred, spat back: 'Of course I do – why should I fight for this stupid capitalist country?'

He was thinking that his loss of temper could develop into a situation that would result in his being kicked out of the army. Charlie was surrounded by soldiers and the officer went across the other side of the room to talk to somebody.

'You are for it now, that's the commanding officer,' said one of the soldiers.

'Richardson, you will sign the Official Secrets Act at once.'

'No, it's a load of bollocks and red tape,' he repeated.

'Don't let this man communicate with anybody. March him to the guardhouse,' ordered the commander.

Charlie felt like laughing out loud. Looking around the room at everybody watching him with speechless expressions on their faces, he couldn't believe the panic he had caused. The sergeant tried to get Charlie marching but he resisted and slouched out of the room. Outside, two soldiers were ordered in front of him, two behind.

'If he refuses to march, kick him in the legs,' bawled the sergeant.

Charlie spun round: 'You try that, soldier, and you'll wish you bloody well hadn't,' he said with surprising force.

He got his way and shambled resentfully across to the guardhouse. An hour later another sergeant slammed back the locks and strode in.

'Don't you worry, laddie, we've got ways of dealing with traitors like you here.'

Throughout the night Charlie was aware of people spying on him through the Judas hole. He felt pleased with the attention that his performance had drawn to himself. 'That will teach them to treat *me* like an idiot,' he thought. He was left until two o'clock the next afternoon when the camp RSM ushered himself noisily into the cell. He was a classic of the breed. He had a huge moustache, a puffed-out chest and a baton under his arm. Charlie laughed at him and said, when asked, that of course he would be prepared to give secrets to the Russians. He again refused to sign the Official Secrets Act. The rest of the afternoon he watched and listened to all the new soldiers being drilled and shouted at. He felt such contempt for them in their badly fitting uniforms. At 5pm he was told the CO wanted to see him in his office. He was ordered to march in. Charlie walked. The officer ordered the other soldiers out. Charlie knew what was coming. It was just like the police 'nice guy' trick.

'Charles Richardson, now what is all this fuss about?' asked the CO. 'I've got two sons myself about your age, have you got any brothers?' He told Charlie how good life in the army could be. When he found out that Charlie would like to be a driver, he promised him that he would see what he could do. 'Now come on, why don't you stop all this nonsense with the form?' he said, putting it in front of Charlie.

'I'm sorry, sir, but I can't sign it. I'd rather go back in the guardhouse. I can't and I won't.'

After more pleading, the commander decided to put Charlie into his company barracks so that he could have a few days to think it over. At the barracks, everybody looked at him strangely. Charlie went and had a cup of tea in the NAAFI. Then he simply got up from the table, walked out of the camp and caught a bus back to London.

His mother was heartbroken. Next morning he was arrested outside the flat. He tried to give the policemen £5 but this didn't work. He was taken to the Whitehall guard-house to await an escort back to Aldershot. He pretended to faint and explained after he had 'come to' that he suffered from blackouts as a result of a car accident.

He ended up shortly afterwards in a military hospital at Woolwich, in a ward of about twenty people, a few genuinely ill, most trying to get a medical discharge like Charlie. At 6pm that night the ward was put under the guard of armed soldiers. Charlie, at the far end of the ward, decided he wanted to go to the lavatory which was just outside the ward past the soldiers. He got out of bed and took huge long strides and wore a crazy look on his face. The guards looked apprehensive. Charlie had made up his mind. He was somehow going to get his medical discharge.

A couple of days later he discovered from another patient that the best way to get out was supposed to be attempted suicide. They discussed how this might be done without too much risk of actual injury. That night, the man took a cord out of his pyjamas and tied it round his neck. He fixed it to a bar on the window and let himself go. After a moment Charlie gave the alarm as arranged. The guards came running. The man was foaming at the mouth and groaning. He was cut down and laid on the bed, which was next to Charlie's. He slept for the next couple of days. Charlie decided that attempted suicide was not for him.

Charlie's attempts to feign madness were not believed, despite some absurd antics. After ten days he was sent back to Aldershot where he was put back in the guardhouse. He still tried to push his story about blackouts, but the army doctor didn't for a minute believe him. He gave him enough codine tablets to last him the next few days. Charlie bought some asprin from the NAAFI and took them all with the codine. He thought that the overdose would give him a genuine blackout and that the doctor would have to believe him then. Before the pills had even begun to have an effect, he was taken into the offices and ordered to sweep them out. A regimental policeman was posted to watch over him. Charlie started to feel hot and dizzy.

'Are you all right?' asked the policeman, seeing that something was wrong.

'It's as if my head is going in and out, as if it's on fire,' replied Charlie, grinning to himself.

The policeman sat him down and was just giving him a glass of water when the large, red-faced RSM barged into the room.

'What's all this?' he bellowed. 'Get to attention!'

Charlie, not feeling nearly as ill as he looked, staggered to his feet.

'At the double, soldier, quick march, quick march.'

Charlie decided to faint. The policeman ran to his aid.

'Don't touch him,' the RSM roared, 'I've seen all this before.'

Charlie was genuinely furious. He could really have been ill, he might even have been dying for all the RSM knew, and he didn't give a damn. The RSM bawled at Charlie to get up off the floor. Then Charlie went berserk. He yelled that he would kill him. The RSM stormed out of the room to get help. It looked to the cowed young policeman as if

Charlie really had gone mad. He set about demolishing the office. He punched holes in the wooden panel walls, smashed the windows with chairs, and only stopped when he got his foot stuck in the wall trying to kick a hole in it.

By this time there was a score of soldiers outside. Charlie had another faint, and was carried to the guardhouse. The doctor who was called for bandaged his bleeding hands and legs, which made Charlie think he was at last being taken seriously. The other soldiers appeared to be rather more sympathetic this time – it was agreed that the door in Charlie's guardhouse cell could be left open, and a cup of tea was brought on the double when Charlie asked for it. Charlie felt very pleased with the performance. He was particularly gratified at the respectful way in which the other boy soldiers dealt with him. They, at least, appeared to think he was mad.

A little later the sergeant came in and asked how he was feeling. He suggested that Charlie come and sit next to the fire and have some tea with the rest of the guards. The sergeant asked about his fainting fits and blackouts. Charlie went into great detail about the crash. He had told the story so often he was getting pretty good at it; as with some of his other alibis, he had almost managed to convince himself that it was true. Charlie asked for a cigarette. About five packets were instantly produced. Charlie chuckled to himself.

'I've got this girl at home that I want to marry. But how can I when I am like this? I might wake up in the middle of the night and strangle her without even knowing it,' he explained.

The soldiers were sympathetic. Charlie started to laugh. He said he felt drunk with the heat of the fire. His laughter now became hysterical. Tears ran down his face. When he did stop, he only had to look at the soldiers' faces and he was off again. In the end he really couldn't control himself. He stood up and went back to his cell. He asked the sergeant not to close his door.

Next morning he was charged with causing malicious damage. The guard may have believed the story, but somebody else did not. Charlie was furious. He had been thinking about his yard in Addington Square and reckoned he might be back there pretty soon. Now it looked like a court martial. He decided that he would simply step up his act. However, there was no court martial. Instead, the CO, despairingly, gave him another fourteen days' detention.

Charlie made sure that he remained the centre of attention. He shredded a pile of newspapers into confetti. When he was aware of being watched through the Judas hole, he would create a mad expression on his face. When his food was passed in, he would leave a little and mix it all up – pudding included – so that the guards thought he had done this with all his meal. And all the time he kept up the hysterical laughter. Charlie thought he could smell the fear of the doctor when he next visited. He was prescribed some exercise. Two guards handcuffed themselves to Charlie, who went where he wanted to go, not where they did. He made them have a rest and give him a cigarette, and they had to plead with him to come back to the guardhouse. From his cell window, Charlie would hurl abuse at officers. He would shout at ordinary soldiers as if he was an officer. Since they could hardly see Charlie, a couple of them really thought the voice was an officer's. Charlie thought this was terrific. He would order them to go and polish their brasses or blanco their belts.

One day the sergeant came into Charlie's cell and asked how he was. Charlie had a mug of tea and a teaspoon in his hand.

'I'm all right, thanks very much,' he said, stirring the tea as fast as he could, splashing it out of the cup and pretending not to notice.

Despite all this, there was still no medical discharge. With only a few days left in the guardhouse, he had to do something about it soon. He remembered what the man in the Woolwich hospital had said. Attempted suicide, that was it. Only Charlie decided he would do it a little less painfully. He piled his uniform, his blankets and newspapers in a corner of his cell, and put two cans of shoe polish over the lot. He got a towel and vest, planning to tie them round his neck to give the impression that he was trying to hang himself.

60

He knew the guard would be round for an inspection at any time, and he thought the fire would probably be discovered before then anyway. He set fire to the heap in the corner and positioned himself near the air vent. It seemed like ages to Charlie before anybody discovered the fire. When he heard people coming, he pulled the towel and vest round his neck and got close to the fire. When the soldiers burst into the room Charlie lay there as if he was dead. By the time Charlie was dragged out of the cell, he really was unconscious. The doctor arrived and slapped him round the face, telling him to wake up. The doctor's patience with Charlie had long since run out.

'Come on, man, wake up, wake up,' he snapped bad-temperedly, while giving Charlie another couple of slaps. 'Come on, you are lying there like a pregnant woman.'

Such scepticism and lack of concern from the doctor was too much for Charlie to take. He leapt up and let out a horrible scream. The doctor came towards him. Charlie lashed out, knocking him to the ground. He picked up a wooden bench and, to his amazement, the soldiers tried to run away. He realized that he had done the wrong thing, let the bench go and collapsed to the floor. He was taken back to another cell and later told he could be court martialed. 'I shouldn't have got violent with the doctor,' he told himself.

Charlie was given an officer to defend him. The officer had long chats with Charlie who told him that he would like to become a soldier, but it was hopeless with his blackouts and brainstorms. Charlie managed to convince him.

His mother and father, although separated, came together to see him. After a lot of effort Charlie managed to persuade his father to go and see the defending officer and confirm the car accident and the brainstorms. His parents said that it would be better for them to plead for a second chance. But Charlie was adamantly against this; it would mean having to go through his act all over again.

'You're mad, Charlie. They'll blinking well certify you and you'll never get out,' said his father, who, within hours, was buying the officer a drink.

'What nice parents you have,' the officer told Charlie when he next saw him.

'I know,' said Charlie. 'It's such a pity I couldn't be a soldier for them.'

Charlie carried on with his act, laughing, fainting, walking madly and pulling faces. He genuinely felt once or twice that he might be unbalancing his mind. He realised that he would have to be careful, but still put on his most exaggerated performance whenever the doctor came. He would make hangman's nooses with string and leave them under his pillow. Whenever there was a search, they were removed. Charlie would make another. Nothing was ever said by anybody.

A couple of weeks before the court martial he was put in a cell with three other prisoners. The sergeant had been getting the three men to clean his kit and boots.

'You can't let them get away with that,' said Charlie to the others.

Next day when the sergeant came to collect his kit, it had been cut up and completely ruined. He never sent it in again. The camp knew that nothing could be done to make Richardson do what he was supposed to.

When the day of the court martial arrived, Charlie refused to smarten up. The sergeant, wanting to help, had his boots cleaned by another soldier. Nevertheless, when Charlie appeared in court he looked like the scruffiest soldier there had ever been. He was sentenced to six months' imprisonment, despite the efforts of his gullible defending officer.

Charlie was delighted. He had got what he really wanted – the court martial also discharged him from the army.

4. The Gathering of the Gang

As on previous occasions when Charlie had been sent away, or been in trouble, he ended up meeting people who broadened the horizons of his criminal vision. At Shepton Mallet prison, to which Charlie was sent, he met Ronnie and Reggie Kray, two hard cases from the East End, who were to become even more notorious than the Richardson gang itself. They had been having the same kind of trouble as Charlie in accepting authority, as had another embryonic gangster called Nash. He and his brothers were the tough guys from the Islington area. All were men of the same calibre: hard as nails and virtually impossible to beat in a fight. Each had ploughed into brawls with relish for most of their lives and had come to understand the full significance of violence. Their days in Shepton Mallet were the villain's equivalent of a special course for high fliers from the civil service or industry. They seemed to recognise each other as kindred spirits.

Charlie listened to what the Krays told him, about the schemes and villainy they were running and how they were doing it. But Charlie was no plagiarist. He was an original thinker who wanted to do his own thing. Unlike the Krays, who used their violence to ponce off other criminals, Charlie was a hard worker, a grafter, who used violence only when necessary.

When he came out of prison he had only been away from home and his yard for eight months. Not once during his rebellion against the army did he think of giving it a try. Once he got the idea in his mind that he wanted a discharge nothing had shaken his determination. And it had paid off. He had taken on the whole system and, in his own terms at least, won.

He threw himself into the running of the yard and within weeks had opened another. It was as if there wasn't enough time in the day, as if he was trying to catch up with lost time. He already had a few thousand saved up, but from the kind of things the Krays had been talking about, he knew he would like much more. He was more reckless than ever about dealing in stolen metal.

Eddie had matured considerably while Charlie was in prison and the army. He had become the number one around home, had his own circle of friends, and had been running the yard. He wasn't so ready to do what Charlie said. There were still some furious slanging matches, but no actual fighting. The rows did not affect the deep loyalty the two brothers felt for each other.

Charlie had been seriously courting Margaret who very soon thought she was pregnant. When she confirmed she was, Charlie did the only thing he thought right: he got married. The wedding, which was white, took place on the first day of 1955 in St Saviour's Church in Denmark Hill, Camberwell. The couple moved to a flat in Holderness House in Champion Hill and a few months later their first son, Charlie, was born.

Charlie had only one thing on his mind, and that was building up his business. Ironically, one of his biggest problems was people stealing scrap from his yard. It didn't matter to Charlie whether or not it had been stolen by him in the first place. A couple of people learnt the hard way what it meant to be caught nicking lead from him.

He attracted a lot of the totters because he offered keener prices than many of the other yards around. He put a large board outside 33a, Addington Square. On Fridays he sometimes bought out the entire stock of other yards. Occasionally, he cut his profit margins very low. That didn't matter, it was the bulk that counted, and getting known as a big dealer locally.

At about this time, Charlie often used to see a little boy aged about thirteen coming into the yard selling any kind of scrap he could lay his hands on. Sometimes he brought it in an old pram. His father had been killed a couple of years earlier while working on the railway near Waterloo Station, and there was no pension. He sold scrap metal, paper and cardboard to help his mother. One day Charlie caught him stealing some copper wire. Little Roy Hall was going to bring it back next day and sell it to the yard. Charlie took Roy up to his office and gave him a fierce shouting at. Roy explained about his mother. Charlie relented: he saw in Roy shades of his own earlier life. He was a youngster prepared to graft, prepared to steal, who knew his way around. Roy started to work for Charlie every day after school. When there was a lot of work on, Roy would take a couple of days off school. He used to work most nights until about 8pm. He came almost to hero-worship Charlie, who paid him well and treated him a bit like a son. A little later on, Charlie, impulsive as usual, was passing a Deptford tailor's shop. He went in and ordered himself a couple of smart suits.

'Do Roy here as well, will you,' he told the fitter.

Roy, like Charlie at his age, wanted a teddy boy suit.

'You don't want any of that rubbish,' Charlie told him. 'You want to look right smart.'

Charlie at this time was also cultivating people at the other end of the social spectrum, particularly well-established businessmen to whom he sold material. There was a kind of mutual fascination. Charlie was constantly trying to find new sources of scrap. Having been taught by previous businessman friends how to write letters properly, he wrote to scores of possible customers, introducing himself and offering good deals. He spent hours on the telephone searching for sources and outlets. Once he got someone interested, he would get in there like any good businessman and offer a terrific price. He would handle every new deal very efficiently, often ending up with a permanent contract with the particular company.

And so it went on. Charlie opened up another yard. He bought himself his first car, a Ford Consul. Eddie established himself as 'King of the Teds' after a fight with the man who had previously held that title. The fight took place on a piece of waste land. It didn't take Eddie long. Once the bloke went down, Eddie walked away. 'He never hit them once they were down,' said a man who knew Eddie. 'He was not a vicious fighter.'

Charlie was building around him a close group of people who were 'on the firm' and who could be trusted in a world where thieving and dishonesty were rampant. His mother still worked in the office doing the books in between helping her parents in the shop. There were Eddie and Roy Hall. An old family friend, Arthur Baron, who for twenty years had worked steadily as a lighterman on the Thames was persuaded to join Charlie. He had lived on the same landing of Cameron House as the Richardsons, and his wife was friendly with Eileen Richardson. He only worked part-time for Charlie, but he was somebody Charlie could trust. The loyalty that Charlie needed had to be returned. Although tight in the way he ran the business, he was generous with the money he made. At the end of each week when scrap had been sold off to the dealers, he would give his closest friends and workers a split of the profits. When there was a lot of work to finish off at the end of the day, he would provide treats to persuade Roy and his mates to carry on. 'If you get those two lorries cleared out and sorted by tonight, I've got some boxing tickets for you.'

By the time Charlie was twenty-two, in 1956, he and his brother had well and truly established themselves on the local scene. Charlie had about £20,000 saved up – a lot of money at this time – and, already with five yards in Camberwell, Tulse Hill and Battersea, decided to open his sixth at Waterloo, in Morley Road. Roy Hall had just left school, and by this time he knew all about metals – how much they were worth, how they could be graded and sorted. Above all, he knew the tricks to look out for. Charlie made him foreman in the new yard at Waterloo. Roy's hard work and blind loyalty to Charlie had been rewarded. There he was at fifteen, running his own yard and earning about £25 a week. Most of his former schoolmates were lucky if they earned £10. Eddie also enjoyed the success. He married Maureen, the girl he had met when he was fifteen, and was rarely short of money.

Charlie was becoming increasingly obsessed with business

efficiency, forever looking for ways of doing the same job for less time and cost. He initiated a new system of sorting and transport. Instead of sorting all the metals out in the yards and then loading up, he arranged for the metals to be sorted straight into the skips and trailers that would deliver them to his buyers. His selling techniques were also becoming more sophisticated: he would sell one lot for a loss in order to get a higher price on other metals.

But he still had a problem with people stealing metal from his own yards. Even Charlie himself came to realise that such thieving couldn't be stopped. He should know – he still received enough stolen gear himself. And this itself was also beginning to cause a problem. He had been making regular payments to the local police to keep them out of the way. He had got to know Albert, a south London bookmaker who was an intermediary between the police and many major villains. Albert knew all the cops, from some of the most senior to the ordinary boys on the ground. If you had a spot of bother with the police, then a visit to Albert would usually result in everything being sorted out – for a price.

Charlie treated money strangely. Although he penny-pinched over every deal, once he got the money in his hands he treated it with abuse. Large bundles of notes would be wrapped up in the *Financial Times* – which was avidly read for market and commodity news – and thrown into a corner. Both Charlie and Eddie always carried large rolls of notes with them. Whenever it came to buying a round of drinks or paying for a deal, they would simply dip into their pockets and unpeel however many notes were needed. If they ran out of money in the yard and needed to pay somebody on the spot, they would nip round to Albert, the bookie, and borrow a couple of hundred. It would always be promptly paid back. Charlie may have been slack on paying bills to people who didn't matter. But to those who had any kind of role to play in his increasingly powerful local organisation, money was always paid on the dot.

If anybody owed money to Charlie and was 'knocking' him, even if it was only a few pounds, the threat of violence always did the trick. One local man who borrowed money from him and only paid it back after such persuasion remembers what happened a few days later. He was walking down the road when Charlie came up to him and said he was still owed money. It was interest on the original money, Charlie explained: about 50 per cent interest. Charlie was threatening and menacing, making it quite clear to the man that he would be beaten up if he didn't pay. He managed to 'hoof it' and kept out of Charlie's way thereafter.

By the end of his twenty-second year, Charlie was a local force to be reckoned with. His six yards had an astonishing £250,000 turnover. The group of dedicated men and relations whom Charlie had around him seemed, some said, to be almost spellbound by him. He kept to himself everything about the running of the yards and what was going on. Business was so good that the Addington Square yard was becoming too small. On top of this, Charlie was beginning to realise that having six yards and employing twenty people had its disadvantages. It was harder to keep a minute-by-minute control over what was happening, and harder to deal with thieving. Six yards also meant that the police had to be paid six times. . . . Charlie decided that he would cut down the number of yards, and move his headquarters round the corner to the old farmhouse building at 50, New Church Road. The lease was for sale from a charitable trust and Charlie snapped it up. The building could be used for offices, and there was much more yard-space. For the next eight years number 50 was the centre of his activities. Even though he ended up with offices in Park Lane, a front for his South African mining interests, it was New Church Road that was the centre of his empire. He called his new company Peckfords Scrap Metals, after the name of the road in which he had his first-ever business.

During this period of rationalisation, a number of other important developments took place. Charlie, having more than successfully established himself in scrap in three years, was beginning to find it all a bit too easy and undemanding. He had been keeping up his reading – he was now a complete bookworm – and was constantly aware of a world opening up before him. He wasn't quite sure what he wanted to do, but he was thinking about it. His father, seeing what a booming business his son had developed, also saw the chance of an easier life. After twenty-five years at sea he had had enough, and it was agreed that he should join in with Charlie. It didn't seem to matter that Eileen was often in the office.

Now that the company had moved round the corner, there was the problem of what to do with 33a, Addington Square. It was Eddie who put the idea into Charlie's mind that they should turn the building into a drinking club. The yard had already become quite a market and meeting place for the totters with their horse and carts, which sometimes used to jam up the road. What better than to have a club where they could all meet after the pubs had shut? Eddie, always the more sociable of the two brothers, liked the idea of running his own club, instead of being in other people's. It could become an important centre for gossip and news, about what was going on, and who was doing what. The ground floor of the small building was turned into a reception area, and the bar was built on the first floor where Charlie had had his office. It was a rough and ready joint, but soon attracted custom, especially on Mondays – traditionally the 'club day' that totters took off and spent drinking and socialising. The family all took turns in working at the bar, but Charlie's father, scoundrel that he was, soon established himself as the main barman.

The club hadn't been going long when it received a visit from a nearby protection gang. They wanted money and free drinks to 'mind' the place – keep order and make sure there was no trouble. Either they were foolhardy or their information about the Richardson set-up was bad. A phone call was made to the yard. Charlie, Eddie, Roy Hall and a couple of others rushed round.

'Right, who's the funny geezer who wants the trouble?'

They set about the man and his thugs and gave them probably the biggest beating of their lives. It wasn't just an ordinary beating. Such a challenge right in the middle of Richardson territory had to be dealt with properly. An example had to be made of the cheapskate gang. Word would have to go out about what happened to them. By the time Charlie and his men had finished, the entire gang had been knocked unconscious, and there were some broken noses and bones. Half the furniture in the club had been demolished and the place looked like a bomb site. But there was never any more trouble with protection. The Richardsons did that themselves.

The club was called the Addington. It became quite a local centre, attracting not only the totters but the street bookies, villains and every kind of wide boy imaginable. Drink was served whenever there were people who wanted to drink in the afternoons and evenings when the pubs had shut. The clientele would buy whole crates of beer at a time and sit round tables with mates drinking into the small hours. The place became known as a safe place to have a drink where you could meet your own kind of people – what they call 'solid' in south London. There was little trouble because the Richardsons policed the place themselves from the yard just 100 yards round the corner. Whenever anybody started getting out of hand, a call went round to the yard and Eddie, who was based there more permanently than Charlie, would come round. Many a reputation bit the dust in this way. Men back from prison, unaware of the name that the young Richardsons were building up, would find themselves flattened in a volley of punches from Eddie. True to form, Eddie would never hit them when they were down. He was, by everybody's reckoning, a clean fighter. They used to say that you didn't need a crane at the yard if you had Eddie, who was renowned for his ability to lift whole car engines single-handed and for his very hard work.

As some older reputations crashed to the floorboards with their owners, so that of Eddie and Charlie grew. A man called Ken, who was serving behind the bar one night, had to deal with somebody who was causing trouble. Ken was no mean fighter himself. But he couldn't deal with this particular tough customer. The call went out to Eddie who arrived covered in grease and in his overalls. A couple of punches lifted the man right off the ground and that was that. When the man came to, Eddie had a drink with him and there was no more trouble from that particular person. It was the kind of language which most of the customers of the club understood. Fights in their particular society were commonplace. Often they were followed by 'a wash and drink up'. But at other times, people got very badly hurt. If hospital treatment was needed, then the form was to make up some excuse – a car accident was one of the favourites – even though the doctors knew exactly what had happened. The one thing you never did was admit a fight when the police were called in by the hospital.

Charlie showed an unusual ability to operate in this kind of society and yet deal impressively with more respectable businessmen. For all his villainy, he was an intelligent man. As well as reading avidly, he had long discussions with the more educated people he met, about almost any subject under the sun. But through the club, he also got to know many of the market street-traders. He was fascinated by their business, involving as it often did the acquisition of goods from dubious sources, and their deals with big wholesale suppliers. Charlie had already got drink for the club through unofficial channels – often the proceeds of whole lorry-loads of drink being stolen – and he wondered if he should go into the wholesale business himself. He was still feeling a bit bored with scrap, which he found so easy, and which seemed almost to run itself thanks to the loyal workers he had around him.

After the success of the Addington, further clubs were opened. There was one in the Albany Road called the Orange, and another in Lordship Lane in East Dulwich called the Cavern. Both these had cafes in the front part and drinking clubs at the back. The Cavern was not so successful perhaps because it was in the wrong area – not so rough as at Addington Square – and it was also too far away, not in Charlie's manor. Charlie had interested the public-school-educated son of a Midlands foundry owner to invest money in the club. When it went wrong and was shut down, the partner didn't get much of his money back.

Charlie also opened an illegal club called the Shirley Anne behind a garage just off Queen's Road in Peckham. The man

71

who ran this for him was known as John West, although his real name was Bradbury. He was a local villain who acquired some lorries and did some haulage work for Charlie. He was what is known down Camberwell way as 'a ducker and diver'. He tried to have his finger in every piece of villainy, although in real terms he was a nobody in the Richardson world. He was also a great ladies' man, although he was extremely jealous of his wife Sheila. He was later to play a vital role in the downfall of the Richardsons.

The Shirley Anne was the kind of place where local men could drink at any time of the day or night, and it was often the next day when they emerged. Customers had to go through a garage to enter it and when they did the booze flowed. The police tried to close it down. But they could never find the owner. One of the men at the local Peckham station at the time was Sergeant Ken Drury, who nearly twenty years later was one of several senior Flying Squad officers sentenced to a long term in prison for corruption in connection with Soho porn. He was a regular visitor at the Bradbury household. When Charlie heard that the police were interested in the club, he ordered the place to be padlocked for a few days. When the police lost interest, the club was re-opened. When they got a tip-off from a bent cop that the place was going to be raided, they put the padlock back on – only to cut it off a couple of nights later and carry on as normal.

Increasingly, working for or with Charlie meant a whole way of life. It wasn't just a job, it was a matter of identity. You got looked after if you were associated with Charlie, or at the very least you felt safer in a slightly dangerous world where you could get arrested or attacked at any time. Charlie maintained his dominance with a ruthless and unhesitating use of violence.

This sense of belonging was undoubtedly enhanced when Eddie and Charlie started a football team that was associated with the Addington Club. Charlie had already shown an interest in starting boys clubs, but nothing had actually got off the ground. Charlie's motive seemed to be a mixture of genuine charity and a desire somehow to exert an

72

influence over the hearts and minds of local boys. When Eddie and a friend heard that a club called the Westminster Boys Club in Battersea was going to close down and suggested taking it over, Charlie seized on the idea. They asked Arthur Baron if he would care to run it. He agreed readily, having always had a strong interest in soccer. Arthur, a quiet and gentle-seeming man, was one of those puzzling characters who run right through the Richardson story: although different from them, he seemed easily to co-exist, almost as if unaware of their more vicious side. The owner agreed to give Arthur the club name and the few players who remained. Charlie helped out in the take-over of the club and a team was made up of people who worked at the yard and friends who were keen on football. They got hold of a couple of good players, one who played for Queens Park Rangers, and another who played for Gravesend. The team's headquarters were at the Addington Club, and the games were played on grounds such as Blackheath and Charlton, which were rented from local councils.

At first the team was a disaster, beaten by ten goals to nil on their first outing in the bottom division of the Sunday League. But then the margins started to narrow and by the end of the first season they were put in at the bottom of the first division. There was great camaraderie surrounding the team; training sessions were keenly attended; there was a following of 200 to 300 fans; and the team started getting quite a name. Its rapid rise attracted more decent local players, and during the next couple of years the team wiped the board in its league. Charlie never played, but he normally turned out to watch.

It was around this time that Roy Hall found out what protection and help being associated with the gang could bring. Still under driving age, Roy was using his own lorry to bring back some stolen lead to the yard when he was stopped by the police, who soon sized up the position. It was a nasty charge, and could possibly have resulted in a small prison sentence. But Charlie got in touch with a police friend. A deal was done: Roy would have to plead guilty to a minor offence – which, of course, he had not committed –

while the much more serious charge was dropped. The cost: £50. 'Can't say fairer than that,' said the policeman to Charlie.

In the summer of 1957 Charlie, his mother and kids – a second child, called Carole, had now been born – went down to Box Hill for the day. During their outing, they looked at some caravans. Charlie, characteristically, bought one on impulse. He had no idea what he was going to do with it, but Margaret, his wife, had mentioned something about 'wouldn't it be nice . . .' . As it happened, a friend of his had some land in Gnats Valley at West Kingsdown in Kent and Charlie bought a couple of acres from him. Next weekend the family, Roy and a couple of others towed the caravan down to its site. They all mucked in cutting the grass and clearing the scrub. They put some chickens in and built a small swimming pool.

Almost every weekend for the next few months the family would go down to stay. All kinds of friends and relations would also turn up; regular guests included Arthur Baron and his wife, and Eddie and some of his friends. There would be trips to Dymchurch Sands, big Sunday lunches and a lot of larking around. During one visit Charlie and Roy saw an advertisement for a gorilla for sale. They went to see the farmer who was selling it.

'It's in there, over in the shed,' said the farmer.

'Can we have a look?' asked Charlie.

'Help yourself.'

Not wanting to show their surprise at this suggestion, Charlie and Roy made their way over. The farmer stayed where he was.

'It must be all right,' said Roy, 'else he wouldn't have let us look at it.'

They opened the door and saw a large old silverblack gorilla in the corner. Charlie stood behind Roy and guided him forward into the dingy shed, his hands on his shoulders. Suddenly, the gorilla got up and started lumbering towards the two, his rotten yellow teeth bared through a snarling mouth. Luckily the poor beast was on a chain. But the way he lurched at both men frightened the life out of them. The farmer thought it was very funny; the gorilla stayed in its shed.

Charlie's spontaneous interest in animals didn't disappear. A few weeks later, at Petticoat Lane, he bought a goat. He arrived back home carrying it on his shoulders and nobody had the faintest idea what to do with it. He also had an odd fascination with shops that sold tricks. He bought a device you could put round your head so that it looked as though you had a dagger embedded in it. He also bought from his favourite Holborn trick shop a book of nudes. Every time anyone opened it, they got an electric shock.

After only a few weeks Charlie came to like West Kingsdown so much that he decided to move Margaret and his two children there permanently, and he started spending weekday nights there himself. But Margaret didn't particularly like it. It was cramped and difficult and she was a town girl at heart anyway. So they moved back to their flat in Holderness House, just using the caravan at weekends.

Back in London one night, Charlie and a couple of friends went across to the East End. They were in a pub when a fight started – nothing to do with them, but inevitably they got involved. There was one particular man who they didn't like the look of. A friend of Charlie's called Ken cracked his jaw with a punch. Next day Ken was approaching the New Church Road yard in his car. He couldn't believe his eyes. There was a whole gang of men walking down the road, armed with guns and sticks. He drove into the yard and found out from Charlie that it was the Krays. The man they had whacked the night before was a Kray man. It looked as though Charlie was going to get some of his own treatment – and perhaps worse. They persuaded the Krays to have a talk. Explanations and apologies followed: it was just one of those things, they had no idea that it was one of their boys. It was a close shave but Charlie understood. An uneasy truce was made.

Despite this climb-down, the sense of belonging to a special firm continued to grow, extending not just to the people immediately involved in the yards and the club but

75

even to those who lived nearby. The older, poorer people who lived in Sears Street just beside the yard, and others like them in the immediate vicinity, were treated to turkeys and chickens at the Christmas of 1957. Some even got a few pounds from Charlie, who laid on a party and with another friend dressed up as a reindeer. Charlie's generosity also took other forms, perhaps reflecting the esteem in which he held himself. Driving down the road one day with a local businessman, he saw a blind man crossing the road. He stopped his car in the middle of the road, got out and stopped all the traffic to let the man across the road.

For the inner circle of Charlie's mob there was extra special treatment. One of the rooms in the old farmhouse offices of Peckfords Metals in New Church Road was turned into a little bar. They called it the Casbar. On Friday nights – traditionally the night when everybody had a good drink and were not expected home by their wives – Charlie and his men would organise a little party after the pubs shut. Girls would be asked back and a record player was put on. The boys, having worked so hard all week, deserved a bit of fun. There was also a lot of larking around. Sometimes, they would hold mock trials.

Charlie, Eddie and other members of the gang also started taking various kinds of pep pills such as purple hearts to give them greater energy and strength and to make them feel good. Sometimes members of the gang became dangerously out of control with a combination of drink and drugs. It was with Charlie in such a state of mind that some of the mock trials were held. Charlie would normally be the prosecution, Eddie the judge, and some less important member of the gang the defence. Although it is said that many of these mock trials were merely innocent fun, some of the punishments could be extremely unpleasant. One man who had offended Charlie's dignity in some minor way was tried and, inevitably, found guilty. He was suspended by his ankles and hung upside down for many hours. Next morning, when Charlie had sobered up, he apologised and gave the man some money. The mock trials seemed to reinforce Charlie's sense of supreme superiority over the men around him. They

76

also served to remind those associated with him of their contemptible insignificance: you do not run a gang such as Charlie's with liberal sentiments. Power is exercised with the threat or use of violence, and, in Charlie's case, with occasional touches of sadistic, psychological punishment.

Even if Charlie had wanted to let a man off for some liberty taken, it would be dangerous for him to do so. The tin-pot villains and criminals around him would start to think he was going soft and perhaps try their luck too. Only by dealing mercilessly and publicly with such people could somebody like Charlie keep complete control. As it happened, the exercise of such authority seemed to come easily to Charlie. Rarely in his life did anybody ever challenge his power. But such behaviour also has its risks. There was always the possibility that someone might try and get his own back. Charlie started becoming security conscious. Nobody could get into his office at Peckfords without first being noticed. He also carried a gun, a .22 pistol. It was occasionally used in a way calculated to strike terror and subservience in the men around him. One day a man called Jimmy was in Charlie's office. He had displeased Charlie over the way he had done a deal. Charlie fired a shot over his head. When the man protested, he fired another. It passed very close to the quaking man.

The same kind of tactics applied when anybody outside Charlie's gang 'took a liberty' with someone inside it. It was one night in the Casbar that Reggie Jones, a friend of the Richardsons, burst into the room with two black eyes. He told Charlie how he had been attacked after going to the aid of a man called Jimmy Brindle, who had been savagely beaten by an Elephant and Castle gang. Jimmy was well known to Charlie's firm. He was the epitome of the solid man. He was a street bookie, and a regular customer at the Addington club. He was also married to Eva, the sister of Frank Fraser, who, although unknown to the Richardsons personally at the time, was known to them as an important villain with West End connections. At this time, Fraser was serving a seven-year sentence for his part in a brutal attack on Jack 'Spot' Comer, who, with a man called Billy Hill, had more or less run the West End.

Reggie Jones told Charlie and his friends what exactly had happened. It sounded like a right liberty to them all. Jimmy was not a man of violence. He was a good bookie and never welched on his commitments. Jimmy had three street pitches, as they were called, one at the Elephant, one at Leroy Street and one in Forest Hill. He, like so many other members of the underworld society in this part of London, made regular payments to the police, who knew all about these illegal pitches. The system was so well institutionalised that everybody knew exactly whose territory was whose and there were strict rules about pirating. Pitches were sold and bought like any other piece of property. The police would come round every two or three weeks to collect their pay — normally about £20. But it didn't stop there. They also needed 'bodies' to charge and bring before the magistrates. The arrangement was that the street bookies would provide 'stickers' — men who for the sum of £10 would pretend to be running a street book, and who would be caught with the dummie bets. The man would normally get fined a few pounds which, of course, were paid for him. It was even better if the police could have a man with more than one booking — it would look impressive to the magistrate.

On this particular Friday night, Jimmy Brindle had been drinking at the Good Intent in East Lane, just off the Walworth Road, with a man called Rosa, who had a big reputation around the Elephant. He had just come out of prison. Jimmy had put him up in his house, but was getting fed up with him and had asked him to find new lodgings. That particular night Rosa asked Jimmy for a lift up to the West End. Jimmy wasn't keen.

'I was promised some bird because I had three convictions for driving,' he recalled. 'Being a street runner, the law didn't like me and I was classed as a scoundrel. They had me down for about eighteen months or two years. I explained this to Rosa and he didn't like it. That was the excuse.'

Rosa and two friends jumped on Jimmy and started beating him up. Reggie Jones, who was in the pub, tried to help Jimmy out. Jimmy wasn't a fighting man, whereas

78

Rosa and his mates were violent. By the time Reggie ran out, he had been hurt himself, and Jimmy lay covered in blood with a broken jaw and a ripped ear.

When Reggie arrived at Charlie's, the pubs were closing. A couple of telephone calls soon established that Rosa and his friends were at a big club at the Elephant and Castle called the Reform. Charlie, Eddie, Roy and a couple of others stormed into the club and set about Rosa and his various friends with unprecedented fury. The victory was easier than ever. After a short time they walked away from what by now was becoming a familiar scene: broken bodies lying groaning among sticks of broken furniture. As Eddie now puts it: 'We went in there and wallop, wallop, wallop, and they were all over the place. We didn't want a reputation but someone had taken a liberty.'

The Richardsons already had a big reputation at the time of this fight. This incident was to enhance that reputation even further. The Elephant gangs were tough, Rosa's was the toughest of all. He had been well known for a number of years, both in and out of prison: during the spell at Broadmoor Prison, from which he came to stay with Jimmy Brindle, he had pulled the governor over his desk and thumped him hard. That's the sort of thing that enhances your standing in the underworld.

After the fight, Charlie and his men went back to the Casbar to finish off the evening. They felt terrific. Honour had been done. One of their firm had been revenged for the liberty that had been taken on him. Never had the feeling of belonging been stronger than on that night. They had the yards, the clubs, the police more or less straightened. They were well and truly established as the big firm on the manor. It seemed as though they were invincible. They felt that they ruled the world, their particular world at least.

5. Watershed

But a few weeks after the Brindle fight, Charlie was brought down to earth with a bump. He had a full stock of lead which he decided to start selling to the lead mills because the price was running quite high. By the end of the day there was trouble. Somebody at the mill noticed that among a lorry load was a bundle of lead pipes all painted different colours. They looked like domestic overflow pipes which somebody had gone round houses cutting off. The police were called and said that was exactly what they were. The piping had come from an estate on the outskirts of London in Middlesex. The local paper had made a song and dance about the business. In one road, every single house had lost its overflow pipes overnight. Charlie had not realised when he brought it in that the metal had been stolen, not, of course, that it would have made any difference. As he now explains it: 'The police wanted to have me for a few quid. I was big-headed at the time and I told them to get knotted. I told them to do what they liked. I cleared them out and they came back the next day and nicked me, Eddie, my driver and driver's mate and they made themselves right busy over it. They still wanted money off me but I didn't want to know.'

One of the police even waited outside Charlie's solicitor's office in Holborn. As Charlie came out, he pointed to his car inside which were four pieces of lead involved in the case. 'You can have them back for £100,' Charlie was told. But he didn't want to know. He really was innocent. He should have known better. But Charlie's ego was so big that he decided he would fight the case with everything he had and teach the police a lesson. When the trial came up at the Middlesex Sessions, he managed to get a re-trial by showing that some of the evidence was prejudicial. But he was fined £80, and Eddie, £40, at the second trial. Charlie's barrister had to plead for him not to be sent to prison. When the judge imposed the fine, Charlie told him that he was innocent and that he would appeal. Appeal he did, but that only cost him another £800 for no result.

Further troubles were soon to follow, but in the meantime Charlie bought himself a house at 2, St Pauls Wood Road, St Pauls Cray in Kent, and moved his family in. If he didn't want to spend the night at home, he simply slept in a bed at the office. This often happened because increasingly Charlie spent expensive nights out in West End clubs like the Astor off Berkeley Square where a mixture of princes, villains and hostesses co-existed. As a result of this social activity he met a girl called Jean Goodman.

Eddie was also reaping the rich rewards of the business and that year at the Motor Show in Earls Court bought himself the latest Impala. He always had liked big cars, especially big American ones.

The fights carried on whenever honour demanded it. One of their workers, Johnnie, was very upset one day. His wife had run off with another man, a well-known villain and fighter. Trouble was, not only did he take Johnnie's wife, he took all the furniture from his house in Peckham Park Road. The boys didn't think much of this. They found out where the man was, took all the furniture back, and gave him a beating. Another local reputation bit the dust.

But the police were hearing of some of the unceremonial ejections from the clubs. Charlie was getting too big for his boots. Policemen who, as lowly constables, Charlie had treated with contempt a few years earlier, had now risen in rank. Some of them thought Charlie was pushing his luck. It was about time he got taught a lesson. Their first opportunity came one night in the Albany Road after shots were fired at somebody in a block of flats. Charlie and several of his friends, including the man they had helped out over the matter of his wife, had been trying to persuade two men, the Roff brothers, not to give evidence in another case in which a friend of the Richardsons had been charged with causing grievous bodily harm. The brothers had refused to do this. So Charlie decided to pay them a visit. He and fourteen men surrounded the Roffs' flat in Albany Road, close to the Richardsons' shop. The Roffs climbed up on to the flat roof of the block of flats. When Charlie saw them there, he pulled out his gun and, it was alleged in court, fired shots.

Nobody was hit, but the police decided to get Charlie. They had already heard rumours about Charlie shooting at somebody called Micky Harris a few weeks before: Harris had more guts than brains and had apparently taken exception to something Charlie had done. He walked round to the yard, demanding to see Charlie, and when he appeared Harris smashed him across the nose with the starting handle of a car. Whatever Charlie then did to the man it hardly mattered – some time later he was to die in a knife fight.

In the case of the Roffs, the police had witnesses willing to give evidence. When Charlie and three of his men appeared at Lambeth Court, the prosecution alleged that there had been gang warfare. Charlie was remanded in prison for a week, and when he next appeared one of the prosecution witnesses miraculously turned hostile. She had been with the men when the shots were fired but her memory seemed to go remarkably blank as she gave her evidence. She couldn't even identify any of the defendants.

After the Roff case the police were furious. They clearly determined that next time they really would get Charlie. They didn't have to wait long.

Charlie had heard that somebody had six sides of stolen bacon for sale. Typically, Charlie also knew someone who would be interested in buying the bacon. He added a percentage for himself and pushed the deal through. But the police had known from the beginning what was going on. Charlie was arrested, and this time he was helpless. There were no witnesses to corrupt, and it was useless trying to buy his way out of trouble. He was sentenced to six months in prison.

The running of the yards was so well organized that the firm was not affected by Charlie's imprisonment. Eddie was completely familiar with the everyday mechanics of the business, and with help from loyal grafters like Roy Hall, business carried on as normal. Charlie was consulted in prison about the business, and told not to worry. With good behaviour he would probably be out in four months. But, as they say in the Richardson world, Charlie 'had the right hump' over his sentence.

However, prison wasn't too hard for Charlie, simply because of who he was. People inside were as keen as they had been on the outside to do him a favour. When you are as big as Charlie on the outside, life inside is much more bearable. Charlie brooded in prison about where he was going. He recognized that he had got a bit out of hand. He felt that the clubs had not helped. They had attracted the wrong sort of attention; they simply caused too much aggravation. When he came out towards the end of 1959 he decided he would close them down.

Charlie had for some time been thinking of getting into the wholesale business, selling to market traders and the like. He had seen the potential for acquiring goods cheaply and he had at the back of his mind the idea to turn the club at 33a, Addington Square into a wholesale and retail outlet. His youngest brother Alan would be an ideal person to run it. Alan, still a gentle type of lad, looked more like Charlie than Eddie, the older brothers hardly resembling each other at all. Charlie and Eddie felt protective towards him, he being so much younger, and Charlie felt the scrap game probably wasn't suitable for him. But before Charlie could get rid of the clubs and start his wholesaling he was in trouble again. This time, coming so soon after his four months in prison, it was very serious.

Almost inevitably, the charge involved scrap – it was alleged that he had received a large quantity of various metals. Charlie appeared at the Magistrates' Court in May 1960 and was bailed for £2000. But he was very worried and did what he often did when in real trouble – he ran away. Nobody knew that Charlie had gone except Johnnie Longman, a local thief and member of the gang who had been in and out of villainy all his life, and who did haulage

83

work for Charlie. He turned up at Eddie's and told him that Charlie had gone to Canada. He had taken all the money out of the yard and also gone was Jean Goodman, with whom he had begun an affair after he came out of prison. She was an attractive, intelligent woman who had started helping out around the office and slept with Charlie in a little bedroom above Peckfords' offices.

Margaret, Charlie's wife, had five children by now. Charlie felt that she had lost any attraction she ever had and he didn't like the way she seemed to be too easy-going with money. While Charlie had been lifting himself up in the world, Margaret had stayed exactly where she had always been, her feet firmly on the ground in the poor working class of south London.

Eddie was angered by Charlie's sudden departure. For a start, there were the two people who had each stood £500 surety for Charlie's bail. One was Reggie Rumble, a close family friend who had a demolition business in Addington Square. The other was Reggie Saunders, 'Reggie the Milkman' as he was known: he had been the milkman on the local round, but Charlie, having got chatting to him one day in characteristic fashion, suggested he worked part-time at the yard. Before long he gave up his milk round, joining the firm full-time.

Everybody rallied around and Eddie started again to take control. Money kept coming in at its usual steady rate, so the two Reggies were given back the surety money which they had lost. After the first few difficult weeks, Eddie rather liked running the show. With Charlie around or even in prison, he had never had the chance before. He had the clubs as well, so was kept well-occupied. Having played number two all his life – albeit under protest sometimes – he surprised himself at the ease with which he became 'the Guv'nor'.

Charlie and Jean Goodman, meanwhile, had arrived in Toronto where within weeks he was back in the scrap business. Charlie found the trade very underdeveloped, with plenty of scope for putting his well-tried techniques into practice. He advertised in papers, put a big board outside the rented yard offering keen prices, and before long he had a thriving business. But after eight months he so missed south London and his business there that he sold up – to people who today still run the company and are millionaires. Using the false passport he had acquired before he left, he slipped back into England and went up to Norwich where he had friends who ran a big waste-paper business. He kept a low profile but popped back to London to keep himself in touch. One business friend walked into his office to find Charlie in dark glasses hiding behind the door. They got into the car, embarrassed as the businessman was, and drove round while Charlie checked up on what was going on in the world.

But as the weeks went by, Charlie grew more careless. He was caught one night as he was leaving a party. But before he was arrested he had 'made himself busy', and a good set of lawyers managed to get him acquitted. After the case he sent a scales of justice to his solicitor who wrote a letter back thanking him for his great generosity.

As on previous occasions when Charlie had been unavoidably detained away from the yards, he set about his life with renewed zeal. A lot of changes were going to be made. The clubs would now definitely be shut down, he would go into wholesaling, and the yards, which only numbered three by this time, could be kept ticking over by trusted workers.

The Addington club was the first to go. It just so happened that there was a small fire, enough to destroy the contents of the club, but not so big as to destroy the structure. The insurance company found no evidence of foul play. The club was completely done up for the wholesale venture, and Alan was installed as manager. Charlie's odd fascination with exotic animals was reflected in its interior: downstairs was caged a selection of animals and birds – there was even a monkey and an animal they called a buffalo. Some of the animals they bought – such as two bears, one of which escaped and had to be chased around the streets of Camberwell before being recaptured. Others they borrowed from a woman called Dolly Legs. She helped Alan feed and care for the beasts, which made the place into quite an attraction. Local mothers brought their kids along, and at the same time they bought goods. The shop had a bit of everything, also selling wholesale to the market traders from East Lane and other local markets.

Charlie's mother, who had worked off and on at the yard for nearly eight years, now took over her parents' newsagent's shop. Charlie thought that Jean Goodman would be better running the office administration and books. Jean quickly established herself in the office, and Charlie delegated more to her than he had ever done to anyone else. Charlie's children hated her. Whenever they turned up at the yard looking for him, she used to tell them that he wasn't there. Often he really wasn't, and this started to cause some friction between Jean and some of the other workers. Jean was not the kind of girl to give a nice big bonus at the end of the week, as Charlie might have done; she couldn't anyway, it wasn't her money. Roy Hall especially got fed up. He had always worked his heart out for Charlie and still did. But with Charlie not around so much, there was less fun and fewer perks with the job. Roy started to feel that he was being taken for granted and one day, after a big row, he walked out. Eddie, too, disliked Jean. 'Shit legs' is what he called her unendearingly behind her back.

Charlie meanwhile decided to move back from St Paul's Cray to Holderness House with his wife Margaret, who by now suspected something was going on. She disliked living away from south London, despite the nice house; she felt too isolated in St Paul's Cray, and didn't get on very well with the neighbours.

The wholesale shop in Addington Square did well enough through the early months of 1961 for Charlie to see the potential of this kind of business. Ideas for getting the goods more cheaply started stirring in his mind. But that summer, tragedy struck the Richardson family.

Charlie had bought a speedboat which he wanted to try out on the Thames. He persuaded Alan to come and help him launch it, even though Alan was only just recovering from severe concussion sustained a month earlier after falling thirty-five feet (he had been trying to climb into the flat because he had lost his keys). Reluctantly, he went with Jean and Charlie to Richmond where the boat was placed in the water. Alan again said he didn't want to come.

'Ah, come on, Alan, get in, we'll put you off at the Tower, and you can go home then,' said Charlie, winning the argument as usual.

They sped up the Thames into central London. Charlie was in excellent spirits. It made him feel very special planing up the river in the boat, which was a symbol of his success. He turned, hair streaming in the wind, to see if Alan was enjoying it as much. He certainly appeared to be. They were just coming up to Blackfriars Bridge having passed under Waterloo, when the boat hit the wash of a pleasure boat going the other way. Charlie was inexperienced. The boat flipped over, throwing its three passengers into the water. They were just scrambling back on to the capsized craft when a large barge went past.

'The boat was upside down and it got sucked under the barge,' recalls Roy Hall, who was one of the few people Charlie ever talked to about the incident. 'Charlie and Jean came up the other side, but Alan didn't.'

Perhaps the concussion from the fall had something to do with Alan's failure to surface. He was normally a strong swimmer and a keen sportsman. He had had a trial for Crystal Palace football club, and, like his two older brothers, was a fine physical specimen. His body, identified by Eddie, turned up ten days later. The drowning stunned Charlie and the whole family. Mrs Richardson was grief-stricken. She had a special bond with her youngest son. In the months to come she consulted spiritualists in the hope that they could contact Alan for her. When she was told he was happy and well and had them all in his thoughts, she felt better. Today, twenty years later, there is still a great reluctance among the family to talk about the accident.

6. Wholesale Robbery

Charlie took many weeks to get over the death of Alan. He shut down the shop that Alan had run and let it remain unused for several months. He wouldn't go near the place: it pained him to recall memories of the shop. But he was still determined to get into the wholesale business. His outlet for goods in East Lane market had been developed through people like John Bradbury, the man who ran his illegal Shirley Anne drinking club in Peckham. The goods for this and other stalls he supplied came from many different sources including lorry-loads hijacked by Charlie's men. On one occasion Bradbury failed to pay Charlie for goods that had been supplied. It was only a matter of £10, but that wasn't the point. Bradbury got a beating. His wife remembers him coming home with a cut lip and black eyes and bruises all over. However, Bradbury, who seemed to regard the beating as an occupational hazard, continued working with Charlie.

It was through people like Bradbury in the market trade that Charlie came into contact with the bigger wholesale suppliers. One of these was Tommy Costello (a pal of Johnnie Longman) who, with his partner, George Westcott, ran W & C Suppliers in Catford. Costello was well connected with much of the wholesale trade and in particular knew people who operated large-scale frauds — known as long firm frauds in the trade, or 'LFs' for short.

The principles of LFs were simple. A company would be launched to buy, or to import or export goods such as stockings, shoes, toiletries, household and fancy goods for the wholesale trade. A local bank account would be opened and money paid in and withdrawn to give the impression of activity. The company would then order smallish quantities of various goods from a range of established manufacturers. The new company would provide the manufacturers with the names of referees at bogus companies who would write and vouch for the new company's reliability.

As soon as the first orders were supplied to the new company the bills would be paid promptly. Then started the slow process of building up trust with various suppliers. The 'front men' running the long firm had to be excellent conmen — it was on their ability to create confidence and trust that the whole fraud ultimately depended. Orders would increase in size and always be paid for on the spot, the goods then being sold off to traders and retailers at cost price. The company would not yet make any profit.

Once confidence had been established with enough manufacturers, the company would move in for the kill. With careful timing, big orders would be placed covered by cheques and plausible explanations about the terrific order that had been won. As soon as the goods arrived they would be sold off at vast reductions — to ensure that everything was bought within hours. It wouldn't matter that the company had issued a cheque worth £10,000 for the goods and sold them for only £5000. By the time the manufacturers presented the cheque, the bank account would have been cleared out bar a few pounds. And when the police or Board of Trade inspectors arrived at the company's premises there would be no trace of anything. The front men, having used false names, would have disappeared into thin air. The men behind the fraud, who put up the initial capital for the bank account and payment for first orders, would probably not be fully known even to the front men. Certainly there would be nothing on paper to connect them with the company concerned.

Charlie started to learn all about the many variations on this type of fraud. Being an intelligent man, he soon got the hang of it, but at first he had to fumble his way around. One of the commodities in plentiful supply at this time was stockings from Italy. Some of the new people Charlie was meeting bought large quantities of these stockings from a Polish wholesaler called Benny Wajcenberg, who had

89

premises in Whites Row in the City of London. Charlie went and saw him and started ordering Italian stockings and knitwear for his wholesaling operation.

Charlie decided to set up his own long firm with some partners. Using front men, they opened a warehouse in Mitre Street in the City. They put in an ex-policeman to manage it. Charlie didn't know exactly who was supplying the stockings, but he knew they came from Milan in Italy. He went out there with a man called Bill Desmond and one of his south London businessman friends to try and start ordering. Desmond had not long joined Charlie. He had specialized in country house robberies with his great friend Ruby Sparks, a Camberwell man who eventually wrote a book about his burglaries at stately homes. Charlie had hired Desmond, a bricklayer by trade, to supervise the building of a weighbridge at Peckfords after he had injured himself in a fall. After that, he was kept on: he was the kind of solid person Charlie liked to have around.

Charlie was able to order some supplies for the fledgling long firm venture. But it annoyed Charlie greatly that he didn't know everything that was going on. He simply could not discover who was who in the stockings racket. He was beginning to move into a world that was peopled by characters entirely different from those he had known before. These were shrewd, clever con-men, with a background and breeding quite unlike the twopenny-halfpenny villains Charlie had found so easy to dominate and control. To these new men, someone like Charlie was good news: he wanted to get in on the act, he had plenty of money with which to buy goods, and he had absolutely no qualms about how the supplies had been acquired.

Another aspect that puzzled Charlie was how many possible buyers for his stockings already seemed to have their own plentiful supply. Unknown to him, they too were being supplied through Wajcenberg and through another man, whom Charlie was soon to meet, and who was to have a major impact on his life.

Nevertheless, he found enough outlets for his Italian goods. One of these was Alf Berman, a flamboyant character given to the good life and sudden tantrums, who ran a large, successful, legitimate wholesale business in Rotherhithe. Despite his inexperience, and the uncertainty about who was who in this new area of activity, Charlie muddled through with dogged persistence. Towards the end of 1962, he and his partners had managed to fill the Mitre Street warehouse with the goods that had been ordered and only partly paid for, or not paid for at all. Many of the suppliers were pressing for payment and it was decided that the time had come for the coup.

They sold off all their stock. Then, instead of disappearing without trace, as in the traditional long firm fraud, they decided to try a variation: they would set fire to the warehouse and get the front men to tell the manufacturers that all the goods had gone up in flames, that because the company had not been insured there was no money for them. In the meantime, they would get the men to try and claim insurance. The plan was hatched. An explosives expert, who himself had money in the company and who was a friend of Charlie, soaked the inside of the warehouse with petrol, closed every window in the building except a small one in the semi-basement, and locked the front door. A few hours later, when the petrol had filled the building with highly inflammable, explosive fumes, he returned. It was an ideal time. The City was deserted. There was minimum risk of people being injured, or of his being spotted. The man and his assistant parked their Mini car near Aldgate and walked into Mitre Street. There was not a soul around. But as they approached the building, the man's jaw dropped. In the doorway was a courting couple. They had to wait for what seemed an age. Eventually the couple left. The men got into their car and drove to within a few yards of the warehouse. The assistant got out and walked up to the building. He lit a standard Guy Fawkes rocket and aimed it at the semi-basement window. As rockets do, the thing went all over the place. But a second rocket found its mark. The blast was enormous. As the assistant tried to scramble back into the car, it was blown down the road. He lost most of his hair and his clothes were badly singed.

The petrol fumes had had so long to develop that the explosion and fire were far greater than planned. As the inferno ripped through the building, a gas main went up in a gigantic secondary explosion. A metal grill on one of the windows of the building was shot across the road, crashing right through the windows of the off-licence opposite. The whole street seemed to erupt. The floors of a factory further down the road collapsed, all the machinery crashing down in a pile of rubble. By the time the fire had been brought under control by twenty-seven fire engines, the street looked like a bomb site. Roads were sealed off and news of the fire was carried on the television news that night. Even the man who had done the job felt amazed as he watched the report. The large wooden doors of a building opposite had scorch marks nearly half an inch deep. Every window in nearby buildings had been blown out. A street lamp had simply buckled into the shape of a question mark in the heat.

This wasn't the only question mark left hanging over the scene. The fire brigade report stated that the circumstances were most suspicious. Damage was put at hundreds of thousands of pounds.

But still, Charlie's first long firm had been a success – one of his former partners reckons a quarter of a million was made out of it. And while it had been moving towards its dramatic end, other changes had been taking place. With Charlie distracted so much by wholesaling and the long firms, Jean Goodman, much to Eddie's annoyance, had been taking over more of the responsibility of the scrapyards. She had started to live in a room at Peckfords that had been turned into a little flat. Margaret, Charlie's wife, could take no more and in September 1962 she walked out, taking the two youngest children. The day after she left, Charlie turned up at her mother's house and took the two children back. He never saw Margaret again.

Jean immediately moved into a new detached house that Charlie had just bought and started looking after the five children as well as helping run the scrap business. The new house was in Acland Crescent in Denmark Hill, just south of Camberwell. It was not a rich area, but it was respectable.

Charlie also decided to open up Addington Square again. A friend of his and Eddie's took the lease, and the premises became another part of Charlie's expanding wholesaling activities. Many of his local wholesaling deals were very profitable. For example, in the course of one transaction he bought a vast quantity of tins of Johnson's furniture polish. The tins had faulty lids, and Charlie was able to buy the vast lot as scrap, for virtually nothing. But instead of removing the polish and then selling off the metal, as he should have done, Charlie disposed of the tens of thousands of tins of polish through the street markets. He reckons he made about £15,000 out of the deal.

During the autumn of 1962, before the Mitre Street fire, Charlie had also become reacquainted with Brian Mottram, the old school pal with whom he had engaged in the daring raids on lorries between Camberwell and Vauxhall. The pair, who had not seen each other for about ten years, got chatting. Mottram then joined in the Mitre Street company, and soon found himself running a long firm in Catford. The firm pulled off a deal involving 70,000 Schick razors. But Mottram had a row with some of the other men involved after the premises, like those at Mitre Street, had been burnt down. Charlie was also cross with Mottram because he had argued over the ending of Mitre Street. Mottram moved the firm to a new base near Charlton football ground, taking with him some of the men from Catford. But he hadn't been there long when Charlie and Eddie turned up looking for Mottram and one of his men who, Charlie reckoned, had tried to pull a fast one.

'We come to give him a whack,' Charlie informed Mottram.

'You can't do that in here,' said Mottram. 'If you want to give him a whack, whack him somewhere else, don't whack him here.'

Charlie, Eddie and another man with them called Jimmy paid no attention. They set about the man with Indian clubs. Mottram, a big strong fellow who had little fear of the Richardsons, went to the man's rescue. He sorted out Jimmy, then started on Eddie. He was more than holding his own when Charlie crept up from behind and smashed him over his head with a club. Mottram was badly hurt, needing many stitches in his head. When he had recovered, he telephoned Charlie and warned him that if he ever turned up at the premises again he would blast him to kingdom come with his shotgun.

Charlie, for once, was unnerved. It wasn't simply that Mottram was very hard. He was also friendly with some extremely heavy men from the Surrey Docks area. In this world, what mattered was not just who you were, but who you had behind you. Charlie understood this perfectly. It was why few people would dare tackle any of his own gang. To have done so would be to risk swift retribution. So Charlie decided he would send down a couple of his tame policemen. Mottram well remembers the exchange that took place.

The detective told him: 'Either you play ball with Charlie, or we will get you some bird.'

'As far as I am concerned you can tell Charlie to go to hell,' Mottram replied.

Mottram was furious. He started terrorising Charlie and some of his henchmen. He put cannisters of lighter gas up the exhausts of their cars, causing explosions after the exhaust had heated up. It wasn't long before Charlie was on the phone.

'Come on, Brian, let's be friendly and have a meet.'

Mottram turned up with a couple of friends for the meeting at the Army and Navy pub between Addington Square and Peckfords. He had also arranged for a couple of other mates to be parked casually at the bar. They, like Mottram, were 'tooled up' – armed with guns. For the first few minutes, territorial politenesses were exchanged. Eventually, Mottram and Charlie sat down at a table.

'Give me that gun,' said Charlie. 'I'll put it on the table and then we can talk straight. What will it take to sort this out?'

'As far as I am concerned you took a right liberty and you ruined a straight business,' said Mottram. 'I want something out of it.'

'OK, Brian, nice one, you're right. We were a bit out of order. I'll give you a nice few quid and we can call it quits.'

'A nice few quid' in this case involved £3000, according to Mottram. Charlie also gave Mottram another long firm to run.

Charlie's early, somewhat amateur attempts at wholesaling frauds were soon to be radically upgraded. He was at Tommy Costello's Catford supply company, ordering goods, when he saw a noisy, fat man who spoke with a foreign accent and behaved as if he owned the place.

'Who's he?' Charlie asked Costello, stabbing his finger irritably towards the man.

'Blimey, don't you know?' said Tommy surprised. 'That's Jack Duval. You ought to meet him.'

Charlie was about to meet the man who in five years' time was to be responsible more, perhaps, than any other person for his conviction. But there was no sign of such dangers as Duval greeted Charlie like some long lost friend. Costello explained to Duval who Charlie was. Charlie listened in amazement as he learnt that Duval was the man who had flooded the English market with nylon stockings from Italy during the past eighteen months. It was Duval who was supplying people like Benny Wajcenberg.

Charlie was overwhelmed. Duval spoke several languages, and seemed to have contacts everywhere. He had the Italian manufacturers of stockings, shoes and knitwear virtually sewn up. Charlie started to realise why he had had some difficulty in selling his own supply of cheap stockings: Duval had been supplying nearly everybody in London, and had imported so many stockings into Britain that he had changed the nature of the market.

It was surprising that Charlie had in fact not already met Duval, not just because of his involvement in the stocking trade, but because Duval had run a fraudulent motor company in 1959 and 1960 in the heart of Richardson territory in Camberwell. Duval had also employed as a driver and general dogsbody a man called Bunny Bridges, a Camberwell man of dapper appearance who had drunk occasionally in the Addington club.

By the time Duval met Charlie he had already led an extraordinary life. After he and his family had escaped as Jews from Russia in 1919, he had lived in France and joined the Foreign Legion, only to desert and join up with the RAF in 1940. After the war he had stayed in Britain and developed into a great con-man under several different names. Before he came to Camberwell in 1959 Duval had owned a club at 52, Great Marlborough Street in the West End. He had also spent two years in jail for a fraud involving air tickets; and he had been sentenced for his part in a notorious case known as the Great Orange Juice Swindle. Whatever he was involved in had always made him a lot of money. But he was never able to hang on to it. He lived lavishly, and whenever he had money he used it to pay off other debts that various people were screaming for.

It was the failure of the Great Marlborough Street club that brought Duval to Camberwell. With him had come a man called Frank Prater, an equally colourful character, perhaps the only real friend Duval ever had. Prater and Duval were indispensable to each other: Prater had the brains and the understanding of the legal, business and banking worlds; Duval had the 'front' to put everything into action. He was the kind of man who could be summoned to a bank to be carpeted by the manager over his overdraft and leave three minutes later with another £2000 facility, the manager all smiles and helpfulness. The Camberwell car operation lasted for nearly eighteen months. By the time the finance company realised that something was very wrong, Duval had fiddled thousands and was declared bankrupt for £24,000.

This kind of disaster was not the kind of thing to worry a man like Jack Duval. He merely moved on to the next con – this time a travel agency called Denbus Travel in Westbourne Grove. He moved in the same way from wife to wife: when he got fed up with any particular wife, he would marry her off to a friend and take up residence with the next female.

A year and a half before Charlie met Duval, Frank Prater

1. Charlie in 1950, aged sixteen, with his mother Eileen outside the family shop.

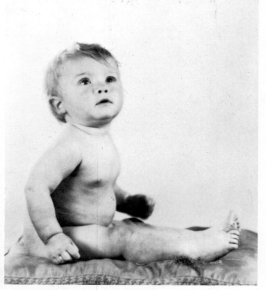

2. Charlie on his first birthday.

3. Charlie (centre) aged eleven, with Alan (left), aged five, and Eddie, aged nine.

4. Charlie's marriage to Margaret in Camberwell, 1 January 1955. Arthur Baron and his wife are on the far left; Charlie's mother is fifth from the left, with his sister Elaine clutching Eileen's handbag; Eddie, with Alan just in front of him, is standing beside Charlie; Eddie's future wife, Maureen, is beside Margaret.

5. Eddie's wedding to Maureen. Charlie and his mother are on the left.

6. The family shop in Wyndham Road. The picture shows Eddie and Maureen, Alan, Eileen and Elaine, and, in the doorway, Charlie's grandparents.

7. The centre of Charlie's scrap empire at 50, New Church Road: Peckford's yard and, to the left, its offices in the old farmhouse, today the site of a block of flats.

had seen an advertisement in one of London's evening papers for agents to sell Italian stockings in Britain. Prater and Duval saw a golden opportunity. A tiny office was hired in an impressive-looking block called Abbey House in Victoria, and the Italian agents were contacted. They came across to see the pair and were met in the smart foyer of Abbey House. The Italians did not get as far as the grubby little box-room of an office that the couple had hired. Instead, they were taken out to an expensive lunch. By the conclusion of the lunch it had been agreed that the agents would send 10,000 dozen pairs of nylons to London. When they arrived a few days later at Heathrow airport, Duval did not even have the money to pay the duty to get them out of the warehouse. But he and Prater managed nevertheless to persuade a forwarding agent to sneak some of the stockings out. They put them in the back of the car and set off to the East End in the hope of finding a wholesaler who would be interested.

Before long, they walked into a little place in Whites Row and there met Benny Wajcenberg. Duval and Wajcenberg hit it off immediately. They both spoke German, were both Jewish, had similar war-time experiences and had lived by their wits in England since. Duval told Wajcenberg that he could supply as many stockings as he wanted at an incredibly low price. Wajcenberg paid some money down, and the rest of the stockings at Heathrow were gradually released.

It became clear to Wajcenberg, and as a result to Duval, that there was a great demand for the stockings at the price for which they were being offered. Duval, not for the first time in his life, saw what he thought was yet another million pounds staring him in the face. He decided to get out to Milan and secure further and cheaper supplies of the micromesh stockings. He took the north Italian city by storm. Within days he had the Italian manufacturers eating out of his hand. Great schemes were promised, vast sales guaranteed. Duval installed himself in great style in the Caveleiri Hotel and entertained the Italians to vast banquets. His friend Bunny Bridges remembers an occasion when Duval received a party of millionaire businessmen while lying in his bath and sipping champagne.

Soon vast quantities of stockings were being freighted to England. Frank Prater estimates that over a million pairs were imported. Everything was paid for on sixty- and ninety-day bills of exchange – meaning that no payment was made until the agreed period was up. This didn't seem to bother the Italians – it was an offence in Italy for anyone to issue a cheque unless they had the funds to meet it. And anyway, Duval was so convincing. Yet Duval was selling off the stockings for around ten shillings a dozen, five shillings less than he was buying them from the Italians. He sent over to Milan a man called Lucien Harris, who had worked for Denbus, and hired a secretary called Dominique Henman.

During this period of late 1961 and early 1962 Duval also acquired a travel agency called Personal Travel with the money he was getting from the stockings. He moved the business from New Bond Street to one of his main bases, Salters Hall in Cannon Street in the City. The great attraction of Personal Travel was that it had an IATA rating, which meant that large quantities of airline tickets could be ordered in advance on credit, with no need for payment until after they had been sold. Duval started selling off tickets in large quantities at such reduced rates that there were plenty of takers. It didn't matter to Duval that he would eventually be required to pay the airlines. He would sort that problem out when it arose. For the moment, he was able to raise money with which to meet some of the pressing demands of the Italian stocking manufacturers. He had to pay them something, after all, so that he could place more orders to meet the voracious demand in London for the stockings.

But Personal Travel was to be the vehicle for a far more incredible fraud than simply selling off underpriced tickets. The fraud was based on the now extinct system by which a businessman who didn't know exactly where he would be travelling, or what he might want to bring back with him, could buy an excess baggage ticket. All he would do initially was pay for the fare to his first destination. He would then use his excess ticket, almost like travellers' cheques, to fly on to wherever else he wanted. The various extra journeys would be marked up on the excess ticket which was presented to the travel agent on return to Britain. It would then be put through the airline, who would send a bill for payment.

Duval, having picked Prater's brains, managed to exploit this system in such a way that they could put a large number of passengers on one excess ticket. As a result of what happened at Personal Travel, and at the Argosy Travel company which the two men also acquired at this time, the system has been long since stopped. But in the meantime, the pair made vast sums of money – the airlines calculated that they lost almost £300,000 – by bringing thousands of Pakistanis into Britain on the excess ticket fiddle. They teamed up with a Birmingham Asian businessman and later claimed they put more Asians into Enoch Powell's former Wolverhampton constituency than anyone else.

It was while so much money was being made from Personal Travel and the Italian imports that Prater and Duval met a twenty-two-stone man called Alex Herbage. He was an unusual character who had his own bank. It had two branches, one in Bournemouth and the other in Shaftesbury Avenue, London. It was, however, in difficulties. Herbage had debts of around £30,000 and no obvious way of paying creditors. Prater suggested to Duval that he should approach Herbage and offer to take over his debts and the bank. This is exactly what happened. Suddenly Duval, the man who had fleeced more banks and kited more cheques than probably any man in London, had his very own bank. Herbage was kept on there, but it was Duval who really ran it. He gasped when he even thought of the potential. The main thing, of course, was that he could issue irrevocable bills of exchange to the Italian manufacturers who wouldn't have the faintest idea that Duval was connected with the bank, which became known as the Bank of Valletta.

With thousands of pounds flowing into the bank every day from the Personal Travel fraud, and flowing out to pay for part, at least, of the larger and larger orders from the Italians, the bank became the pivotal centre for Duval's monstrous frauds. He was in his element ordering bigger and bigger quantities of tickets and stockings, just paying enough in time to be able to persuade people to provide more of whatever commodity he wanted.

It wasn't long, however, before Prater and Duval nearly had their heads blown off. This time it was Prater's fault. He had imported a consignment of shoes and stockings for his own company, Swiss Straps. He had sent out a Bank of Valletta cheque thinking that he had more than enough funds in his account. Little did he know that Duval had not put the money into the account in the way he had claimed. Unfortunately, the company which had supplied Prater with the goods was a Mafia-controlled organisation. He, Duval and the twenty-two-stone former owner of the Bank of Valletta were upstairs in the office when the three Italian gentlemen burst in. One of them pointed a revolver at Prater.

'You have ruined me,' he said. 'I have no reason left for you living. You will die.'

Herbage, despite his size, dived under the desk. Duval bolted out of the room like a frightened rabbit, spluttering something about getting the money – about £5000. Prater managed to command greater control of himself and the situation.

'I was in Italy for three years during the war and 20 million of your people tried to kill me,' he announced to the astonished gunman. 'And so you want to be a hero, do you?'

'But you have ruined me and my business,' protested the man as Herbage shifted nervously under the desk. The two Mafia men looked twitchy.

'Look,' said Prater sensibly, 'let's calm down, shall we? We had advance warning of your visit, and if you look outside you will see that the place is surrounded.'

By sheer chance a group of men were standing around outside. The Italians seemed convinced that they were the police.

'If you do anything silly you'll never get back to Italy,' Prater reasoned with the gunmen. 'Let's go down to the counter and see what we can do.'

It was just as well that Duval came running in through the front door clutching £100 as Prater and the Italians arrived at the foyer. There was no money in the bank that day. He had got it from one of the neighbouring shops by writing out a cheque for £120.

'Take this,' said Duval, thrusting the money into the leader's hands. 'At least that will pay your expenses.'

Prater added: 'If you re-present the cheque, I guarantee it will be met.'

They did, a few days later. But it was never honoured.

Duval soon got over the incident and returned to Italy. He now had a permanent suite in the Cavelieri Hotel and continued in his flamboyant lifestyle. He also started a branch of Personal Travel in Milan, operating the same gigantic swindle with air tickets as he had in London. He regularly invited his London friends across on free tickets. When they arrived, all without exception were amazed at Duval's luxurious lifestyle. He lavished money on women, made regular gambling trips to Switzerland, didn't drink much but ate vast quantities of food. He was sufficiently vain to feel concern about his ever increasing weight. Dieting, however, was not for Jack Duval. He decided to have an operation to have fat removed from his stomach and called Frank Prater over – again on free tickets – to hold his hand. The operation took place on a Friday in Milan. It left a scar like an inverted cross. And with this chunk of flesh removed, Jack Duval was trimmed down and ready for his next mission. . . .

7. On the Firm

When Tommy Costello introduced Jack Duval to Charlie
Richardson, Duval was just about at the height of his complicated web of frauds involving the Italian stockings, the
Bank of Valletta and the air tickets. Charlie made his mind
up on that first meeting to get involved with him. He seemed
to Charlie to live in another world. Here were sophisticated
men who spoke foreign languages, had their own banks, who
seemed to know people everywhere and even had free air
tickets with which to visit them. It wasn't often that Charlie
felt in awe of anybody, but this meeting was one of those
occasions. Jack, he decided, would help him get into
wholesaling and fraud in a really big way. Charlie asked him
for a further meeting.

'Of course,' said Duval benignly. 'Why don't you come
around to my flat in Dolphin Square?' Duval was as
interested in the potential of Charlie and his money as
Charlie was in Jack.

Charlie turned up at the flat – not actually owned by
Duval – with a couple of his mates, determined to pull off a
deal with Duval. But Duval had other plans. He had asked
Frank Prater along and decided to throw a tantrum at
Prater's expense. It was all new ground for Charlie, who had
become accustomed to his presence having, if not an
intimidating effect, then one which produced respect. He
smiled coolly as Duval flew into an emotional rage with
Prater, complaining about the way the Italian operation was
going. It ended with Duval banging a glass coffee table with
his hand so hard – to emphasise the point he was making –
that the table shattered.

After Prater left, Duval and Charlie talked. Duval agreed
that he would send supplies across to Charlie on his next

trip. He said that his Denbus wholesaling company at Cannon Street was now running into a few difficulties and that he was thinking of setting up a completely new company to do the buying from Italy.

'Perhaps you would like to put some money up and come in as a director?' Duval asked Charlie.

Charlie agreed, but as he left the flat he felt uneasy. The meeting had not been what he expected. Duval was flattering and full of ideas. But it appeared to Charlie that Duval would be difficult to control, unpredictable. And that wasn't the way Charlie liked working: he had always been used to total control. Charlie decided this would have to be corrected. He called on his explosives friend and explained the situation. He wanted to put a small bomb outside Duval's flat – just enough to scare the wits out of him and bring him in line. Charlie had guessed correctly that Duval was not a brave man. Nor was he used to violence.

Charlie's man was not too happy. He was still concerned about the Mitre Street fire which he had organised. Police investigations had come perilously close. Now he was to blow up a flat in a large and prestigious block, where MPs and other well-known people stayed. There was a terrible risk that others might get killed or seriously injured. No amount of payment would stop the police if that had happened.

The man waited until Duval had left the flat. He entered the block and made his way to Duval's corridor. He placed a five-pound charge of gelignite right outside Duval's door. Had such a charge gone off in such a confined space, it would have caused considerable damage, and, no doubt, death and injury. To blow in Duval's flat, all he needed was about four ounces of the explosive, he says today. But the man had no intention of causing an explosion. He wanted to make it appear that he had tried to blow up the flat, but that it had gone wrong. When he placed the bomb, he took the fuse in his hands and snapped it almost in half. Then he lit the fuse and ran off. By the time the flame reached the place where the fuse lead had nearly been broken, it petered out, as the man knew it would.

Duval was terrified when he found out about the bomb. But his problems were only just beginning. In February 1963, the goings on at the Bank of Valletta started to hit the headlines, and three airlines, Pan Am, BOAC and TWA, had begun to discover what had been happening at Personal Travel. On Sunday, 3 February the *People* newspaper carried a sensational report by Roy East. It stated:

> A man who, five days ago, resigned as chairman of a London bank, last night offered to help Scotland Yard in its inquiries into a £500,000 fraud plot. He is 33-year-old Mr Alex Herbage, of the Merchant Guaranty Bank, and former chairman of the Bank of Valletta.
>
> The frauds involved forgery of cheques and drafts drawn on the Bank of Valletta and of bills of exchange purported to have been backed by the bank.
>
> These documents were used by a London gang to obtain vast quantities of merchandise from several foreign countries.
>
> Now the foreign businessmen have discovered that the documents were false. Their losses have been gigantic.

Herbage was quoted as saying: 'Things went on in connection with bills of exchange, bankers' drafts and cheques issued on the Bank of Valletta while I was in charge, which have horrified me. I have not the faintest doubt that I am in greater danger now that I have decided to assist the police. I am going into hiding.'

A Fraud Squad detective was also quoted: 'This is the most far-reaching plan for large-scale fraud we have ever had to probe.'

Further newspaper reports followed. Some mentioned 'recent bomb incidents' and 'confrontations with the Mafia'. And it was only a few days after the revelations about the bank that reports also started to appear about the police looking into a connection between the bank and a £300,000 air ticket swindle. . . .

Duval was now in real trouble. He couldn't even turn to Frank Prater to get him out of difficulty as he so often had done in the past. Prater was just coming to trial over a fraud he had been connected with the previous summer involving a casino racket. Thousands of posters were put up all over the country promising a £5-a-week return on every £100 invested – in other words, a 250-per-cent annual interest rate. The scheme attracted many investors – including a top airline pilot who put in thousands. They were never paid. Thousands of people lost hundreds of pounds. The *News of the World* exposed the fraud in the autumn of 1962. They referred to the man behind the scheme as having disappeared to Milan. Prater and the others were brought to trial in March 1963 and he was sentenced to three years in prison. On top of this, Duval was declared an undischarged bankrupt in March 1963 over his West End club in Great Marlborough Street and his Camberwell car company with its subsidiary in the New Kent Road, which had finally caught up with him.

Duval did what Charlie perhaps would have done in such a tight situation – he ran. He went to Milan where, despite his dire circumstances, he set himself up in a palatial flat. Through an accountant and solicitor he reorganised the Denbus company into Lyons Continental and based it at Salters Hall, Cannon Street, in the City of London. Charlie became a director of this company and put some money in to finance Duval's ordering of fresh supplies of stockings. Duval was quickly back to his old tricks. He now had a new company with which to buy the Italian goods, and some fresh money – from Charlie – with which to pay off the most pressing debts. He also still had his various outlets for stockings. So he started to trade again. The air tickets fiddle in Milan had not yet been affected by the troubles of the Bank of Valletta and Personal Travel in London. He was to send over about £20,000-worth of air tickets from Milan during this period.

Back in London, Charlie was preparing for his supply of stockings from Duval. He lined up several buyers. When he heard that Benny Wajcenberg, the man who had originally sold him Duval's stockings, was closing down his premises, he took John Bradbury along to meet him. Wajcenberg agreed to allow Bradbury to sub-let the premises. Charlie set up a company called Park Lane Galleries for Bradbury to run for him from Whites Row. Wajcenberg introduced Bradbury to his bank manager and went off for six weeks' holiday. When he came back, he discovered that the landlords were furious. They hadn't given permission for the sub-letting and there had been no rent from the new tenant. Wajcenberg sorted it out, and Park Lane Galleries, trading in stockings and other wholesale goods, was moved to new offices near Waterloo Station.

Wajcenberg then had a visit from Charlie, his father and Johnnie Longman. With them came Enrico Manyanni, a Milan stockings agent from whom Duval had bought thousands of stockings. Charlie wanted to know the name and address of a firm which owed Manyanni money. He thought that collecting the debt would be a good way of getting in with the Italians. Wajcenberg supplied the name and address of the firm, and Charlie went round to see them. After abuse and threats he came away with two cheques, then returned to Wajcenberg's. He persuaded Wajcenberg to pay Manyanni, and Charlie, having taken £200 commission on the £1200 debt, gave Wajcenberg the cheques he had collected. Far from being impressed, Enrico Manyanni told a friend later that he thought Charlie was a madman.

With his organisation now prepared, Charlie received his first consignment of stockings from Duval in Milan. There were a lot of seconds among the batch, but, Charlie was told, that was to be expected. The second consignment arrived soon after, and it seemed to Charlie that things were now really getting under way. But then, suddenly, the supply dried up. Charlie had not been paying for the thousands of pairs he had already received. Duval had been using Charlie's initial investment to pay off earlier debts, as well as pay for some of the stockings he was purchasing for Charlie and other people. He was having difficulty in getting more supplies.

Eddie and a couple of others went out to Milan to see what was happening. Free tickets were sent across to him by

106

Duval. Like previous visitors to Duval, they were amazed at the lifestyle and his regular trips to the gambling casinos just the other side of the Swiss border – an hour's drive from Milan. It was on the return from a gambling expedition in Lugarno on the Swiss border that Eddie flared up with Duval. Eddie, always much more cautious than Charlie, reckoned Duval was a con-man, and didn't trust him. On this particular night, Eddie suspected Duval had taken them up to Lugarno only to use them as cover to bring back diamonds from Switzerland. Eddie stopped the car, searched it, got hold of Duval and shook him about, threatening to half-kill him if he ever did anything similar again. Duval shrugged the incident off. He also managed to placate Charlie about the supply of stockings by promising that supplies would start again.

But Eddie had been right about Duval and the diamonds. Jack had become involved with the Mafia in a scheme to defraud a Swiss jeweller. The local Mafia don had put up money for Jack to open an account in a local bank. Jack then told the jeweller, who was based in Lucerne, that he was a dealer. He bought small quantities of jewels from him, paying by cheques against the Mafia money in his account. He was operating a variation on the long firm fraud technique. By the time Duval had finished, the poor Lucerne jeweller was £50,000 worse off.

Duval's dangerous lifestyle became even more perilous shortly after the visit of Eddie and his party. He was paid a visit by the Kray twins, Ronnie and Reggie, who by this time had established themselves as the top gangsters of the East End of London. The twins, whose information had always been very good, and who were also, like Charlie, taking a great interest in long firm frauds, had heard about Duval. They had turned up earlier at the Cannon Street offices of his dubious empire where they found Lucien Harris, the well-spoken and mild-mannered man who had worked with Duval throughout. As well as being associated with Duval, Harris was a compiler of crosswords for various newspapers.

The Kray twins, like the Richardsons, were not the kind of people to mince their words. They told Harris that they had decided to take over the company. They were particularly interested, Harris recalls, because the Krays thought the company had a bogus purchase tax number. This meant that the 25 per cent purchase tax didn't have to be paid on the goods before they were brought in by the wholesaler. Harris, with considerable presence of mind, told them bluntly that they had got it all wrong. The company was dead and there was no purchase tax number.

The Krays seemed satisfied and went away, only to turn up at Duval's headquarters in Milan. As well as being interested in stockings, they told him they wanted to buy art treasures and paintings stolen from churches. Duval, not the slightest bit frightened, saw an opportunity for a deal. He was always at his best when confronted with men who had insatiable greed. Anyone with the desire to make a fast and dishonest buck was good news for Duval. But, he had little idea what a good painting was. He got hold of some ghastly daubs and displayed them in an old shed in the back streets of Milan. Even the Krays could see they were rubbish and they left muttering dark oaths.

Duval was perhaps lucky to get away so lightly for trying to con the Krays. But his luck was soon to run out altogether. It was time for some chickens to come home to roost.

For nearly two years, Duval had been operating a series of frauds at an extraordinary level. He had got himself so involved that one thing had led to another. He had had to start up some new scheme to generate immediate money to pay off huge debts left by the manner in which he had run a previous scheme. Already the London police and the airlines were on the trail of his tickets and Bank of Valletta operation. There were dozens of manufacturers in northern Italy who had fallen again for the evil charms of the Duval technique. And Charlie, back in London, was getting angry that none of the newly promised stockings had started to arrive.

But it was the Mafia who first caught up with Duval. Foolishly, he had not paid them the £20,000 they considered their share of the jewel fraud in Switzerland. Duval was just

108

climbing into his marble bathroom when the Mafia burst into his flat. Duval told them he hadn't got a penny. Under the pretence of ringing around to see if he could raise money, he arranged with a manufacturer friend of his to be waiting outside his flat at 2am the next morning. The Mafia decided to hold him in his flat for the time being and left two people there to guard him. Duval plied them with wine and with all the charm and flattery he could muster in his broken Italian, reassuring them that everything would be all right. By 2am the guards were asleep. Duval packed two cases and lowered himself out of the window. He borrowed the manufacturer's car and drove through the night to Basle.

By first light, the seriousness of his position had begun to dawn on Duval. For just about the first time in his life he felt something vaguely akin to worry. This time, he had nowhere to run. The Mafia were after him, the Swiss Police were after him, the British police were after him, and of course there was Charlie. Duval understood the nature of Charlie pretty well by now: he had found out about the bomb, and heard of other people getting beaten. Duval had a fair idea of what Charlie would do to him when they next met. He decided to make for Brussels and lie low.

Duval had been right. Charlie was hopping mad about his disappearance. This was not the way that Charlie had planned events. Duval should have been the key to his own massive string of frauds. Instead, he had had nothing but trouble from the man. Charlie called everyone who might know where Duval was. None of them had any idea. They understood Duval better than Charlie did, and guessed what must have happened.

Charlie forged ahead on his own with his various wholesaling enterprises. But Eddie was becoming more and more unhappy with the way things were going. He did not share Charlie's faith in the new breed of men who were coming into their lives. Charlie was ready to rush into anything that sounded good; he was always confident that he could impress himself on the situation and take control. Eddie, on the other hand, had a deep-seated suspicion of anything new. Of the two brothers, Charlie was perhaps more thrusting and imaginative, but Eddie's instincts were far superior.

Eddie's disenchantment with Jean Goodman at the scrapyard had also worsened. The close-knit, inward-looking world in which the scrapyards and clubs had developed now seemed to be breaking apart, as Charlie looked to greater things. Eddie decided at last that he would try and make it on his own. Charlie tried to stop him leaving, without success – but there was no animosity. It was decided that in future they should work in loose association rather than together.

Eddie first tried working at the races with a couple of bookmaker friends. He came into contact with some of the bigger names from the West End, but he found that he could not make anything like the kind of money to which he had long-since grown accustomed. So he set up his own wholesale business with the friend who had been running the premises at Addington Square for the past few months. Eddie and his new-found partner acquired large premises in Deptford High Street and set up a wholesale and retail business called Revvon. It was a large walk-around supermarket selling to the public and to the trade. It soon started doing well.

Not long after Eddie left, Charlie managed to bring Roy Hall back to work in the yards. While he had been away, Hall had worked in Covent Garden fruit market, and as a lorry driver. With Addington Square again unused, Charlie brought John Bradbury over from Park Lane Galleries to set up a new company. It was called Bradbury Trading – Charlie not, of course, being connected with it in any way on paper – and it was soon to become one of the centres of his wholesaling and long firm enterprises.

Very quickly the new company was immersed in a large fiddle involving transistor radios. Bradbury started ordering thousands of them from various manufacturers. Charlie also managed to interest Benny Wajcenberg in the scheme. The Pole had his own purchase tax number which Charlie wanted to use so that when Bradbury Trading ordered the radios it need not pay the 25-per-cent tax to the manufacturers. Since the company had its 'own' purchase tax number, it was supposed to pay the 25 per cent itself. This naturally did not happen. The result was that Bradbury Trading could sell the radios to the market traders and their suppliers at a cheaper rate than anyone else, but still have a greater profit margin than other, more honest suppliers.

During this period, in the middle of 1963, Charlie also pulled off a typical scrap deal. He tendered successfully for a 2 million lot of Christmas cards which the manufacturers wanted to jettison because their design was too out of date. The cards were bought for a pittance. Charlie employed a handful of girls to box them up in premises just behind Addington Square in Caldew Street. He sold them all to various suppliers, managing to make a lot out of the deal.

Life had not been going so well, however, for Duval, whom Charlie still wanted to see. He had got up to all his old tricks while in hiding in Europe. Having nearly been caught several times, in the end he decided to chance his arm again in London. He rang up Tommy Costello, describing his plight and incredible near-escapes. Costello felt sorry for him and agreed to have him to stay. He took him down to Brighton for a day out one Sunday. They went to a club called the Jokers. But Duval's noisy, boastful manner annoyed three men nearby. They chucked their beer over him and there followed a fight in which Duval was badly hurt. Costello had tried to help Duval, but Duval had simply run out, leaving Costello to fend for himself. As a result, Costello told him to leave his house. Duval went to stay in Brighton with his old friend Bunny Bridges in a bungalow he was borrowing, and together they planned to set up another long firm.

But Charlie heard about the fight at the Jokers club from Costello who, not realising that Charlie was after Duval, also told Charlie where Duval was staying. Charlie picked up the phone and called the Brighton number. He was perfectly friendly towards Duval, asking how he had been getting on and listening to Duval's account of his problems and his many escapes from the people who were after him.

'Nice one, nice one,' Charlie kept repeating as he listened to Duval's various stories.

'Now what about our little bit of business, Jack?' Charlie asked towards the end of the conversation. 'Why don't we have a meet at the yard tomorrow and we can get something going again.'

Both men knew that this wasn't so much an invitation as an order. And it occurred to Duval that Charlie might be just the source of money he needed to get going again.

Next afternoon Duval set off for Peckfords from Bridges' flat in Sidcup. Charlie had planned the meeting carefully. He arranged for Eddie and Bradbury to be waiting for Duval when he arrived. Charlie was too busy to see him yet, he was told. Both men took Duval round the corner to Bradbury Trading in 33a, Addington Square, it was explained later in court. Bradbury held the poor fat Duval while Eddie punched him a couple of times in the face and stomach. He went down on the ground and Bradbury set about him. Duval lost a tooth which he had had expensively crowned in Milan. As south London beatings went, it was very mild.

When Eddie and Bradbury took Duval back to Peckfords, Charlie was with Benny Wajcenberg, with whom he had been discussing transistor radio deals. Charlie had especially asked Wajcenberg to stay. 'Have a cup of tea. A friend of yours will be here soon, you might as well wait.' Eddie and Bradbury opened the door and wheeled Duval in. He had red eyes and a bruised face, he had blood over his shirt and was crying.

'Why aren't you a good boy?' Charlie asked Duval. 'Why don't you behave yourself? Why do you put people in prison?' he asked, referring to somebody whom Charlie heard had received a twelve-month sentence through Duval. 'Can't you work properly? Must you put people behind bars?'

Charlie was more reproachful than angry. Eddie having done the dirty work, Charlie was now going to be the nice

112

guy. He still had great plans for Duval. But the man had to be taught that nobody messes Charlie Richardson around. If you work for Charlie, you do exactly what you are told, or take the consequences.

Charlie gave Duval a drink and suggested that he have a wash. He then took him out with Wajcenberg and bought him a new shirt, then to the local chemist, well known in Camberwell for being better than most doctors in the neighbourhood. When Duval emerged, he had been patched and bandaged up. Charlie took him back to his office, apologised and explained to Duval that he shouldn't have run him around like he had in Milan. They talked about various business ideas. Charlie told him to find somewhere to stay.

'Here's some money,' he said, giving him a bundle of notes. 'Have a rest over a couple of days and come down here next Monday.'

Duval, for once not having been able to talk and charm his way out of trouble, was now well and truly on the Richardson firm. Whether he liked it or not.

8. Jack the Chequeman

Wajcenberg – Benny the Borrower as he was known – drove his friend Duval to the White House near Regents Park after his beating. Duval booked himself into a single-bedroom flat and went to bed to nurse his wounds. He felt bad, but not bad enough to call a doctor. He had, after all, been treated by the renowned Camberwell chemist. What worried him most as he lay in his bed talking to Wajcenberg was that he had nowhere to turn. If only Frank Prater was around he could have discussed things with him. He had always come up with some new-fangled scheme in the past. He had usually managed to get him out of trouble. Both men mused over the possibilities. They knew Charlie quite well by now. Neither man liked him, but they felt that he was a bit of a mug who could be used. He had the money, and, most importantly, the greed. They would have to watch the violence, though; Charlie could not be fobbed off like so many of Duval's other victims. Duval decided that he would turn up at Charlie's as arranged and see how things developed. Perhaps he would be able to interest him in a new project.

The first few days, he merely hung around Peckfords discussing various ideas. Charlie was friendly but careful. 'You toe the line, Jack, and everything will be all right,' he told him several times. Charlie was keen to impress upon Duval the fact he was not to be taken for a fool again. Above all, Charlie was determined to be able to use Duval for his expanding wholesaling empire. For the time being, Charlie put Duval in Park Lane Galleries.

In fact, Charlie had very ambitious plans. These he confided one night to Roy Hall. 'I want to have the biggest supermarket business in the country,' he revealed. Charlie never did things in half measures. His experiences in the wholesale business had, despite the problems, filled him with grandiose ideas. He had Eddie with his shop over in Deptford High Street. There was Bradbury running the place in Addington Square. Park Lane Galleries was ticking over. Charlie had also got to know the main wholesalers and retailers on the south London scene. Above all, he had Duval working for him. He, Charlie thought, would be able to supply vast amounts of goods from foreign suppliers. Huge profits could be made. The potential for expansion seemed endless.

In the particular circumstances, Charlie and Duval suited each other perfectly. They got talking and decided to set up a new company for importing European goods. Duval would change his name to Longman, using the false passport he had had with him during his escape. He could buy all manner of merchandise, he said. This time he would try Germany. His German was excellent and he was not known to the manufacturers there. Both men got more and more excited about their plans. This was just the kind of talk that Charlie had wanted to hear on that first full meeting in Dolphin Square. Duval was now working entirely for him; there would be no repeat of the kind of trouble there had been before. Charlie was pleased when Duval suggested that they base the new company at his headquarters in Cannon Street. 'Nice City address,' Charlie thought to himself, feeling that Duval really had come over to him now. A few months before, Charlie had bought a company called the Northlands Street Traders. It was decided to use this for the operation, renamed Common Market Merchants. It was a very good name.

Charlie naturally wanted to use Duval as the main buyer. Duval suggested that Wajcenberg should come into the deal as well, and Charlie agreed. Benny, he knew from his dealings with him already, was no mean operator. Finally, they would need some money invested in the company. This was settled when Charlie interested a magistrate from south London, whom he had befriended. Charlie's ability to lead a double life, one as underworld villain, the other as the charming, clever scrap dealer making good, had been increasing all the time.

It was precisely this characteristic which had also helped him to bring into Peckfords a man called Ken Nicholson, a relative of one of Charlie's businessman friends. A former owner of a small engineering company, he was a well-spoken educated man who Charlie thought would be very useful in providing a respectable front for some of his exploits. In fact, Nicholson was slightly burnt out. He had a drink problem which annoyed Charlie, especially when Nicholson stole Charlie's own scotch, which he did once too often. Charlie laced a bottle with a powerful drug. The next morning the cleaning lady discovered Nicholson unconscious on the office floor. Half dead, he was rushed to hospital. He never nicked any of Charlie's scotch again.

Nicholson came to be known at the yard as 'Rednose'. Some of the lads thought he was a 'right toffee-nosed git'. But they tolerated him because of Charlie who, after all, knew what he was up to. They couldn't *understand* what he was doing; but such was their faith and admiration for the guv'nor that they didn't question his decisions.

Nicholson helped with the formation of the new company Duval and Charlie had agreed on. By November 1963, the stage was almost set. Duval had come up with a complex arrangement for evading purchase tax on a scale even bigger than was normally possible. Wajcenberg would provide his own purchase tax number; but they would need another if the scheme were to work in a foolproof way. Charlie, Duval and Wajcenberg therefore turned up at Tommy Costello's, and outlined what they had in mind. They asked for the use of his purchase tax number. But Costello refused. He knew Duval and Wajcenberg only too well; their latest plot would almost certainly end in trouble and he didn't want to be involved. Charlie was furious.

In this mood, a few days later Charlie had an extraordinary row with Wajcenberg. It was about the commission which the Pole expected on all the transistor radio transactions he had been arranging for Charlie and the Bradbury Trading company during the previous few months. He

116

turned up at Peckfords one day in December 1963 hoping to collect some money. A row developed. Charlie accused Wajcenberg of ratting on him to a policeman friend of his in the City. Then he decided that Wajcenberg owed him money – to be precise, £5000, according to court evidence. He accused Wajcenberg of going behind Bradbury's back with his purchase tax number and of trying to get Bradbury into trouble. Wajcenberg protested his innocence and appealed to Nicholson, who was present with Duval and a couple of others, to check the books. This was done. The books apparently showed that Wajcenberg indeed owed no money. But Charlie felt convinced he was being taken on again by the smart men. He stood up across his desk and grabbed Wajcenberg by the lapels. He shook him hard and threatened him violently, demanding all the money. Wajcenberg, having already seen what happened to Duval, didn't equivocate. He made some telephone calls and went off and borrowed over £1000 from a business contact known as 'Tolla'. Later that evening he borrowed some more money from another friend called Stander and handed the money over to Johnnie Longman, who had followed him.

Wajcenberg left the country next morning and spent Christmas in Munich before going on to stay with relations of his wife in Austria who were building an hotel at Lake Verdun. Such was his fear of Charlie that he didn't dare return to England until he had Charlie's clearance to do so. He rang him up (reversing the charges, which infuriated Charlie) and wrote to him, and only after Duval promised that Charlie had no evil intentions towards him did he come back, in February 1964, and work again in Common Markets.

Some strange latent paranoid force seemed to be stirring in Charlie. He had a remarkable capacity for twisting the facts when problems arose in his wild schemes, and for convincing himself that they were somebody else's fault. That person would then have to be sorted out and taught that nobody, but nobody, took a liberty with Charlie Richardson. He had an extraordinary self-righteous manner when dealing out the harsh and often unfair treatment. Once he

117

had convinced himself of something, nobody would distract him from what he felt. He would go into a frenzy of crazed activity until he felt what he called justice had been done.

Such a frenzy was still raging in his mind on Christmas Day, 1963 – just a couple of days after the row with Wajcenberg – when Charlie decided to pay Tommy Costello another visit. With Roy Hall, Eddie and Johnnie Longman, Charlie turned up at the Rabbit club in Catford, where Costello was enjoying a Christmas Day drink. Charlie was looking for an excuse for a fight with Costello, who saw the signs instantly. 'I don't know what was going wrong with him,' he recalled later. 'He was a one-hundred-per-cent bloke before all this wholesaling stuff started.' As it happened, Costello had for years been friendly with Longman. They had spent many nights at the Catford Dogs together, and it was perhaps this that saved him from 'the treatment', as Charlie's violent punishments were by now becoming known. Costello managed to wriggle out of danger. As he left he told Charlie: 'Shrewd as you are, Charlie, I know Duval. You had better watch him.'

Even if the circumstances of this advice had been more favourable, Charlie would not have listened. Nobody could tell Charlie what to do these days.

Charlie didn't remember the advice even when his magistrate friend resigned from Common Market Merchants a few days later on 10 January 1964. He told Charlie that he didn't trust Duval, and that he certainly didn't like the way things appeared to be run at Cannon Street. Charlie put it down to a clash of personality between the magistrate and Duval – two very different men anyway. Secretly, he felt it was a good sign. It probably meant that Duval was getting up to his good old tricks again – but this time for Charlie.

Charlie, who had put Duval up at his home for Christmas – the kids had called him Uncle Jack – decided he would try and get Phil Wilson, a black man he knew, to put up some money in place of the magistrate. Wilson had made a name for himself in the south of London by running a very successful bingo hall called the Riverlea. All the old girls loved him. One of the reasons for his bingo's popularity was the generous raffles and prizes he gave away. Most of these were bought from the kind of wholesaling places that Charlie was now involved in. On one visit to Bradbury Trading he had been short of money, and met Charlie. 'Don't worry about it,' said Charlie, 'pay me tomorrow.' He did, and the two became chatty. Charlie, as always, was interested in anything new. Wilson ran a highly successful business and Charlie wanted to know all about it. Charlie, as he so easily could, showed his good side. Wilson, like many others, felt he was a perfectly reasonable man and a good businessman.

The day after the magistrate cleared out of Common Markets, Duval and Charlie turned up at Wilson's place. Duval did most of the talking.

'He said he had four or five business people like myself who had agreed to put up money, with no bother about returns for four or five years,' Wilson recalls. 'He said he had persuaded Charlie to put up money and that after a few years we would have a count up and open a merchant bank.'

Duval's smooth talk flowed effortlessly and convincingly. It would start with one company based in the City, and the plan was to open up a whole group of companies. Fortunes were guaranteed for everybody involved. Charlie agreed. Wilson was taken round to Cannon Street and introduced to the office manager, a man called Wade. There was a typist, and everything looked pretty good. Duval and Charlie asked him to become a director. Wilson said he didn't know a thing about companies or how to run them. Duval soon got over that possible obstacle. He told him that he would be more of an investment director, and if he was worried about the money he might put in, then he would be made the sole signatory of all the cheques which were cashed by the company. It seemed pretty good to Wilson who went and told Tommy Costello all about it.

'You're mad, Phil,' said Costello. 'You'll lose every penny you put in.'

'How can I when I'm the only one who can sign the cheques?'

Wilson had coughed up £1400 in cash and Charlie put in nearly £4000. Duval had brought two friends of his into the company, one Jimmy Bloor,* the other Harry Waterman. It was now time to start work. In February of that year, 1964, Duval and Waterman set off on their first expedition. They went first to Israel where they managed to buy a fur coat on a false cheque. They tried defrauding a jeweller but it didn't work. They came back to Germany, and Duval started ordering all manner of supplies, from electrical goods to cutlery. He had bank references for the new company and, with his smooth talking, soon large consignments were heading back to Common Markets.

Charlie distributed them all very eagerly and easily through his outlets. While Duval had been getting Common Markets under way, Charlie had been further expanding his wholesale interests. He had heard through Johnnie Longman that a man called Dicky Deare was planning to sell his shop in Atlantic Road, Brixton. Charlie bought the freehold, spent £3000 on doing it up and, together with other premises he bought next to the police station in Camberwell, formed a company called Sales Associates. Longman, who by now was one of Charlie's inner circle, was given the company to run. Longman was so blindly loyal to Charlie, he would do almost anything for him without question. Some called him Charlie's lapdog. In the company of Charlie he felt a somebody: it felt good and safe to be on the firm. Sales Associates was another important milestone in Charlie's wholesaling empire. The two businesses sold direct to the public the goods that had been acquired through a mixture of legitimate and dubious means. The company also dealt with the wholesale trade.

Meanwhile, Bradbury Trading was coming to the end of its natural life. The Board of Trade had started taking an interest in some complaints about it and when the bailiffs turned up on the doorstep one morning, Charlie decided that was it. The whole shooting match was closed down overnight. Officials investigating over the next few weeks found

* Sometimes spelt 'Blore'.

it impossible to trace anybody connected with it.

As Bradbury Trading disappeared off the face of the earth, so a new company called Twelve Estates appeared, as if by magic. There was to be nothing subtle about this company: in the next few months it became a naked long firm fraud operation.

While Charlie was still very much tied up with his own wholesaling ventures, he was also making new inroads with his scrap business. Peckfords had started getting large jobs from the Ministry of Works. Charlie was now tendering for some of the biggest scrap jobs in London. He would go along with Roy Hall and between them they would work out what was involved. Very often the company was to be paid for simply removing the scrap. Such were the difficulties of removing huge old boilers in the deepest recesses of office blocks, for example, that a great deal of work was involved just to get the stuff out. The scrap value of the material was a kind of bonus at the end, on top of the money charged for removal.

Peckfords had by this time started acquiring some of its own heavy plant, such as cranes and the low loader transporters to carry them. The company scored time and time again thanks to the combined entrepreneural skills of both Roy and Charlie. They would go to jobs from which others had shied away because of the difficulties in getting at the scrap. 'What d'you think, Roy,' Charlie would ask, 'can we do it in a weekend?' Roy wouldn't hesitate in saying yes. 'No sweat.' He would regard any other answer as an admission of failure, not only to himself, but to Charlie. He took a great sense of pride in never letting him down, never finding anything impossible. The stocky little Roy would often have to work his very heart out to accomplish what he had said could be so easily achieved. But Charlie appreciated it. Roy was a good boy. He wasn't like so many others in the world who were forever finding difficulties with Charlie's plans. In this way, Roy organised and helped in the clearing out of massive cellars in the Department of the Environment, and in stripping out all the old wires from the Public Record

Office at Kew. Roy was amazed at the dangerous state of the wires in such a place. 'The whole lot could have gone up just like that.'

It was because of Roy's eagerness and incredible hard work that Charlie was so often able to get away with the low tenders he put in for these kind of jobs. There was considerable pride in the new work the firm was doing. The company's letterheads were altered: 'Peckford Scrap Metal Company Ltd. Contractors to HM Ministry of Supply, Air Ministry and War Office.'

But if the new ground being broken by Peckford's took the company as close to legitimate operation as it had ever been, there was no shortage of villainy and skulduggery back at the newly formed Twelve Estates, the company which had sprung up as magically at Addington Square as Bradbury Trading had disappeared. Charlie's name, naturally, was nowhere to be connected to the company. A couple of soft front men were appointed secretary and director, including an unwitting Asian gentleman who was to be used considerably in the various long firms that were to follow. It was Bradbury, who had done so well at Bradbury Trading, and Jimmy Bloor, whom Duval had brought on to the scene through Common Market Merchants, who were to get the company off the ground. Already Duval had arranged for his long-time friend and associate Bunny Bridges to set up a company called Exmosdale at Welling, in Kent, with almost the sole purpose of providing bogus references for Twelve Estates.

In April 1964, Twelve Estates took its first tentative steps into fraudulent activity. It started ordering quantities of bleach, detergent and disinfectant – always a favourite cheap buy at market stalls – from the large Snow Glow company in Strood, Kent. Mr Frank Sales, a salesman from Snow Glow, said later in court that he responded to an inquiry from Twelve Estates and was amazed when he turned up at their address. Only a couple of weeks before, he had supplied goods to Bradbury at the very same address. Bloor, the man he saw, smooth-talked his way round the

122

problem and ordered 75 dozen bottles of Spring disinfectant. Mr Sales was given bankers' and company references, which seemed to be in order. Once delivered, the goods were quickly rattled out to the traders – very cut-price – and Bloor was back with another order of the same size just over a month later. He got on well this time with Mr Sales, and later the same day put in another order. This time it was for 100 dozen bottles of the disinfectant. Three days later there was an even bigger order: 100 dozen bottles of Snow Glow bleach, plus 100 dozen bottles of washing up liquid. The day after, 15 May 1964, an order went in for 150 dozen bottles of what seemed to be the firm favourite – Spring disinfectant. Later the same day came an order for 200 dozen bottles of the Snow Glow bleach.

Mr Sales's brother Albert, a director of the company, suddenly realized that they had had no money at all yet from Twelve Estates. Frank Sales therefore called round and asked Bloor for some money. Bloor said of course he would pay him. A total of £415 was owed – quite a lot of money in 1964. But then he discovered that he didn't have enough ready money. 'Would £100 be all right now? We'll pay the rest as soon as we can.'

Mr Sales was to get no more. In view of what was to come, he was perhaps lucky to get even £100. He made frequent visits subsequently to try and get the money. But whenever he called, Bloor never seemed to be there. The few people around simply had no idea where he was. They were always 'just workers'. All Mr Sales would see were the other goods lying around in the premises: transistor radios, toys, shoes and fancy goods.

It was a successful first sortie for the new company. They were able to find plenty of buyers because the company was offering the goods to the traders at less than wholesale price. Their profit was still big enough because they had paid less than a quarter of the full wholesale price. The other legitimate wholesalers in the area simply couldn't compete.

At the same time as Twelve Estates were taking Snow Glow for a ride, Bloor saw an advertisement in one of the trade papers for transistor radios for immediate supply. He called the company, Cannon Supplies Ltd of Rich Bell Place, London WC1, spoke to a Mr Peter Sharp, and told him he wanted 40 dozen radios. Mr Sharp asked for references, it was later stated in court. Bloor gave the names of Lloyds Bank in Hammersmith – as far as they could see the company was an active one and in the black – and Exmosdale, the company set up by Bunny Bridges. Bridges, who had changed his name to James Bernard, wrote in response to Mr Sharp's inquiries about Twelve Estates: 'Re: Mr Bloor, Twelve Estates Ltd. 33a Addington Square, Camberwell SE5. Dear Sirs, I have known this gentleman for a number of years and have done business with him and found him trustworthy reliable and punctual with his commitments. Yours faithfully, J. Bernard.' It was the perfect kind of reference. Short and to the point, and with no hint of oversell. It's a pity Mr Sharp couldn't have checked out Exmosdale.

Bloor found the radios sold extremely well, and, wanting to place a further order, paid off most of the first account. He ordered a further 80 dozen sets. They sold even faster at the price they were pushed out to the traders. By the beginning of June, when Twelve Estates had not paid the bill, Mr Sharp tried to contact the intrepid Bloor by phone. He was, of course, always out. A further barrage of letters and telephone calls followed, but the company was never to get back its £402.

Had somebody dared to 'knock' Charlie like this, if it had been one of the buyers from Twelve Estates who were not paying, it would no doubt have been sorted out in the way Charlie had already proved so effective: a visit from him and a few of his heavies, and the naked threat or use of violence. For one who was so sensitive about his own customers paying their bills, Charlie was remarkably reluctant to settle his own debts.

Since the life of a good long firm always had to be short, the knack was to get as many individual deals going all at the same time. Bloor thought he would have a crack at Sellotape Products Limited. Their agent, a Mr Peter Hubbert, arrived to see Bloor, who placed an order for £27-

worth of sellotape. Mr Hubbert, as he later told magistrates, took references, passing them on, as laid down by Sellotape, to the credit sanction advisor. He in turn checked with one of the references given, Lloyds Bank at Hammersmith, then, dissatisfied with what he learnt, took up the other reference given, Exmosdale.

On 26 May Bridges, again under the name of Bernard, wrote the familiar letter: 'I have known Mr Bloor for a number of years and have had various business dealings with him and have always found him to be reliable and trustworthy and good for his commitments.' This letter did the trick and Sellotape despatched the first order. The credit limit given to Twelve Estates by Sellotape was £250. But the little back-street company was soon to exceed that vastly. By the time Sellotape found out what was happening, it was, as usual, far too late.

After the first order had been delivered on 29 May, Bloor did the decent thing and waited for three weeks. He then put in a very similar order, £50-worth, on 19 June. By 6 July the order started going up, but not too much. This time it was £67. Bloor, having realised that Sellotape had been initially suspicious, was careful. He waited another three weeks and put in another order for £67. It all helped to establish a pattern of a moderately successful company doing a steady trade. In fact, Bloor couldn't get enough. Sellotape, especially at the prices he was putting it out, was in demand in the markets and by the other wholesalers. The next order, on 12 August, was again £67-worth. By the time of the August order, Bloor and his associates were sure that the time was right for the kill. On the same day, on the pretext of a big and sudden order for the special Christmas sellotape, Twelve Estates banged in an order for £228. It was supplied without a murmur. And so it went on: £67, £134, £268, £6, £134, £165, £82, £47, £75, £111, until the total owed to Sellotape reached the staggering total of £1595.

When Sellotape turned up demanding their money – the usual phone calls and letters had not worked – they found nobody at all at the warehouse. When Mr Hubbert looked through the windows he could see boxes of the latest unpaid-for delivery. Twelve Estates had had enough sellotape to go round the circumference of the globe several times. Yet they hadn't paid a single penny. They had got rid of tens of thousands of rolls of the stuff. Many a south London Christmas present that year was wrapped in stolen sellotape, although the innocent customers, of course, had paid something pretty close to the real price.

It was during the earlier stages of Twelve Estates that Bloor was joined by a local man called George Green, a shifty little south London villain. He was released from Wandsworth Prison on 22 May 1964 having served two years of a three-year sentence for fraud. There had been eleven different counts on the charge, and Green was perhaps lucky not to have got longer than he did. Before that he had been in various troubles for car thefts and shopbreaking. Such a person was an ideal man for Charlie, especially with his qualifications in fraud. Like most released prisoners, Green had nowhere to go, no work arranged, and would naturally be grateful for almost any job at all. A friend of his called Boysie Jones took him along to see Charlie and asked if there was anything available.

'We'll see if we can get something sorted out for you,' Charlie told him. He gave Green £20. 'This will keep you going for a bit.' It was a tradition to give a man just out of prison a small sum of money if you were somebody like Charlie.

As they were talking in Charlie's office, Duval walked in – behaving, as usual, as if he owned the place. 'This is George,' said Charlie to Duval. 'He wants to know if we can put him to work.' Duval introduced himself immodestly as Charlie's partner. Charlie said nothing. As Green was leaving Peckford's, Duval asked him to drive him up to Cooks travel agency in the West End. Duval wanted Green to change an open Common Market cheque which had been signed by Phil Wilson. Duval waited outside while Green changed the cheque for nearly 2000 dollars for him. He gave him £5 for his troubles. Green was on the firm. Soon he

126

started full-time work at Twelve Estates, telephoning sales agents and placing orders for their goods. Supplies of radios, lamps, books, toys and even flippers were arranged.

Other faces were also joining the Richardsons at this period, some old, some new. One of the most important of the new group was a man called George Cornell. Under his original name of Myers, he had waged wars with the Kray gang in the East End. He was one of the few members of the East End underworld who had no fear of the Krays; he had taunted Ronnie, a psychopathic homosexual, many a time. But a long firm he had been running was crushed by the Krays. He decided to move south of the Thames and put himself among the Richardson crowd. Cornell was a strong, hard man, who would resort to violence at the slightest excuse. It wasn't often that he came unstuck. With him at the same period came a more familiar face, Brian Mottram, whom Charlie had paid off after their earlier disagreement. He and Cornell became friends and were to set up a long firm with Charlie just around the corner from Addington Square in Caldew Street.

At Cannon Street, Common Market Merchants had been going along under Duval and Wajcenberg in a manner similar to Twelve Estates — which on several occasions had provided false references for the company. But with Duval and his cronies involved, it was done with veritable style compared to the way amateurs like Green were performing down at Twelve Estates. But they didn't just use the company for stealing merchandise. They used it to provide themselves with air tickets, the best seats at the theatre, foreign currency and meals out, all fraudulently acquired through various agencies.

On 20 March 1964, Common Markets wrote to a Derby company called F. Longdon, manufacturers of elastic and woven knitwear, expressing interest in quantities of Brinylon stretch fabrics. Longdon replied a few days later and Common Markets placed an order for 5000 yards of different coloured material, according to magistrates court evidence given later. The letter confirming the order on 13 April was signed by a Mr Len Rugg. It stressed the urgency

127

of the order. Rugg by this time had been interested in Common Markets by Duval and Richardson, and had invested £14,000. Among the list of companies he quoted in the letter for references was one called Bi-Rite Stores Ltd. That was his own company. As soon as Longdon's received this reference, they started delivering. By the time they had started to get worried about non-payment, there had been eleven deliveries to the value of £2695. Mr Arthur Varley, a director of Longdon's, made several telephone calls to Common Markets, but never got an answer. He decided to visit Common Markets in Cannon Street. The offices were closed, but he spoke to a neighbouring tenant in the building and managed to get access. There he found five cartons of his products, which had been sent down in the last two deliveries. He took those away with him. But he never received a penny of the outstanding sum, £2338.

Radios were always a favourite of the Richardson-Duval long firm. On 23 April 1964, Len Rugg telephoned Winter Trading in Ladbroke Grove, London, and told them how interested his company was in purchasing radios, it was said in court later. They had a ready outlet who couldn't get enough of them, he said. The following day a letter went in ordering 2000 Imperial Transistor 6 radios at 43/6d each, less 25 per cent purchase tax. Winter Trading hesitated in supplying the ordered goods. They weren't sure of the new company and nobody they dealt with regularly had ever heard of it. This didn't bother Common Markets, and they let the matter ride. There was no point in appearing to be too keen or earnest. Eventually Len Rugg telephoned Winter Trading and casually asked what had happened to the order. The following day Rugg and Duval, in the name of White, paid a visit to the company, giving them all the assurances necessary. Two days later, they placed an order for 1000 radios. They quoted their purchase tax number, Central 4/6439, and paid the £1741 bill on the nail. At the same time, they placed another order for a further 1000 radios. That bill of course was never paid. Common Markets had obtained 2000 radios at half price, even more if the unpaid purchase tax is taken into consideration.

Shirts were another popular item — as they indeed are today in the markets — and Common Markets turned its avaricious eyes on a Londonderry company called J. Hamilton and Sons. Jack Duval telephoned their London agent, a Mr Harry Davey, and a meeting was arranged. Duval was at his smooth-talking best, his foreign accent somehow making him seem even more impressive. An order for 1400 shirts was placed, magistrates heard later. Len Rugg's Bi-Rite was again among the references quoted, for the urgent order. Hamilton's took up the references and decided that they wanted payment on delivery. This was not good enough for Common Markets. On 5 May Rugg wrote an abrupt little letter to Hamilton's stating: 'We are unable to agree to accepting these goods on Pro Forma Invoice as it is our practice to give credit terms to our customers whose reputations are of the highest repute. It is unnecessary to quote any other terms on orders. Unless you can revise the method of payment from Pro Forma to the usual credit basis, we are unable to confirm the order given to you.' If only Hamilton's had heeded their initial suspicions. They didn't, and lost £666.

Charlie was quite pleased with the way Common Markets was progressing. Goods were coming through at a steady rate and the whole operation seemed to be setting itself up nicely. But all was not what it appeared. Nearly £20,000 had been invested in the company by people like Len Rugg, Charlie and Phil Wilson. That, it appeared, is what Duval really had his eyes on.

Unfortunately for Duval, Phil Wilson took an amateurish interest in the new company. It was something completely novel for him and he spent far more time in the office than anybody had expected he would. He felt completely safe as a result of the fact that he was the sole signatory of cheques issued by the company. But Duval got round that problem with consummate ease. He would come flapping in to see Wilson, carrying a cheque and having a tantrum about some non-existent problem. During his tirade he would slip a cheque under Wilson's nose. 'Sign this,' he would say, 'for ze wages. It all seemed perfectly normal to Wilson. Wages had,

129

after all, to be paid. The next time, there might be half a dozen representatives due to come to the office. Duval would get Wilson to sign half a dozen cheques − not filled in − on the pretext that they would be needed for purchasing samples. 'I didn't know what they were for, but I was letting the professionals get on with their business,' he recalls.

But Wilson hadn't been around for many weeks when he found out something that worried him: Mr Wade, the office manager, was working under a false name. He went immediately to see Duval.

'I thought you said this company was straight?'

'It is, it is,' said Duval.

'Well, how come Eric Wade is there with a false name?'

Duval realized he was caught. 'I should have told you, Eric is an undischarged bankrupt. I suppose I will have to tell him to go.'

Wilson did not argue with the suggestion and Wade indeed left. It was soon after that Len Rugg had been brought into the company.

About a month after this Wilson was at the office when Len Rugg explained he had to go out to court because his company, Bi-Rite, had been accused of receiving stolen material. Wilson was left holding the fort. A phone rang.

'Is Mr Rugg there?'

'No, but he won't be long,' said Wilson.

'This is the bank manager. I want £2500 in the bank before 2.30pm or else.'

'I'll tell Mr Rugg to get in touch as soon as he comes back,' said Wilson, slightly surprised.

While he was trying to work out how on earth the company could be owing that kind of money when nearly £20,000 had been invested, the phone rang again. It was the manager of another bank. Wilson couldn't believe it. This time he wanted £1500 paid in before the end of the day. The poor hapless Wilson was staggered. But worse was to come. By the time Rugg returned, there had been another two calls from two further banks, all demanding instant settlement of debts. Duval had not only been emptying the main Common Markets account, but he had opened up others. All those

130

cheques that he and Wade had got Wilson to sign had been cashed for themselves. In Duval's case, most of the money had been used for meeting other pressing debts.

The first thing Wilson did was go and see Charlie. He explained what happened but Charlie didn't – or perhaps couldn't – believe it. He eventually got in touch with Duval who talked his way out of the problem with ease. Charlie appeared satisfied and the matter, to Wilson's dissatisfaction, was dropped.

A few days later Duval turned up at Wilson's with Jimmy Bloor, the man who was running Twelve Estates with George Green. 'I know you don't feel good towards the company,' said Duval. 'Do you want out?' Wilson, who had been wondering exactly what it was he had let himself in for, jumped at the offer. A price of £2500 was agreed for his shares. Wilson, thinking that perhaps things weren't turning out so badly after all, signed the necessary paperwork.

Wilson never got a farthing. It was small wonder that some of Duval's friends called him 'Jack the Rat' or 'Jack the Chequeman'.

9. A Couple of Right-handers

When Charlie a few days later found out exactly what had been happening at Common Markets, he plunged into one of his dangerous frenzies. He had been made a fool of by Duval. He couldn't comprehend how the man could have dared. All the warnings about Duval from people such as the magistrate, Costello and Wilson came rushing back. Duval, instead of being the master operator behind Charlie's empire of fraud, had resorted to his old tricks — the very thing which Charlie was convinced he had stopped.

At 4.30 on Friday afternoon of 12 June 1964, Charlie picked up the phone and called Duval. He asked him to come down to the yard. There was nothing untoward about this to Duval — such meetings took place several times a week. Charlie also asked Jimmy Bloor to come to Peckford's at the same time.

As Duval walked into the office Charlie rushed at him from the side of the room and smashed him across the nose with his fist, the Old Bailey heard later. Duval staggered and his nose started bleeding.

'Nice few fucking quid you've had out of this,' Charlie yelled at him, releasing a battery of hard punches to the face and stomach.

Duval lay groaning. Charlie picked up the phone and called Phil Wilson. Charlie had always been a great user of the phone, making call after call until he got hold of the person he wanted.

'We've got Duval and Bloor down at the yard. You'd better come down,' he told Wilson.

'I can't. The bingo is just about to start.'

'You bloody well get somebody to look after the bingo. Your fucking liberty's at stake.'

132

By the time Duval had come to, he was sitting in a chair facing Charlie across his desk. He was covered in blood. He noticed that Charlie had taken his wallet and put the contents on the desk. He had also removed his watch and his ring. Duval saw his wig on the desk.

'Right, we're going to sort this little lot out,' said Charlie, as Jimmy Bloor was brought into the office by Mottram, Cornell and Bradbury.

Bloor was sat down on another chair.

'Who's the guv'nor? I'm the guv'nor!' screamed Richardson at the terrified man.

'What have I done for Christ's sake Charlie?' he spluttered. 'What's going on, what's this all about?'

Bloor's mistake was to be a friend of Duval and associated in Charlie's mind with the tricks that had been played at Common Market Merchants. Charlie picked up a knife from a canteen of cutlery. It was part of a consignment of 6000 canteens which had been acquired by Richardson. He took aim and hurled it towards Bloor. It struck him in the arm.

'Don't do it, don't do it!' screamed Bloor. 'What have I done? What have I done?'

Duval sat insignificantly on his chair, as if trying to vanish. Charlie slowly picked another knife from the canteen. It cut through the air and struck Bloor's arm again. Bloor started crying.

'I'm the boss, you take orders from me, you bastards,' Richardson bawled, selecting another knife and toying with it.

Soon Bloor was covered in blood. There was an eerie expression on Charlie's face. It was a sort of a smile, but it wasn't. One man who saw Charlie handing out 'the treatment' likened the expression on his face to that on the face of a man having sex.

Wilson, meanwhile, had arrived downstairs. He entered the office to find both men covered in blood. His arrival eased the tension. Duval and Bloor started wiping the blood off themselves. Charlie asked them what was going to be done. He was softening.

'You've put men's liberties at stake,' he said with an air of justification in his voice. 'What's going to happen to all the money? What's going to happen to the company? Phil here has lost a lot of money. What are you going to do about it?'

All of them started to talk matters over. Duval was full of explanations and reasons. He couldn't talk fast enough. Everything was all right. Somebody had got it all wrong. There was a lot of stuff in transit. Some was at the docks, other goods had been sent out but not paid for. He was so impressive that Charlie started almost to believe him. Phil Wilson wasn't so sure . . .

Something had to be done that night to remove the risk of getting into trouble with the company. Wilson had already told the Fraud Squad in Holborn what had happened. Charlie decided the best thing was to clear out the whole of Common Markets. He despatched Bradbury and Cornell to rob the premises. They arrived with a lorry at around 6.30pm. In the next hour they cleared out the entire office. They took all the goods that were kept in a basement store, and removed all the books, files and paperwork. Their orders were not to leave a trace of anything. They then set off for Duval's flat in Park West Mansions in the Edgware Road, just above Marble Arch. Using Duval's own key, which Charlie had removed from him along with his other possessions, they entered the flat. Again, everything that might shed any light on Common Market Merchants was removed.

Phil Wilson was not the only person who had talked to the police: Mr Varley of Longdon's, one of the many firms owed money by the company, had also gone to the local station after he had turned up at Cannon Street to find the office shut down. And while Bradbury and Cornell had been robbing the office, they were noticed by a fellow tenant of the building, who was having a drink in the pub nearby. He had called the police, saying something suspicious was going on. But they arrived too late. When Charlie later realised that the police were deep into their investigations, he contacted a senior officer he had known for some time. He paid over £1500, and thereafter the police investigations didn't seem to get very far.

Half an hour after the clear-out, Bradbury and Cornell

arrived back at Peckford's. Duval and Bloor were still there with Charlie. The blood on their faces was congealing. The atmosphere was much calmer, however. Duval was chattering away about a scheme for getting all the money back, and more. Charlie asked Cornell whether they had got everything.

'I got the lot,' he said, almost proudly. 'Books, gear, everything.'

Charlie was pleased. 'Take him to Tommy's [the chemist] and get him fixed,' he told Mottram, pointing to Bloor.

Bloor was brought back half an hour later. Charlie reminded both men that he was the boss and only he. They were to take his orders – or else. It was arranged that they would all meet up next morning in the yard to work out the details of how to salvage the situation.

Duval cleaned himself up and left – minus 200 dollars Charlie had taken from his wallet. He called a girlfriend and asked her to book a certain room in an hotel in Russell Square in Bloomsbury. He got into his car and drove to the Sales Associates shop that Johnnie Longman was running for Charlie. He cashed a cheque for £350 from Longman, who wasn't the slightest bit suspicious because Duval had done this many times in the past. Duval then left Johnnie Longman and went over to Alfie Berman, the wholesaler friend of Charlie in Bermondsey. He cashed two further cheques for more than £1000. Duval knew full well that all three cheques could not be honoured. He was pushing his luck, dangerously. He then drove to the hotel in Russell Square. He was wearing dark glasses. He drove into the underground car park. He took the lift to his room. His girlfriend was there. She put him to bed and tended his injuries. He was visited by Lucien Harris and Bunny Bridges, whom he swore to secrecy.

Next morning, Saturday, Bloor turned up at Charlie's offices at 11am as arranged. Duval did not appear. By 11.30 Charlie was beside himself with raging fury. He picked up the phone. He called anybody and everybody who he thought might know where Duval was. One of those he called quickly contacted Duval and told him that Charlie was going berserk. Duval moved out of the hotel, not paying the bill, and went to hide at a friend's house in Swiss Cottage. There was a secret room in the house and Duval felt safe there. He arranged through Harris and Bridges for a travel agent friend called Martin to visit him. When Martin arrived, Duval arranged for him to pick him up in the early hours of the next morning. He drove him to Birmingham airport. Duval caught the first plane to Brussels. He stayed there a month, and then went to Israel for a year. The next time he saw Charlie was in the dock at Bow Street Magistrates' Court in the autumn of 1966.

Charlie's fury intensified over the weekend. That dreadful paranoid force was whirring wildly inside some unfathomable part of his being. Then, the following week, Charlie discovered that Duval had cashed the three cheques after his beating, and that they had bounced. Charlie was so wild with anger that had he got hold of Duval, he probably would have killed him. Not only had Duval taken him on and conned him out of many thousands. He had now turned round and jammed two fingers up his nose. And this after he had been beaten. It took Charlie many hours to calm down. When he did, he decided he would again try and locate Duval. One of his first calls was to Lucien Harris, now running a West End company called Inter City.

Harris had kept in touch throughout this period with Duval, who had been paid some money by Inter City. Harris admired Duval in many ways. And he had, of course, worked with him previously at Denbus, and at Lyons Continental. Harris had also had an account at Duval's Bank of Valletta. When he first started Inter City, his address had been Salters Hall at 104, Cannon Street — the base for so many of Duval's master frauds. It was then moved to 230, Great Portland Street, but had not succeeded. The company had run up debts of £17,500. When Charlie heard about this, he took over the company. After the deal, Charlie had asked Harris to hang around the premises for a few days while Brian Mottram took over the company. And it was during the period when Harris was minding the shop that

136

Duval had had his latest beating from Charlie. On 17 June, five days after the beating, Johnnie Longman turned up at Inter City.

'Charlie's sent us. He wants to know where Duval is,' said Longman, who was accompanied by another of Charlie's heavies. Harris, who had seen Duval only four days before, and knew that he had left the country, realised that even the slightest clue about the whereabouts of Duval would put Duval in danger. Harris decided to call Charlie on the telephone. He told him that he had no idea where Duval was. He also made an appointment to see Charlie the next day to pick up the money he was owed for his few days' work. Lucien Harris wanted to get out.

On 18 June, the day of Harris's appointment with Charlie, he arrived at the yard in the late afternoon, the Old Bailey heard later. He had brought his secretary and partner, Miss Henman, with him from Great Portland Street. She lived a couple of miles south of Camberwell and Harris thought he would be able to drop her off after he had collected his money from Charlie. He parked his car opposite the premises and walked in. He was told that Charlie wasn't available. He apparently was up at Luton airport, where Roy Hall and others were undertaking the cutting up and the scrapping of several planes. Harris and Miss Henman sat down and were given coffee. Harris had a chat with Jimmy Bloor who, despite his beating, was still working at Twelve Estates. Eventually John Bradbury came in. He suggested that they go and meet Charlie who had now arrived and was over at Addington Square. Miss Henman rose to come too, but Bradbury told her to stay. 'We'll only be five minutes at the most,' he said. 'Charlie just wants to have a quiet chat with Lucien.'

Bradbury drove Harris to 33a, Addington Square – about fifty yards away. They went up to the first-floor office. Charlie appeared. He greeted Harris warmly. 'Come in here and we can have a little chat.' Charlie was hoping he could get information out of Harris without violence. He had no compunction about using violence against his own kind, south London villains, but somebody like Harris was different. He was well-spoken, had a degree – he had 'a right good education on him' – and was not a man of the slightest violence. He told Harris about the cheque, and about Duval.

'Do you know where he is?' Charlie asked nicely.

'I haven't got a clue, and I know nothing at all about the cheque. ... You were naive to get involved with Duval,' Harris observed in a somewhat supercilious manner.

This was too much for Charlie. He was still frantic with rage about the way Duval had conned him and taken him for a fool. Now Harris was not only not helping him, but poking fun at him. Or so it appeared to Charlie.

'I like you, Lucien,' said Charlie menacingly, 'I don't want to hurt you. Tell me where Duval is.'

'I really don't know, I haven't seen him for weeks. Can't you understand that?'

'Somebody told me that you were seen with him last night?'

'That can't be right. You must be mistaken, Charles. I have no idea where he is or what he is doing.'

Charlie asked him again, this time much more fiercely. Bradbury and another man came into the room.

'Really, I simply don't know where Jack Duval is,' said Harris. 'You can turn me inside out.'

'We very probably will,' Bradbury reassured him.

Charlie asked the question again. Harris, tiresomely, said that he didn't know. Charlie left the room. Bradbury, who had been looming around the back of the chair on which Harris was sitting, spun round and punched Harris hard in the middle of his stomach.

Harris, dazed, recovered his wind. 'Look,' he said, much more emphatically than before, and with the first audible sign of any desperation in his voice, 'I have already explained I don't know where Jack is.'

Bradbury stood over Harris with a pleased and stupid expression on his face. He punched him several times more. 'See if that helps you to remember,' he quipped.

Charlie appeared again with two other men. He emptied out Harris's pockets, placing the comb, pen and address book on his desk. He ordered Harris to place the rest of his

138

possessions next to them. Charlie was particularly interested in the address book. He thumbed through it.

'Who's this?' he demanded to know. 'And who's 'e?'

Charlie got out of his seat behind the desk. He walked around the room cleaning his finger nails with a knife he had taken from the drawer. He rounded on Harris and held the knife quivering right next to his cheek. He put his face close to Harris's. 'You'll get some of this if you don't fucking tell me where that cunt is,' he threatened.

At that moment, Eddie arrived and joined the others. 'Is it going to take long?' he asked. 'There's something I want to watch on the tele.'

Charlie walked round to Harris on the other side of the desk. Quick as a flash, he lifted his leg and brought his heel hard down on Harris's hand, which was resting on the arm of the chair. Luckily, it hit his wrist watch. It shattered, and bits fell on to the floor. As it did so, Roy Hall came into the room carrying an odd-looking wooden box. It had two thick wires sticking out of it and a handle on the side. Hall, fresh from cutting up the Luton airport planes, placed the box on the ground. Charlie returned to the seat at his desk.

'Go and get some scampi for us,' he told one of the men in the room.

Charlie's sense of the dramatic was considerable. It was going to be more than just a spontaneous outburst of violence that Harris was to suffer. Charlie would savour it. Consider what to do next. He had an innate understanding of the finer points of the psychology of fear. He would let Harris wait, think, wonder . . .

When the scampi arrived, the assembled group took a short break. They sat around munching their scampi, joking among themselves and ignoring Harris, who was left out of the impromptu feast. Charlie, scampi in newspaper in hand, got up and walked over to Harris. He thrust a piece of scampi into Harris's eye. He turned his thumb sadistically. Harris screamed, tears pouring out of the eye.

'Take 'is shoes and socks off,' Charlie ordered Roy Hall.

The leads of the wooden box contraption were held to each of Harris's big toes. Hall turned the handle. Harris

139

bumped violently out of his seat. The contraption was an electricity generator, scrapped from one of the jobs that Peckford's had done. Harris crashed down on the floor and screamed in terror. It wasn't just the pain or the shock, it was as much sheer bewilderment.

Hall wound the handle again, Harris bumped up and over the floor. The others laughed. 'Poxy little cunt, serve him right,' said one of the brighter, more sensitive types. Charlie remained impassive, watching with that eerie half-smiling look on his face.

'Take the rest of his clothes off,' he ordered coldly.

The box was operated again. Harris was jerked involuntarily across the floor by the contractions in his muscles caused by the electricity.

'It doesn't seem to be working right,' observed Charlie, dissatisfied. 'Get a bottle of that orange squash.'

The squash was poured over him – to increase the conductivity of Harris's aching body. The box was operated again. The pain was visibly greater. Charlie looked more content.

'Stop the cunt screaming,' he ordered.

A handkerchief was stuffed in Harris's mouth. A further dirty piece of cloth was placed on his mouth, and was bound tightly with a narrow strip of material. His hands were tied behind his back. This time the leads were held to different parts of Harris's body. The bare-wire ends were held on his calves, his thighs, his chest and his temple. Lastly, one was placed on his penis, the other thrust up his backside.

'You're lying, you're lying,' Charlie screamed as Harris underwent the excruciating and humiliating treatment. 'You're lying!'

The torture had gone on for what seemed an age before Harris was untied and ungagged.

'Put your clothes on,' Charlie told him.

While the numbed Harris was shakily trying to get dressed, Charlie started talking to Hall and one of the others present.

'It's no good. He ain't going to talk. I think we better knock 'im off and dump him in the marshes.'

140

Harris, petrified, was sitting on the floor doing up his shoes. One of the men present came across to him and thrust a knife right into his left foot. Harris yelled again. He was surprised, though, that he didn't feel greater pain.

Amazingly – characteristically – Charlie suddenly changed. 'I think I got it wrong, Lucien,' was all he said. 'I'm sorry. You took it well.'

They both sat down; some of the others left.

'If you wanted to find Duval, how would you go about it?' Charlie inquired as if nothing had happened.

'I would telephone anybody who knew Jack and see if he was with them,' said Harris.

'Nice one,' said Charlie. 'There's the phone.'

Harris, understandably, was in no mood to argue. He felt numb and bewildered. He called three people who knew Duval. He knew it wouldn't matter because Jack was already out of the country. Charlie made him hold the earpiece of the phone slightly away from his ear so that he too could listen. Harris was then allowed to call his wife.

'Would you like a drink?' Charlie asked Harris.

Bradbury was sent out for a bottle of Scotch. Charlie ordered a bowl of water and a towel. He apologised profusely to Harris. He seemed genuinely sorry. The storm that had raged inside his head was easing, temporarily at least. Charlie poured Harris another drink.

'Have you got any money, Lucien?'

'No, I haven't,' Harris replied.

Charlie pulled a bundle of notes out of his pocket and gave Harris £150. It was what he was owed anyway.

'I'm sorry, Lucien,' said Charlie. 'I'm really sorry.' He was anxious that Harris should tell nobody about what had happened.

Bradbury drove Harris back around the corner to the yard. Miss Henman was angry that she had been kept waiting so long. She was so cross, in fact, that she looked straight ahead of her and didn't notice anything unusual about Harris. But then she saw that his eye was troubling him and saw in the lights from other cars that the white of his eye was completely red. He told her that his eye was bad,

141

he didn't know why. Harris then drove himself from Norbury, where he dropped Miss Henman, right across the southern half of London to his home in Teddington.

Next morning, he went to Inter City offices to collect his belongings. Unknown to Harris, or anybody else at this time, an investigator from Customs and Excise had been keeping watch on Inter City. They suspected that Inter City had been involved in purchase tax evasion. As Harris left the building at twelve minutes past eleven on that Friday morning, James Cooney, the Customs investigator, took some pictures. He wrote in his notebook: 'Harris was walking very slowly, with a noticeable limp. He was supporting himself with what appeared to be a rolled umbrella. He was wearing dark glasses and was very pale.'

The next day, Harris was still feeling so poorly that his wife decided he should go to their doctor, a man called Marsden Ryle. Harris had been unwilling to do this earlier because he knew that the doctor would want to call the police in. So his wife now arranged for him to see the reluctant doctor in secret. He gave him some sedatives and patched him up. He took no notes, according to Harris, because of the nature of the visit.

The following day, Sunday, Tommy Costello and his wife paid Harris a visit. 'His foot was bandaged up and he looked in a bad way,' Costello recalled years later. 'He told me it was Bradbury who had stabbed him through the foot. Whenever I met Bradbury after this, it always reminded me of the incident. I used to think to myself: "You're the swine that stabbed poor old Lucien." '

More than three years after the Harris beating, during the course of the Richardson trial, Charlie flatly denied in court that he had laid a single finger on Harris. Today, however, Charlie admits that there was some kind of altercation. But he insists that 'it was just a matter of a couple of right-handers. . . . '

The day after Harris's beating, Charlie was on the warpath again. He repeatedly called everybody who might have any idea where Duval was. Charlie was never the man to give up or let matters rest. He had developed an obsessive desire to catch Duval. Nothing would stop him, nobody dared to persuade him otherwise. As the word got around that Charlie was on the rampage, people disappeared from sight – hoping that the storm would pass. When Charlie was in one of these moods, life became unpredictable, dangerous. But Bunny Bridges was not one of those who managed to keep out of the way. He had obliged Charlie's long firm companies with false references from Exmosdale. This hadn't only been done because he knew there would be trouble if he didn't. It was also because Duval, with whom Bridges had been friendly for many years, had become directly involved with Charlie.

It was only a couple of days after Harris's beating that Bridges was asked to turn up at Peckford's to see Charlie. The message had come from a south London man called Spud. He knew Charlie, but was working at the time with Bridges in the Exmosdale business.

'There's no way I am going round there, Spud,' Bridges said when he got the message. 'You know what he did to Jack.'

'There's no problem,' said Spud. 'He's as good as gold. He just wants to have a chat with you.' Spud genuinely thought there were no problems. 'Jack only got whacked 'cos he took Charlie on. I tell you he took a right liberty, he deserved what 'e got.'

Bridges thought that he had better turn up. If he didn't, there would be trouble for sure. If he did, perhaps things would be all right, as Spud suggested.

The Old Bailey heard later that he arrived at the yard late the next afternoon and asked for Charlie. He was kept waiting for about half an hour. It was a bad sign. To those in the know, this was usually the way Charlie started his 'treatments'. Keep the man waiting, let him start thinking. But Bridges saw nothing sinister in the delay. He did not know the set-up that well. Then George Cornell called Bridges into the upstairs office. Charlie was sitting there behind the desk.

'Hello, Bunny, where's your great friend Jack Duval?'

'I don't know,' said the smartly dressed Bridges. 'The last time I saw him was in the hotel off Russell Square the other day. He told me he was going abroad.'

'Where?' demanded Cornell, aggressively. 'Where's the fucking rat gone?'

'I don't know. I haven't the faintest idea,' said Bridges, now realising that trouble was looming. 'All I know is that he told me he was going to leg it abroad. He didn't say where he was going.'

Charlie knew that Bridges was telling the truth. By this time, he had found out that Duval had gone to the Russell Square hotel after his beating. But he assumed that Bridges was just being clever, making his story sound good by giving away true, but by now useless information. He was a smooth-polished salesman, after all.

'Where is he?' Charlie demanded forcibly.

'Come on, Charlie, I've told you I don't know. Straight up. That's the truth. I've got no idea where he is. Really. On my kid's life.'

Charlie looked at Cornell. That sinister half-grin was spreading over his face.

Cornell asked once more. 'Where's Duval?'

'I don't bloody well know.'

The first punch hit Bridges in the neck. The rest, delivered with the considerable power of the Cornell body behind them, went all over. Cornell had other talents as well: he kicked at Bridges as if he were a soggy football. Charlie sat motionless, coldly gazing on. Bridges started to try and pick himself up off the floor. As he did, Cornell went into him again. He caught him with such force that he was punched through the glass door in the office. The broken glass cut through his suit and shirt, and slashed his arm. It wasn't a bad cut.

'Where's Duval?' Charlie and Cornell kept asking.

'I don't know, I don't know, for God's sake. Can't you understand that?' Bridges kept repeating.

But this was just the opening of the proceedings. After a few more punches to the head and body, Bradbury and Roy Hall walked in. Hall carried the electrical box. He walked

144

over to Bridges and placed it at his feet. Nothing was said. Bridges was undressed. He was dazed, flabberghasted, submissive. Bridges had some rags stuffed in his mouth. He was tied up with a white flex. It was tied so hard around his hands that it burnt his wrists. He was sat on a chair. Hall grabbed the two thick wires – on the parts where they were insulated – and held the ends to each of Bridges's feet. Bradbury cranked the handle. Bridges got a severe electric shock. It bumped him, but not sufficiently to make him jump out of the chair as Harris had done.

'Where's Duval?' they all kept shrieking, while Bridges endured the pain and humiliation the best he could. Even if he had known, and had wanted to tell them, he couldn't have done so because of the gag tied tightly around his mouth. The only sounds coming from him were deeply muffled groans.

'Something's wrong with that bloody thing,' Charlie observed after a while, referring to the box.

Charlie decided that Bridges should be taken upstairs. This was done by Hall and Bradbury. Charlie searched through Bridges' jacket and wallet. He also removed his briefcase from his car. He found some very interesting papers in it, relating to the sale of cheap heavy plant in the north of England. 'I'll have some of that,' Charlie thought to himself, going upstairs to see how the boys were doing.

Bridges had received a couple more bouts of kicks and punches. 'The boys' were becoming more ambitious with the box. The wires were now being held to other parts of his body, including his backside and penis. Charlie walked in and stood, motionless, watching it. Bradbury stopped turning the handle. Bridges tried to recover himself and sit back in the chair. Charlie walked up and jabbed his finger into Bridges' eyes. Each time there was an excrutiating twist. That was the most painful thing of all. It blinded him temporarily and caused his eyes to water profusely. Charlie left again and the treatment carried on. Periodically Charlie would return and demand to know where Duval was. Charlie wasn't going to be bothered with supervising the torture of a man like Bridges. He had more important things

145

to do. Walking in and out of the office gave him the same kind of detached feeling that making telephone calls or eating scampi had during previous torture sessions. Eventually Bridges could stand no more. He indicated by nodding his head that he wanted to talk. The gag was removed roughly from his mouth.

'Well?' said Charlie, without the slightest trace of concern or pity.

'The only place I can think he might be is up in Manchester, with his ex-wife,' said Bridges with difficulty.

Bridges was untied. He was taken downstairs, where he had a wash. He was given a new shirt and underpants, and his suit back. Charlie gave him £15 'for expenses'. He wanted him to drive to Sale in Manchester that night. 'Phone Bradbury at this number when you get there,' Charlie said. There were to be no apologies to Bridges. He wasn't like Harris, whom Charlie treated with a certain degree of interest and respect because of the different environment in which he had grown up. Bridges was a local man. As such, he was a complete nobody.

It wasn't Bridges' night. When he staggered out of Peckford's after midnight, he found that his car wouldn't start. He called a friend, who came round in another car which Bridges borrowed. After dropping off his friend, he set off through the night for Manchester in the blue automatic Jaguar. Bridges had always been a shocking driver. His latest disqualification had been ordered by Tower Bridge Court only the year before. He had been banned for ten years for dangerous driving while under the influence of alcohol. This hadn't stopped him driving, and it was the least of his worries this particular night. Bridges knew full well that Duval would not be in Sale, or anywhere else in the country for that matter. His pointless drive up to Manchester, in the middle of the night and in the exhausted state he was in, was yet another indication of the grip Charlie had over the minds of the men who were in any way associated with him. Bridges felt he just had to go through with it. It was simply too risky not to. One never knew who might spot him and report it to Charlie if he stayed in London.

When he arrived in Sale it was just after 7am. He knocked on the door and woke up Duval's ex-wife and her new husband. She was two months pregnant. She liked Bridges – with his dapper appearance and gentle manner he had always been a favourite with the women – and asked him in for a cup of tea. She was surpised that Bridges should even dream that Duval would be with her. She noticed that he was limping slightly, and wondered why he was wearing sun-glasses. But Bridges said nothing.

Bridges left and called Bradbury at the number he had been given. 'He's not here,' he told him wearily.

'OK, well get back down to the yard, Charlie wants another word with you,' he was told, without any concern being expressed over his condition.

Bridges had a sleep in his car before setting back for London. When he arrived he was still exhausted. Almost automaton-like, he presented himself at Peckford's. There was no long wait this time, and Bridges told Charlie that he couldn't find a trace of Duval.

'All right,' said Charlie. 'Fair enough. Call back here tomorrow morning. I want to discuss this heavy plant with you.'

Bridges offered not the slightest protest. The papers Charlie had stolen from his case related to a deal Bridges had been setting up for the past couple of weeks. A man called Williams had a lot of heavy plant machinery for sale. It was up at Newcastle-under-Lyme and had belonged to a company that had gone into liquidation. The machinery had been bought cheap, and Bridges had already got a buyer who was based not far away from Charlie in Camberwell. Such details were not the kind of thing to worry Charlie. He wanted the machines.

Bridges returned home. His wife was horrified. He looked like death warmed up. He had scratches all over him from the ends of the heavy wire of the electric box. All Bridges wanted to do was sleep. But first he had a bath and cleaned his teeth; he was very particular about personal cleanliness.

He was woken next morning with a call from Cornell. 'You're wanted down the yard by Charlie, you're late.'

Charlie was going to have the machinery. It was becoming a point of principle. If he couldn't get Duval via Bridges, then at least he would make a few quid on the side. Charlie had been developing new business interests. The machinery would come in very handy, especially at these prices. Bridges was very angry. He thought of getting hold of a gun and shooting Charlie. Then he realised that he would have to shoot Charlie *and* Cornell, otherwise there would be comebacks. He had a little girl of three, and a wife whom he cherished and adored. The risks were too great. He didn't have a gun anyway. One of Charlie's men would be bound to get him and his family. But he had no greater wish in his head that morning as he made his way to the yard than to gun down Charlie and his henchmen.

Charlie was brisk and to the point. He made no reference to the beating and torture. 'Just how much gear is up there?' he asked.

Bridges took him along to see the man called Williams who was handling the sale. Bradbury came too. He was a mechanic, among other things, and would be able to examine the condition of the machines. There was always a man for every kind of work on Charlie's firm. Whenever there was something wrong with Charlie's car, a large Rover at this stage, he would simply send for Bradbury. 'Have a look at me motor will you, Johnnie?' was all that was needed to send him scampering under the car.

A second meeting was arranged with Williams, long-time associate of Duval and Bridges. It was agreed that Charlie would pay so much for a small lot of the machines available. In the next few days, the entire stock of plant – cranes, bulldozers and tractors – was cleared out. Williams was speechless. But he couldn't go to the police – he had his own problems, and he also had heard about Charlie. And anyway, Charlie wanted the machines.

148

10. 'Mad' Frankie

Slowly it dawned on Charlie that he was not going to be able to reach Duval. It is a good job that he didn't, in view of what he had done to those whom he thought might merely lead them to the man. That terrifying part of Charlie's nature started to creep back into its dark, inner recess. Charlie started getting back to normal — working on his long firms, his scrapyard and various other schemes that were developing.

Eddie, who at the beginning of June had adopted a little girl, had taken virtually no part in the latest round of beatings. Indeed, he had been conspicuous by his absence. His only appearance had been at the Harris beating. His main concern then seemed to be to get back home and watch television. 'Turn it up,' he had said during the course of Harris's ordeal, meaning 'ease off'.

But Eddie had been up to plenty himself during this period. Sinister developments were taking place in his career. For more than a year he and his friend had been running their wholesale and retail business in Deptford. It had been going very well and there had been none of the problems that Charlie was experiencing as a result of his ambitions with Jack Duval.

But it was while Charlie was involved with Common Market Merchants and the other long firms that a man called Frank Fraser had been released from prison. He had been sentenced to seven years for his part in a brutal attack on a man called Jack Comer, known universally as Jack Spot. With another man, called Billy Hill, he had virtually run the West End underworld. But the two, whose reign had gone on for years and years, fell out. This caused all kinds of jockeying for power in the top end of the underworld; the

Kray gang had decided to back Jack Spot, in their attempt to get into the West End in a big way. Fraser, meanwhile, had aligned himself to Billy Hill.

By the time Fraser was released, he was a man with a big reputation. He had spent so much of his life in prison that he was known in criminal and related circles the length and breadth of the country. The authorities, finding it impossible to control him in prison, moved him round the country at regular and short intervals. He would take on the warders at the slightest affront to his dignity, not thinking twice about attacking a prison officer if he was maltreating another fellow prisoner. He was one of those immensely well-connected villains, who seemed to know everybody who was anybody in his particular world. If anybody offended his highly developed – although highly distorted – sense of honour and dignity, Fraser would deal out merciless punishment. It was perhaps no surprise that by the time he was released from prison the newspapers were calling him 'Mad Frankie'. During the latter part of his sentence, he had been courted by the Kray twins, despite the earlier differences there had been over the Spot/Hill bust-up. With their ambitions still to get into the West End, somebody like Frank Fraser would have been a great asset to the firm.

The Krays had sought out Fraser through Eva Brindle, his loyal sister, wife of Jimmy Brindle, whose savage beating at the hands of Jackie Rosa at the Elephant and Castle the Richardsons had revenged. The Krays started to take Eva in their big American car down to whatever prison Fraser happened to be in. They treated her like a lady, made a big fuss of her, and when they couldn't drive her down themselves, they laid on train tickets. As soon as Fraser was released, the Krays organised a homecoming party at one of the big West End clubs. It was a mighty occasion and the underworld knew that Frank was back.

The Richardsons knew all about Fraser by the time of his release, but had never met him. An introduction was arranged by Alby Woods, a south London haulage contractor, who had been friends with Fraser for years. Frank willingly agreed to a meeting: he had heard about the

150

Richardson's rapid growth. He had also been told how the Richardsons had helped his brother-in-law Jimmy Brindle. That was the kind of thing which really went down well with a man like Fraser. Very quickly Fraser and Eddie became close friends. They were both the kind of men who liked the club life of the West End. They were both fighters, and much more sociable than Charlie. They respected each other from the start. Frank Fraser became a member of the gang. He was an important – and disastrous – recruit.

When he met Fraser, Eddie had for some time been toying with the idea of a fruit machine business. He had already got to know a few of the club owners. The explosion in the popularity of fruit machines with the changing betting laws was just starting, and Eddie knew that the machines involved a highly lucrative business. With Eddie's inclination towards the world of boxing, racing and night clubs, it was a natural direction for him to move in. He had money coming in from his Deptford business and was attracted to the more glamorous world of the West End. You needed to be tough to move in this circle. Eddie was ideally qualified; his reputation as a 'hard nut' had long since reached the West End from the wastelands of south London.

It was decided soon after the meeting with Fraser that they would form a fruit machine business, aimed at exploiting the clubs and the pubs. A company was set up called Atlantic Machines, and a man called Sir Noel Dryden was duped into heading the company and giving it a respectable front. Fraser and Eddie made ideal partners: Fraser had the contacts where they mattered, and Eddie had the money. And both were extremely tough characters. One of Fraser's most important contacts was a man called Albert Dimes, known as Dimsey. He had a betting shop in Frith Street in Soho and was the unofficial banker of many an imprisoned criminal. He was a kind of social worker for West End villains. Many disputes were settled by him, he was known and universally respected throughout Soho. He knew all the gossip and gave the new business an important edge. Some of Eddie's friends from the boxing world were also brought into the new company. With this combination, business started going well from the beginning. Some of the machines the company bought cost £400 each. But some were also taking up to £100 a week in sixpences from the better and more popular clubs.

For Eddie's company to get a machine into a club, it would often mean that somebody else's would have to be removed. This was no problem. The company would offer a better share of the takings to the owner. Where before he might have been getting a 35-per-cent split, Atlantic machines would offer him 40-per-cent. The club would also be offered a better service — in accordance with good orthodox business practice. Eddie proudly boasted a guaranteed round-the-clock service, as well as the latest and best machinery. But more important than this was a more subtle benefit that was bestowed to a club which had Eddie's and Fraser's machines. With an Atlantic machine went a kind of unwritten guarantee that there would be no trouble in the club. For anybody to cause trouble, or try to force a club using Eddie's machines to pay protection money, was to confront, head on, Eddie and Mad Frank. Few people were foolhardy enough to do that, especially since they were associated with Albert Dimes. It gave many a club owner a warm, safe feeling to see Eddie and Frank drift into their premises and park themselves at the bar to sip drinks. They would rarely take a free drink — those were for the minions who worked for them. Atlantic Machines quickly established itself as a good company to do business with. The service was good, Eddie was straight in his dealings, and it was an advantageous firm to be associated with because of the protection from trouble it afforded.

One of Fraser's friends was a man who owned several clubs all over the country, including Charlie Chester's in the West End. He was having some trouble with fiddling at a club called the Horseshoe in Southport. It was decided that Atlantic would sort it out and put their own machines in. Eddie and Frank turned up at the club a day after the beating of Jack Duval. They drank steadily throughout the night, sizing up the place and watching what was going on. A man called Peter the Greek, a key man in the club, was running the gambling tables. Eddie walked up to him. 'We are taking over this town. We are going to warn a few of your friends and show them what we can do,' he told him. 'Would you like to come outside?' When the man, whose proper name is Peter Joannides, refused, Eddie said: 'Well, if you are not coming outside, we'll do you in here.'

A fight started but was quickly stopped by club stewards. Joannides went across to the bar and ordered himself a drink. He had been there for a couple of minutes when Eddie walked across to him and rammed a broken glass in his face. Joannides' face spouted with blood from three half-inch cuts that had been gouged into his face. The rest of the club heavies turned on Eddie and Frank. They were chased out into their car pursued by an Alsation dog which managed to get in the car with them. It calmed down inside as Eddie and Frank screeched off down the road. As soon as they got clear of the club they stopped to let the dog out and made their way to the house of the club owner where they had been staying.

The boys from London had not done very well. What was worse, they had the provincial police to deal with. The local police weren't used to this sort of action and started immediate inquiries. It was a serious position for both men. There was no bookmaker friend up in Lancashire with a list of tame coppers only too happy to take a 'drink' for dropping evidence. The Richardsons put into action their only alternative − intimidating or paying witnesses. Several members of the firm were despatched to 'make themselves busy' including Harry Waterman, the man Charlie had met through Duval, and with whom he had become more friendly. He contacted one of the major witnesses and promised him £500 if he forgot what he had seen. Other possible witnesses were seen and the problem was squared.

By the time the case came to court in August 1964 the police had to tell the magistrates that they would have to drop the charges because of intimidation of witnesses. The head of the local CID said that several witnesses had received telephone calls inviting them not to take part in the proceedings. Eddie had been charged with causing grievous

153

bodily harm and had only been given bail – for £15,000 – after his solicitor had promised magistrates that there would be no intimidation. Peter the Greek, appearing in court with a scarred face as a result of the incident, gave evidence saying he couldn't even remember the man who had caused his injury. He looked round the court, past Eddie, 'I am rather vague,' he said. 'I was under the influence of drink.' A friend of Joannides, who was at the club with him on the night, also had the same trouble with his memory. He said he saw the fight, but that he didn't recognise the man involved in the court. One witness even said that Joannides was the aggressor, that Eddie had behaved quite correctly. A waiter called Guido said all that he saw was Joannides holding his face. He didn't recognise Eddie either.

The court found that there was no case to answer and the charge was dropped. Eddie was delighted, but the police and others were left extremely concerned about what had happened. Mr George Brown, then deputy leader of the Labour Party, made a public statement. 'This seems to be a case that needs to be looked into further,' he said. He and Captain Henry Kirby, MP, called on the Home Secretary, Henry Brooke, to hold a full investigation into the police allegations about intimidation of witnesses. But nothing further came of the case. Eddie was freed, and Atlantic Machines went on to gain rights in over fifty clubs. There was to be considerable trouble with the police and other gangs over territory. In a little under two years a shocking affray at another of the clubs owned by the man who owned the Horseshoe was to be the beginning of the end for the Richardson empire.

But the Richardson empire had a lot more expansion ahead of it yet. After Charlie had cooled off from the latest round of beatings, he started forging ahead with new schemes. He had been in the process of forming a heavy plant company when he had helped himself to much of the Newcastle-under-Lyme machines. Some of these machines found an immediate use in the scrap business, which was getting more and more jobs from the Ministry of Works. A huge boiler had to be removed from a government building in Russell Square. A low loader crane was driven up there on Sunday morning. Traffic had to be diverted as Roy Hall supervised the tricky operation. An even more complicated job was to follow with another govenment building on the Thames near Vauxhall. This time a barge had to be brought alongside while a massive crane lifted out the old boiler.

But Charlie was soon to find a new and greater use for his newly acquired scrap. Through Harry Waterman he had met a Welshman called Richard Aubrey, who seemed to have his finger in every pie. He said he was a scriptwriter and a film producer as well as a businessman involved in all sorts of deals. One such deal involved a coalslag heap at Ruabon just outside Wrexham in North Wales.

A Canadian working from Cardiff had already made a million by extracting usable coal from the coal tips. Aubrey said he could help Charlie get a similar deal on a large tip at Ruabon. A team of Charlie's men, including Ken Nicholson, was sent up to the site, together with quantities of machines. The local paper reported that a large London consortium was going to set up an operation. Charlie's men took over the local hotel and it all looked very promising. But after a month it became clear that it was not a viable operation commercially and Charlie pulled out.

Back in Camberwell, the long firm frauds continued. Common Market Merchants had gone with Duval — Wajcenberg had also fled to Austria again after his friend's beating — but Brian Mottram was doing nicely at Inter City. He pulled off a classic long firm coup in July. On the eighth of that month he telephoned Olivetti, the typewriter manufacturers, and talked to a Mr George Cooper. He ordered four Studio 44 machines, and as soon as they were delivered, paid the bill promptly. Seven days later Mottram called Olivetti again. He had an urgent order for ninety-six of the machines. They had to be delivered as quickly as possible if there was to be a deal, because they had to catch a ship for South Africa. Olivetti had already taken references, and in view of the prompt payment of the previous bill obliged, delivering the goods and a bill for £2800.

Within a week Olivetti had a report that some of their machines were being sold in the Liverpool area at £21 a time. This was £9 under the £30 a machine for which they had been sold to Inter City. Olivetti, having checked the serial numbers of a few of the machines on offer in Liverpool discovered that they were from the batch delivered so urgently to Inter City. Mr Cooper went to see Mottram to ask for an explanation, pointing out that the machines were being sold at a big loss, magistrates were told.

'It's complete news to me,' said Mottram. 'As far as I am concerned, the machines have been shipped. I'll get up to this Liverpool company and look into the matter straight away.'

Two days later Mr Cooper saw him again.

'You're right,' he said. 'They are being sold in Liverpool like you say. I can't do anything more about it, the director has taken the matter out of my hands.'

Olivetti did not get its money. It had to content itself with sending a letter of complaint on 30 July.

There was many a commercial fraud like this yet to come in Charlie's life. But by now he was turning his mind to the biggest proposition he had ever had in his life. Everything else palled into insignificance. The proposition was to change the direction of his life. . . .

11. South Africa

While Charlie had been exploring the Welsh coal tips, Richard Aubrey, the man who had introduced him to the idea, also told him about extensive mining rights in South Africa with which he had a connection. Charlie listened as Aubrey explained that he was involved with a group of people who owned the mineral prospecting rights to 4 million acres in a place called Namaqualand. They were short of money, and needed somebody to back them. A lot of money would be needed, but there was every prospect of making a fortune.

It was the kind of project that would intimidate even a big company. But the whole thing excited Charlie intensely. He discussed the idea with a new and important friend he had made from the respectable upper-middle-class establishment, the late Major Herbert Nicholson. The Major was a director of several large British companies. He, too, thought the proposal sounded most interesting and used his influential contacts to do some checking out for Charlie.

Nicholson was to play an important role in Charlie's life. He had been introduced to Charlie by another of the respectable business people Charlie had befriended. The Major was a relation of this friend. It wasn't just the business connections of Nicholson that were to be important to Charlie. The Major was a Conservative Alderman in Bedford. He had captained the local and East Midlands rugby teams during his youth, and had become a prominent member of the local Conservative Party. During his time as local Conservative Party agent, he had helped out with MPs' surgeries. Among those whom he knew was Christopher Soames, now Lord Soames, who was MP for Bedford from 1950 to 1966. Soames remembers him well to this day. He called him Nick

Nicholson, and he appreciated the invaluable work he did in the constituency.

Charlie also consulted a firm of lawyers in Victoria which specialized in South African law. He showed them a document which Aubrey had given him outlining the nature of the mining rights. The rights concerned did indeed seem incredible. They had been granted by the South African Mining Commission to a man called Thomas Waldeck the previous year on 9 August 1963. The reference numbers to the concessions were 5659 to 5773 inclusive. Waldeck had then formed a joint venture operation on 5 September 1963 with three other men to exploit the prospecting rights — which appeared to cover a vast range of semi-precious and base minerals. The Victoria lawyers told him that everything seemed to be in order. That was enough for Charlie, never the kind of man to prevaricate or worry about the detail. The scheme really seemed to him to be what Aubrey had said it was — a once-in-a-lifetime chance to make a fortune, and a legitimate fortune at that. Well, more or less.

Charlie moved quickly. He decided to go to South Africa, and asked Major Nicholson to accompany him. The Major refused: he had other pressing commitments which he could not get out of. Instead, he told Charlie that he would get one of his political chums to write to the British Embassy in South Africa. The letter asked that the Embassy give Charlie and his team all the help it could by way of introductions and support. The hapless friend of Nicholson who wrote the letter had no real idea what the scheme was all about, or who exactly was involved in it. It was quite sufficient that the request for help had come from the Major, a liked and trusted friend. The Major himself was equally unaware of the wider nature of Charlie. He had seen only the best side of the man, the intelligent, inquisitive, charming and eager south London scrap dealer who was trying to raise himself in the world. The letter of introduction was worth its weight in gold to Charlie. It indicated the immense value of friendly contact with respectable, well-placed people like the Major to people like Charlie. Every well-organised gang leader needed such men.

Full of hope, Charlie took off from Heathrow on 24 August 1964 with his common law wife Jean Goodman, Richard Aubrey, Ken 'Rednose' Nicholson – the other Nicholson in his life – and his brother Eddie, fresh from his narrow escape over the fight at the Southport club. Any notions of respectability that Charlie entertained about South Africa were obviously being reserved for the future: Charlie and his party flew out on tickets fraudulently acquired from a travel agency. Charlie was in high spirits as the plane headed south to Johannesburg on its twelve-hour journey. He chatted incessantly to Aubrey, who did nothing to discourage his enthusiasm. It appeared to Charlie as if all the minerals and semi-precious stones were there for the taking. All it seemed to need was some money and drive. Charlie had both of these requirements in large quantities. Ahead lay a fortune and respectability. But, perhaps inevitably, as he settled himself into BOAC's hospitality Charlie was not altogether aware of exactly what was involved in the vague deal he had been offered through Aubrey. . . .

For a start, there was Aubrey himself. He was in many ways a delightful character. Welsh, witty and devious, he was a fabulous raconteur, and had made a name for himself as a scriptwriter and film producer. But there also seemed to be a shady side to his character. Aubrey had arrived in South Africa around 1963 at the invitation of an eccentric millionaire who had a poetic streak and wanted to learn to write properly. Aubrey was to be his tutor and guide. He took to the role with relish, having a strong dose of that didactic streak which seems to run through many a Welshman. He showed no respect or fear for the millionaire's wealth or position. He threw tantrums and fits of temper at the drop of a hat. Such was the behaviour of great artists, the indulgent millionaire reassuringly told himself. On one occasion, Aubrey took his eager pupil out early one morning in the car. He made him stop, take his shoes and socks off and then walk in the soaking grass. 'If you want to be an artist, you have got to feel with every one of your senses,' he reportedly explained. On another

159

occasion, he threw himself out of the man's car in anger after a disagreement. Although the millionaire never went on to write anything of genius, he did finish up financing and helping with films, one of which starred Stanley Baker.

While Aubrey was on this mission, he had met Thomas Waldeck, the man who had originally been granted the mineral prospecting rights. Aubrey got to know him reasonably well. He found out a number of fascinating things about him which suggested that Waldeck was very well-connected and that he had the key to a fortune. Waldeck was a member of the Broederbond, the immensely powerful secret South African society. To liken the society to the Masons in Britain would be a gross understatement. The Broederbond, or Band of Brothers, runs South Africa. According to a book by two South African journalists, Ivor Wilkins and Hans Strydom, published in 1978, it is the most powerful secret society in the world. Based on absolute secrecy, it has about 12,000 members in 800 cells from every walk of South African life, which it utterly dominates. The previous South African Prime Minister was a member, as were all but two of the cabinet. The members are all white, Africaans, male and protestant. It was formed in 1918 to counteract the hated influence of Jews and the British.

But Aubrey discovered that there was more to Waldeck than just this. The extensive Namaqualand rights that he had acquired had resulted from an arrangement with an official in the government body that dealt with mining. The official, himself a Broederbonder, had enabled Waldeck to get the Namaqualand rights despite the fact that the area had been closed to prospecting since 1928. In return, the official was to get a 20- to 30-per-cent cut of any profits that Waldeck made out of his development of the area. Even more importantly, Waldeck hoped that, unofficially, he would be able to prospect for diamonds. The rights he had been granted only allowed him to prospect for base and semi-precious minerals. But the arrangement was that he would be able to use this as a cover for looking for diamonds. If he found any, he would have been able to claim discoverer's rights. And the indications were that in some

160

areas of Namaqualand, diamonds were in abundance.

During his 1963 trip to South Africa, Aubrey had also bumped into an old friend of his called Gordon Winter, himself another extraordinary character. The two men had shared a flat in London in the early 1950s when Winter, a Yorkshireman son of a publican, was engaged in a life of crime, specializing in jewel thefts and in seducing rich women. But Winter's luck had run out. He was convicted three times and spent twenty-one months in jail. By the time he was released, he knew many of the important names in the underworld. Winter decided to emigrate to South Africa to try and make a new and honest life for himself. He arrived there in 1960, became a reporter on the South African *Sunday Express*, and quickly established himself as one of the country's top crime journalists. For Winter this was relatively easy: he had an intrinsic understanding of the criminal mind. He was able to befriend villains whom no other reporter could even approach. He did deals with them and with the police and soon started producing a battery of sensational front-page scoops.

But Winter didn't just stick to crime reporting. Through a rich woman he knew, he met John Vorster, at the time Minister of Justice, but soon, in 1966, to become the Prime Minister after the assassination of Dr Verwoerd. He developed a close and trusted journalistic contact with Vorster, who provided him with numerous stories, and allowed Winter to interview him on the radio. Because the *Sunday Express* was a liberal paper, by South African standards, Winter also came into contact with many blacks. Much of the abundant information which he gained from them about their plans he passed on to the police. 'The only way to get police contacts is to shop people,' says Winter today, 'which is what I did: provide the police with bodies and convictions.'

Winter became so trusted by the South African authorities that in 1963 he was recruited to work as a spy. He joined a body called Republican Intelligence. It was the forerunner to the present-day BOSS, the dreaded Bureau of State Security, into which Republican Intelligence merged

161

in 1968. According to Winter, Republican Intelligence was based on an idea of the late Sir Percy Sillitoe, a former head of Britain's MI5. He had written a memorandum which suggested that journalists would make excellent agents, especially those working on liberal papers, as they came into contact with all kinds of people whom the state had a potential interest in. The idea had been developed by Hendrik van den Bergh, who set up Republican Intelligence and who was later, as General van den Bergh, to become the head of BOSS. Van den Bergh himself recruited Winter, who went on to become one of his most valued men. Winter was the seventh reporter to be enlisted. His code number was RO17, and he wreaked havoc wherever he went. 'I spied on blacks, on visiting journalists from overseas, I used to set people up and do terrible things. People lost their lives, people hanged themselves, people committed suicide, people were tortured to death,' he says today, with shame.

When Aubrey bumped into Winter by complete chance in 1963, the two men were equally delighted to see each other. They went back to Winter's flat and caught up with each other's lives. Winter told Aubrey how he had been recruited. He trusted the man enough to do this. In his turn, Aubrey told Winter what he had been getting up to in South Africa. He explained about Tom Waldeck and the mining rights, telling Winter that he was about to set off to London to try and raise money for the under-funded Waldeck venture.

'I'm going to approach both the Richardsons and the Krays,' he told Winter, who knew exactly who both gangs were.

'Why?' asked Winter, surprised.

'Well, they both have bags of money and they are the type of people who would love to invest in a reputable business deal where there are millions to be made. They can give up crime and go and live in villas in Bermuda.'

'What a marvellous idea,' said Winter. 'Ingenious.'

Charlie, as he jetted towards South Africa, knew little of all this. He thought merely that the mining venture needed money. Although he was extremely interested in the proposition, he knew it might all come to nothing. But he wanted to come out and have a look for himself. If nothing else, the trip would be a nice break for himself, Jean and Eddie.

The day after he arrived, Gordon Winter came over to see Aubrey and, as a result, met Charlie and Eddie at the Ambassador Hotel in Pretoria Street in Hillbrow. Winter, as a crime reporter, was keen to keep his tabs on the secret visit of the Richardsons. And he was interested in the mining project, from which he felt millions could be made. He thought that perhaps a few crumbs might fall from the rich-man's table. . . .

The group took tea on the hotel balcony in the warm sun of the August afternoon. Winter was tickled by the man whose reputation he knew only too well. Charlie tried to put on a bit of an accent, wanting to hide his cockney origins. He was well-dressed, well-spoken and perfectly charming.

Later that day a meeting took place between Charlie, Aubrey and a Johannesburg businessman friend of Waldeck. Charlie learnt that this man had a scheme for smuggling out of the country illicit diamonds that might be found in Nama-qualand. The idea was to insert the contraband stones into fish before they were frozen for export. Once out at sea, the diamonds would be removed. It was a wonderfully simple plot to beat South Africa's very tough diamond regulations.

Charlie liked the sound of the plan very much indeed. This kind of work was second nature to him. He promised that when he got back to London he would make inquiries about fishing vessels which the businessman said would be needed.

A couple of days after this meeting, Charlie met Tom Waldeck, the man he really wanted to see. He was a tall, gangling, difficult person whose cropped hair exposed a boney skull. He was an ex-farm manager who had run a transport business and who had ventured unsuccessfully into previous mining ventures. By the time he met Charlie, his great hopes for Namaqualand were beginning to fade a little. The company he had set up with his three partners, Concordia Developments (Propreity) Ltd, had not been able to raise sufficient capital, and there had been increasingly bad arguments between the four men. Waldeck was by far the most important man in the group. He was a good practical geologist, had all his government and Broederbond connections, and was also in a position to acquire further prospecting rights to other areas.

The first thing that Charlie wanted to talk about was diamonds. But Waldeck was cool, and worried that Charlie appeared to know so much. But slowly the two men started to get on, and further meetings followed. They agreed in principle that Charlie would invest money in Concordia in return for a half-share of Waldeck's interests. Charlie even started to forget the question of diamonds. Waldeck told him that there were dozens of minerals and semi-precious stones which they had the right to look for. It could all be done completely legally, and there would still be lots of money to be made.

Charlie met Gordon Winter again and accepted an invitation to tea. Charlie was already beginning to size up the position in Johannesburg and realised that Winter was an important man to know, especially from the point of view of good publicity. He had established quickly that Winter was a man who could be trusted. Earlier on in the visit the fact that Winter was a journalist had caused some problems, especially with Eddie: Charlie and his party had been having lunch with Winter at the Halfway House, between Pretoria and Johannesburg. The atmosphere was difficult and strained. Eddie kept jabbing his knife into a roast potato. 'Imagine that,' he said to Charlie, almost mumbling, and with a sullen expression on his face, 'bloody crime reporter. It's almost as bad as being Old Bill.'

Winter got the message. He took immediate control of the situation. He told them about his own previous record back in London. He named the right names and places, to show that he wasn't just making it up. And he promised that he would never write anything about Charlie or Eddie unless they wanted him to. As if by magic the problem vanished. It wasn't so much that Winter had made a promise. It was more that he had given Charlie some information which he could use to embarrass Winter greatly if ever he acted 'out of

164

order'. In subsequent days, Winter had shown Charlie round. He took him and Jean to the zoo, and to a small Zulu village outside Pretoria. He was also to introduce Charlie to Winnie Mandela, wife of Nelson Mandela, the famous black South African political prisoner, who had been tried in the much-publicised Rivonia treason trial. Charlie was described as a journalist from London. He chatted politely to Mrs Mandela and praised the speech her husband had made in his defence.

Charlie arrived with Jean Goodman at Winter's flat for tea. He was shown in and met Winter's wife, Jean La Grange. It was love at first sight. Charlie found her stunningly attractive; he felt instantly drawn towards her. Jean La Grange had prepared a lovely tea for them all, with dainty cakes and finely cut sandwiches. She played the perfect hostess, paying particular attention to Charlie, who couldn't take his eyes off her or stop trying to monopolise her.

Jean Goodman was jealous, but Winter appeared not to give a damn. His work as a journalist-cum-spy had long since extinguished the passion of his love. After a hard day's work at the paper, he would often stay up until the early hours writing up his reports for Republican Intelligence. When Jean La Grange had moaned about the hours he worked, Winter had got permission from van den Bergh to tell his wife about his intelligence work. She was a good Africaaner girl, after all, who loved black children but hated all black adults, thinking they were savages. Her father was town clerk at a prosperous suburb of Johannesburg called Bedfordview, and he, too, was a friend of John Vorster. But Winter's news had done little to help the marriage. The result was that Jack Kemp, Winter's immediate handler for Republican Intelligence, started taking her out on jobs where he needed a female companion. He had started using her for little intelligence errands: in a restaurant she would slip upstairs to have a snoop around, under the cover of looking for the lavatory. And by the time she met Charlie she was doing a lot of this kind of intelligence work.

It was not often that Charlie got on so quickly or so well

165

with a woman. She flirted with him outrageously in a little-girl kind of way. But Jean La Grange was no fool. She appeared so elegant, so feminine, so beguilingly feminine . . . The next night, on the eve of his return to London, Charlie again met Jean La Grange, at a party thrown by one of the businessmen associated with the Waldeck mining venture. He hardly left her side. They talked all night to each other. It appeared that her marriage to Winter was on the rocks. Charlie felt numbed by her presence. He wanted her as much as he wanted the Thomas Waldeck mining rights. He almost told her that he loved her, but held back. The south London gang leader, who instilled fear and dread in all those who were associated with him, was almost like a little boy who had fallen in love for the first time.

Charlie returned to London, leaving Ken Nicholson – and his heart – in Johannesburg. But once back in Camberwell, he knuckled down and started preparing details for a partnership agreement with Waldeck. He was such a determined, single-minded man, that he started to forget the distracting infatuation he felt. He began searching out books on geology, mining and South Africa. He read them all avidly, sucking in every single fact and detail. South Africa, he was coming firmly to realise, could change his life out of all recognition. The possibilities were mind-boggling, the potential too large fully to comprehend. . . .

Waldeck, too, was turning things over in his mind. He realised how valuable and important was the free-and-easy offer of capital that Charlie had made. At last, he felt, he would really be able to get into the big league. Like Charlie, he was a relatively young man, just into his thirties. But he felt that his life so far had not been a great success. He had ambitions for wealth and position. He had the mining rights and now, with Charlie, the means for the first time of turning them into riches. He had got on surprisingly well with Charlie. So often in his past, he had been unable to connect with people, and had almost invariably ended up disliking them – as had happened with the other three men he was involved with. The possiblity of a partnership with Charlie offered an opportunity to break with them. He

became keener and keener on the idea of the new partnership. Remembering how Charlie had first been so interested
in diamonds, he decided to ring him up. He was anxious that
Charlie should not lose interest. He revealed to a delighted
Charlie that he also had rights to a 48,000-acre area in a
place called Meir near the Kalahari Desert on the borders of
what was then Bechuanaland. These rights, Waldeck
announced, included the right to prospect for diamonds.

Charlie was heading back to South Africa within a matter
of days. This time, he took with him a man called Brian
Oseman, whom he wanted to join up with Ken Nicholson
and help look after the developing South African interests.

A series of enthusiastic meetings took place between
Charlie and Waldeck. It was hard to say which of the two
men was the keener. To Charlie, Waldeck was indispensable
because only through him could he get at the minerals he
wanted to develop. To Waldeck, Charlie was an all-
important foreign investor whom he felt he would therefore
be able to control.

This time, Charlie also found out about the contact
Waldeck had with the government official. Waldeck told him
that he would have to be paid something fairly quickly to
keep him sweet. It was the kind of corruption that is today
so rampant in many overseas countries where big contracts
and deals are at stake. It meant nothing to Charlie – who
readily agreed that he would make some money available.
His basic intention was still to make an honest fortune. All
that the graft entailed was getting access to the mining and
prospecting rights. There would still be a mammoth task
ahead in actually developing and exploiting the resources
successfully.

Charlie and Waldeck agreed the final details of a partnership. The deal was that Charlie would pay Waldeck
£10,000, half of it on the nail, the rest when they had got a
viable proposition under way. Charlie would have to finance
all operations that the partnership developed and provide all
the equipment that was necessary for the work that lay
ahead. The agreement would last for five years. In return,
Charlie got half all Waldeck's rights, and was guaranteed

167

half all new rights that Waldeck acquired, as he was more than likely to do. Both men would split equally all the profits of any of their various enterprises in South Africa.

It was a good deal for both men, neither of whom could have survived without the other. Charlie, who was just thirty, had got a foothold in South Africa. He was convinced that there was a fortune to be made. He still didn't know exactly how, but he just knew it was there. He had already come to the conclusion that the South Africans were too slow and easy going. He felt that he could show them how to do it – by fair means or foul.

But Charlie was singularly unprepared for what he was taking on. He knew little of South Africa, nothing of mining. He talked casually of sums of £100,000 being available when in reality he did not have ready access to that kind of money.

He returned to London for the second time in less than six weeks. He had been so consumed with the Waldeck partnership that this time he hadn't seen Jean La Grange. Before leaving he briefed Ken Nicholson and Brian Oseman on the latest developments. They were to oversee the formal signing of his agreement and generally to start setting up Charlie's interests in the country. Back in Camberwell, Charlie set about his task with ferocious energy. The first priority was getting machinery out to South Africa so that prospecting could start. Areas to which Waldeck had rights also had to be repegged, to retain his rights.

Soon after his return he received a telegram from Ken Nicholson. It was marked urgent and dated 24 October 1964. It stated: 'Reward served.' The money for the government official had been paid over.

Around the same time, he made inquiries about fishing vessels – for the diamond smuggling. Several vessels were offered to him. One shipbuilder had for sale two trawlers that were lying in Milford Haven. His letter to Charlie ended: 'We would appreciate it if you would kindly treat this matter as confidential, so far as it is possible, as the owner does not want local publicity at the present moment.' If they had known the intended use of the trawlers, they would have

168

had far more to worry about than simply local publicity. As it was, the diamond smuggling scheme gradually faded away; it never became a viable crime.

Charlie had far greater ideas stirring in his mind anyway. He was coming to realise that there were so many possible minerals he could develop in South Africa – Waldeck had also told him about large kaolin deposits they could get as well – that Charlie was now thinking in terms of launching a gigantic public company. It would be floated on the London and Johannesburg stock exchanges. Vast sums of money could be raised from the public. And Charlie would become an international tycoon.

12. Tycoon Charlie

Charlie indeed came quite close to becoming such a tycoon. In the next few months his plans were to develop steadily, despite some set-backs. Had it not been for certain later events, he might today be one of the world's richer men.

It was with this very notion in mind that he frantically rushed around in Camberwell in the autumn months of 1964. He set up a company to deal specifically with the question of organising heavy plant and machinery for export to South Africa. The company was called the Anglo-American Engineering Corporation Ltd. He had bought the company, which had been dormant for several years. It sounded impressively like the huge South African concern run by Harry Oppenheimer, the diamond magnate. Charlie put into it all the plant that he had acquired through the man called Williams after the Bridges beating. It was based first at the Peckford's scrap metal yard at 50, New Church Road, but soon was moved to new premises at 231, Rotherhithe New Road in Bermondsey. The site had offices and a large yard under some railway arches. John Bradbury was brought in to service, repair and renovate all the machinery that was to start rolling in. Charlie thought Bradbury was a first-rate diesel mechanic. A number of interesting people were to join the company as figurehead directors, including the late Sir Noel Dryden, a descendant of the poet by that name and already a director of the Richardsons' Atlantic Machines; Ken Nicholson; and a clever lawyer's clerk called Michael Leaworthy. Another company was also set up to receive the plant sent to South Africa. It was called Orange River Enterprises, with offices in Johannesburg and Durban. Ken Nicholson had seen what he thought was a good market for hiring and selling a range of heavy plant in South Africa. The idea was that the company would trade in its own right as a plant company, as well as supply the equipment for Charlie's venture. Much of the equipment that passed through Anglo-American was to be stolen from motorway and construction sites all over Britain during the next few months. A former friend of the Richardsons recalls how they used to make getaways down the motorway — flat out at 5mph! Stolen bulldozers, earth scrappers, compressors and every kind of plant was to find its way into Anglo-American.

Raising capital was the most pressing problem for Charlie at this time. He contacted the Iranian Bank of Saderat asking for a short-term loan of £50,000. He presented his proposal with style and conviction. He had long since learnt the art and the importance of presentation in the world of business. On 10 October 1964, he wrote to the bank's British headquarters in Fenchurch Street about his plans for 'the development of the whole of the Coloured Areas in South Africa in respect of minerals and rare earths'. He declared: 'As intimated I have complete faith and confidence in the project supported as it is by irrefutable documentation published by the South African government, the White Paper being deposited and perused by you — further documents, agreements are confirmed by Attorneys of the Supreme Court of South Africa, covering both South African and British law.'

For some reason, the bank refused the loan. So Charlie approached a merchant of substance. With his persuasive ways and massive enthusiasm, Charlie did not take long to convince the man that he should put money into the venture. He agreed that he would invest as much as Charlie did, pound for pound. In return, he would take half of all Charlie's profits from South Africa.

A few days later, Charlie was approached by an American company based in the Bahamas which had heard about his South Africa interests. They told him that they might be interested in investing some money with him. Charlie was pleased. It was a change for somebody to be seeking him out, rather than for him having to go begging from the banks.

He gave them a confident outline of what he had going and it was agreed that the company would get in touch soon. Also at this time, another marvellous possibility was apparently beginning to emerge: it was a year after the Great Train Robbery, and there was a lot of money lying around the south London underworld crying out to be laundered. Where better for it be invested than in South Africa, by the king of the south London underworld himself?

Charlie had also been setting up what was to become his main English company dealing with South Africa, and the one which embraced his agreement with Thomas Waldeck. He called it Concordia Developments (Namaqualand) Ltd, similar in name to Waldeck's earlier company. The new company was set up with the help in South Africa of one of the country's best and most respected firms of solicitors, Cliffe Dekker and Todd. The introduction to this influential firm at 94, Main Street, Johannesburg, had come via the Major Nicholson connection. During the formation of the company, which was initially based at New Church Road, the other Nicholson, Ken, had written to Charlie from South Africa telling him that he had called on Mr James Gordon Dekker. 'Very nice elderly and wise *gentleman* (Top rating in SA) and it appears that we have done quite a deal,' Nicholson stated, concluding on a note of high confidence: it's all nice and tidy under British Law, he said, urging Charlie to 'handle this your *very* self'.

Charlie was pleased with the way his masterplan was developing. He had completely sewn up Waldeck and his rights. More were likely to be granted soon. He had two of his men – Ken Nicholson and Brian Oseman – handling his affairs out in South Africa, and they had set up an office for him in Johannesburg. He had the best solicitors. Waldeck had friends in high places. Some plant was already on the way out and it seemed that he would be able to raise enough money – on top of all his own that was coming in from the scrapyards and the other numerous activities of his gang.

But Charlie was not so pleased with the latest antics of Aubrey, who seemed to him to be an increasingly unpredictable and temperamental character. Waldeck had told

Charlie that he didn't think much of him. And Charlie's patience was soon to run out. Aubrey had been furious at the way he had been completely left out of the Waldeck agreement. He had started to demand a large percentage of all profits from the venture as an introduction fee. His demands were excessive but perhaps understandable since he stood to gain nothing from the valuable introduction he had made.

Charlie finally broke with Aubrey after he received a letter from Brian Oseman on 20 October 1964 stating that Aubrey, who was staying with Gordon Winter, had pestered Waldeck for the diamond rights, and had claimed that he had power of attorney for Charlie. Charlie simply cut Aubrey right out of his plans. There had been no place for him anyway. Charlie wanted to keep as much of the venture to himself as he could. Aubrey had served his purpose with the introduction to Waldeck.

Only a few days after this, Waldeck was approached by another South African prospector called Eddie Kruger. Kruger had the usual prospector problem – lack of capital with which to develop his discoveries. But he had heard that Waldeck had some English money behind him. He told him that he had found vast quantities of an amazing new building material called perlite. It was sited in Natal on the Nxwala Estate, at a place called Mkuse, near the Ghost Mountain. He wanted to know whether Waldeck and his backers would like to invest. Waldeck knew little about the material. But he telephoned Charlie and explained to him exactly what had been offered. Charlie was interested; it could be yet another mineral to put into his planned public company. He was not the sort of man to be cowed by what was already a daunting challenge. He was prepared to take on just about anything.

He told Waldeck to do nothing yet except try and find out more about perlite. And Charlie himself did his own research. He discovered that perlite was a new kind of building material which was in its early days of development, mainly in America. It was a volcanic rock that had a high water content. In its raw condition it was of little use to anyone. But when heated to high temperatures through a process called exfoliation, the water was driven out and the material expanded to many times its initial size. The end product was an incredibly light and strong material that had superb insulation properties. It had many possible applications in the building and construction industries. There was clearly vast potential.

The more Charlie found out about perlite, the keener he became. His luck seemed to be running so well that he began to feel that he couldn't put a foot wrong. It was a dangerous sign — in the past such feelings of over-confidence had often presaged bad mistakes. He called Waldeck on the phone and told him to start negotiating for the Kruger rights. He asked him to come over to London with some samples. There were a lot of things that they had to discuss. Charlie also contacted the American company who had approached him and told them about the perlite. Their appetite had already been whetted. The latest news only increased their interest.

Before Waldeck set off for London, he met John Bradbury, who had been sent out to South Africa by Charlie on 4 November 1964 to help Ken Nicholson with the heavy plant company, Orange River Enterprises. Bradbury's presence in Camberwell had also become a possible embarrassment. Police and Board of Trade inquiries into the tens of thousands of transistor radios that had been sold through the firm in Bradbury's name without purchase tax were getting too close for comfort. The company owed nearly £50,000 by the time Bradbury stepped off the plane at Jan Smuts airport. It didn't bother Charlie because his name could not be linked with the company. He had made sure that there was nothing on paper.

Bradbury introduced himself to Waldeck, who thought he was a bit of an odd character. But Waldeck's wife, Corris, thought he seemed a nice man. Bradbury also handed over some money from Charlie to Waldeck to be paid to the government official.

Waldeck then himself set off for London. He told Charlie as much as he had been able to find out about the perlite deposit at Mkuse. Both men grew more and more excited as

174

they discussed the potential for the perlite and the other various mineral rights they had. Both thought fortunes lay ahead of them. Waldeck was wined and dined. He approved. It was the kind of life he felt he should be leading: flying to London, eating at expensive restaurants and being taken seriously by his financial backers. He was introduced to Major Nicholson, who gave him a conducted tour of the House of Commons. They lunched at the House with another of Nicholson's political friends.

To people like Major Nicholson and his cronies, Charlie's operation appeared somewhat unorthodox. But the old boy had no real idea who Charlie was. He had a slightly affectionate, patronising attitude towards him and his associates. Charlie, he thought, had come up the hard way. But he was making good, thrusting ahead, with an enthusiasm and energy he admired. He was a wonderful example of Tory philosophy in action. A self-made man who had defied all the obstacles, who might in time become a millionaire and an important member of the Conservative Party. One of Nicholson's MP friends even suggested to Charlie that he should go into politics. Had Charlie applied his undoubted drive and talents in a less criminal way, he probably would have succeeded. He certainly would not have been content sitting on the back benches. He had all the deviousness and pragmatism needed to do well in politics, or the City.

While Waldeck was enjoying himself in London, the American company got in touch. They wanted a meeting as quickly as possible. Charlie and Waldeck flew out to Miami to meet one of the directors. From there they went on to Nassau in the Bahamas for a series of further meetings. Charlie and Waldeck were offered a million pounds for their venture. Charlie acted with incredible coolness. His face showed not a flicker of any reaction whatsoever.

'We'll think about it,' he said. 'Thank you very much.'

Secretly, Charlie was amazed. Staggered. Overwhelmed. He flew back to London with Waldeck, who also had been winded by the size of the offer. But he told Charlie he thought their project could be worth even more than that.

175

And Charlie agreed — wholeheartedly. It wasn't just the perlite. There was still Namaqualand to be exploited, there was the possibility of diamond and mineral mining involvement in Meir, and there were other minerals in other parts of South Africa to which Waldeck felt sure he could acquire the rights.

A few days later the American company arranged another meeting wtih Charlie and Waldeck, this time in Rome. Charlie played it cool again. He listened to what the Americans were adding to reinforce their offer: not just money; there was also to be payment in bonds and shares in banana plantations the company owned around the world. It couldn't have been made more attractive. The time came for Charlie to make up his mind.

'Gentlemen, I thank you for your offer. I'm afraid, however, I am going to have to turn it down.'

As Charlie left the room one of the American negotiators whom he had befriended pressed a card into his hand. 'You will never forget the day you were offered a million pounds and turned it down,' he had written. Charlie smiled quietly to himself. If ever he had arrived, this was the moment. The American company was immensely rich. One of its directors was ex-General Motors. It had courted him round the world. He had held his own with experienced top international executives. And he had turned down their offer in a manner which they had seemed to respect.

Charlie felt genuinely that he could make much more money than the Americans had offered. Charlie's financial partner, who had pushed keenly for the idea of selling out to the Americans, was soon to pull out. It didn't matter to Charlie. In the previous few weeks he had reportedly secured the deal that had been mounted with men looking after the interests of some of the Great Train Robbers, some of whom he knew. It had been agreed that Charlie would have in the region of £100,000 to put into South Africa. (It was the share of one of the robbers in particular.) The sum would be repaid with interest when the mining operation was making money. The deal was perfect for both sides. One of Charlie's associates remembers seeing him sometime later in the Langham Hotel in Johannesburg. 'I saw several suitcases. They were packed with £5 and £10 notes and there was a huge amount of money in those suitcases. I actually saw this with my own eyes. Charlie said this was the money he was investing in South Africa. I gather far in excess of £100,000 was in the cases ... I heard from somebody else that this money was some of the proceeds of the Great Train Robbery.' Other people who were working with Charlie around this period also say that Great Train Robber money was invested in South Africa. The deal for this money had been clinched at the very time that Charlie and Waldeck had been about to leave for their meeting with the American company in Miami. Charlie had had to leave early from a champagne party he had thrown for the relatives and friends of the train robbers at his house in Acland Crescent, in order to catch his plane. The party was to celebrate the fact that the people campaigning for the train robbers had managed to secure a new court hearing in which they hoped to challenge the evidence of one of the more important witnesses.

During this period of November 1964, Charlie had also been trying to raise money through contacts of Major Nicholson in the City. His great desire now was to float a public company. There was no stone that Charlie left unturned. On 25 November 1964, the Major had written to one of his financier friends outlining the mining venture and the plans to go public. He told him that the concessions in Namaqualand were at Richtersveld, Steinkopf, Concordia, Komaggas and Lesliefontein, and contained precious and semi-precious stones and base minerals. He said it was the view of the founders of the company, and particularly that of Mr Waldeck, 'who is a ranking expert', that the concessions contained fifty-three easily extractable minerals as well as precious and semi-precious stones. Nicholson explained that the company had access to £100,000, and stated that £35,000 was already in the company's bank. But to extend the scale of operations, Concordia needed to raise a substantial sum of money for the public floatation.

The following Monday, the Major and Charlie had lunch

177

with the financier to discuss this. It went well and, on the Major's advice, and with his help, Charlie wrote a letter of thanks, repeating his desire to form a public company. He added as a 'PS' that since writing the letter he had received confirmation that his deposits of kaolin exceeded 50,000,000 tons.

The financier found the claims hard to believe. So, too, did Frank Fraser, the man tied up with Eddie and the fruit machines and who Charlie was later to try and pretend he hardly knew. He went out with him one night during this period to the Astor Club. Charlie never forgot his roots; his head may have been in the clouds as a result of all the new high-powered people he was meeting, but his feet stayed firmly on Camberwell ground. He told Fraser enthusiastically about all the latest developments. But Mad Frankie thought the whole thing sounded suspicious. 'If it's so bloody marvellous, why do they want to give it all away to a bleedin' foreigner?' he asked with some perception. Charlie shrugged it off, refusing to let anything distract him. He took Fraser to Victoria where he caught his train to Brighton, home of many a successful London villain. Fraser was later to claim that he had a strange encounter on the station with a judge while waiting for the tain.

After the American offer had been turned down, Waldeck went back to South Africa to buy up Kruger's rights. It was agreed that Kruger would sell 75 per cent of his perlite and other mineral interests at Mkuse in return for £3000 and a car of his choice. He chose a Citroen. Waldeck prepared to set up a company to operate the various rights Kruger had ceded for such a bargain price. The company was to be known as Lebombo Mineral Developments Limited. But then Waldeck was brought down to earth with a bump. His wife, Corris, confessed to him one night in December that while he had been away in London, she had had what she later called 'a romantic episode' with John Bradbury.

Bradbury, although insanely jealous of his own wife, was a constant womaniser. He was a physically attractive man, tall and lean with short, dark hair. He always wore smart dark suits and had a flashy style for which many women

178

seemed to fall. He had professed to Mrs Waldeck that he loved her. She felt at the time that the feeling was mutual. When she told her husband what had happened, he went wild with rage. She tried to tell him it was all a foolish business from which she had completely recovered. But Waldeck became so depressed that he told his wife he was thinking of committing suicide. After all the excitement and sense of importance he had felt during the American negotiations the affair made him feel thoroughly wretched and belittled.

He summoned Bradbury to his house and told him that if he ever made another advance to his wife, he would break his neck. Waldeck then telephoned Charlie and said he could no longer work in any way with Bradbury. Waldeck demanded that Charlie sack him. Charlie, with so much at stake, readily agreed. Bradbury anyway was in that class of persons who to Charlie were complete nobodies: two-halfpenny tin-pot villains, from whom there was a plentiful supply to choose.

Charlie was also growing impatient with 'Rednose' Nicholson. Not only did Waldeck dislike him because of his drinking, but he had not been getting things done in the way Charlie wanted. The connection was loosened. Both Nicholson and Bradbury, however, remained in South Africa. Charlie sent out a man called Colin Riddoch in Nicholson's place. He was a middle-class professional businessman whose job was to check the company side of the venture. Charlie was pleased to hear that Waldeck at least got on well with Brian Oseman. From his address in Cardiff Road, Parkswood, Johannesburg, Waldeck wrote to Charlie on 21 December. He ended the letter: 'P.S. Brian O. is a *great guy*.' Charlie was never the man to tolerate for long the kind of squabbling and in-fighting there had been between nearly all the people involved so far in his South African venture. Waldeck in particular seemed to take a dislike to most of Charlie's men. But Charlie was able to accept this: Waldeck held the key to everything Charlie hoped for.

In the next few weeks, events seemed to settle down and

179

progress steadily. Two new companies were formed to help deal with different aspects of the South African venture. One was called Thomas Waldeck Holdings, the other, Namaqualand Enterprises. Colin Riddoch also started trying to acquire a public company called Tati Goldfields Ltd. On 11 January 1965, he wrote to the lawyer acting for the company, outlining proposals for Charlie to acquire the unissued capital of the company of 1 million shares. He suggested this could be done by giving Tati Goldfields £100,000-worth of mineral assets owned by Charlie and Waldeck. He also wanted the company's directors to assign 75 per cent of their share holding. Tati Goldfields was an ideal company for Concordia to acquire. It was solvent and was quoted on the London Stock Market at only a few pence per share. It was a mining company and therefore completely suitable for Charlie's purposes. Its only main asset was shares in a few other private companies, and it had a tax loss position of £118,000.

Waldeck, meanwhile, had travelled to Mkuse with a geologist called Tom Edwards to start prospecting for the perlite in earnest. While in London, Waldeck had arranged with Charlie that he would send tape recordings giving accounts of what was going on. His first tape in January 1965 was quietly optimistic. He confirmed that the agreement for Kruger's rights was now ready for final signing, adding that he thought Concordia would eventually acquire a 100-per-cent holding. 'We don't want to wield the big stick with Kruger at this stage, as a result of peculiar conditions in South Africa, but I am confident we can regard this whole project as if we were, in fact, in control of 100 per cent of the shares.' Waldeck reported that a bulldozer had been sent up to Mkuse to uncover the thin layer of earth of the perlite deposit. 'We have found in fact that the quantity of material available exceeds all expectations. It is quite obvious from visits to the site that where we originally anticipated that this would be, say, *a* deposit, that there are several deposits of this material still on our ground and we are now in a position to get a full independent appraisal of the quantity.'

Waldeck told Charlie that he was instructing a Professor

Van Biljon, South Africa's foremost sedimentary rocks expert, to carry out a full assessment. A problem with a farmer called Mormon who didn't want to give access to his land was being sorted out satisfactorily, as was resistance to the development of the Mkuse Game Reserve by conservationists belonging to a body called Fauna and Flora. In general, Waldeck was confident that he and Charlie could become the sole owners of perlite in South Africa. There was also considerable interest in the perlite from several major construction companies.

Waldeck excited Charlie even more with news of diamonds and pearls at Mkuse. 'The suspicion exists that there are possibly diamonds in this area, and we have now learned that there is a fissure running through our particular property. Here we have to be extremely careful . . . however, dealing with diamonds and the possible discovery of diamonds in this particular area or other minerals of that particular nature, there seems to be some slight confusion as to what are the possibilities down there. First, we have found that we are, in fact, in the oyster beds. In other words, the likelihood of discovering pearls and other semi-precious stones are very imminent. We are only about 15 miles from the coast. Now, in South West Africa, we work sometimes up to 150 miles away from the present shore level and we are still in the oyster beds . . . it does not mean that you have to be close to the coast in order to have that particular commodity.'

Yet Waldeck was cautious about the diamonds: 'When you dig for diamonds, you do not just dig out 500 tons of material and carefully sift and sort this material and in that way you find our diamonds. No. You do it right the other way round. You actually acquire your material by way of mining or explosives or otherwise and then you establish a washing plant. Now in the washing plant you can range from an investment of £50 to something in the region of £10,000 to £50,000. That is the only way in which diamonds are generally recovered. Now the method is very complicated and involved. You rarely find any diamonds just by turning the gravel over and by just sorting the gravel out.

181

Once you go into the question of looking for diamonds, before you do that you must be quite sure that your security precautions are 100 per cent in that you can't just send down people to start digging and ostensibly working in the area as if they were looking for something else whilst they are in fact looking for diamonds. The Illegal Diamond Division of our country over here are acutely aware of the methods that people have adopted in the past in order to recover diamonds under a veil of secrecy of looking for some other material, and once they find that, in fact, that these people are not purely and simply interested at this stage in perlite but that they are using this method to get to the diamonds, we will run into difficulties. ... Should we discover diamonds, we should be in a very strong, and a very fortunate position. But there must be no confusion about the question of diamonds. It is not something where we send a few men of ours in there and they start digging and oh, oh, they've got a diamond in a few days of operation. It is something which is to be carefully considered, carefully planned and then done in the proper manner ... with a complete and comprehensive security programme.'

Waldeck, on this particular tape-recorded message, also referred to the staff situation, which he clearly felt was now much better. 'As you probably gathered, the intrigue and the nonsense that we've experienced here with various people has come to an end and quite frankly we have not got the time to waste with people who are very childish.'

Charlie accepted Waldeck's caution. He was prepared, rarely for him, to wait, to play it by ear for the time being. He wanted to do nothing that might rock the boat.

Charlie had also arranged with Brian Oseman that he too should send over detailed tape-recorded reports to him. From the Oxford Hotel in Rosebank, Johannesburg, Oseman told Charlie that he had been 'running around like a blue-arsed fly'. He reported on Waldeck, confirming exactly what had been said on the tape. 'There are a lot of things that Tom has stopped me doing. His explanations have always seemed just, so I have complied with his wishes. Take the diamonds, for example. When we found that place near the perlite I wanted to start digging right away. Tom told me that you don't dig for them, you get a washing plant and wash for them. Now we have only got the base mineral rights on this area so Tom says we can't go in there with all the equipment — diamond prospecting — until we have made a bit of a show on the perlite. Don't worry, nobody else can discover the diamonds. Tom has been very firm and doesn't want any publicity at this stage. He doesn't want the big mining houses to know just yet. He says he wants to creep in through the back door. Don't think I let him have all his own way, Charlie, because I don't, but I know you will understand when I tell you I can't go too strong.'

Charlie also received a tape from Oseman in February 1965. He described in detail the first trip he had made to Mkuse with Waldeck. 'Hello Chas, today is 12 February. Last night we left Johannesburg for Natal. We left in two vehicles, fully packed and self-supporting with plenty of supplies. We arrived at Ghost Mountain Inn in Mkuse at 2.30am this morning. The weather is very hot, sub-tropical to be exact.'

Next day he recorded a further message: 'Today we pushed on to Sbwana Bay, six of us travelling in a Land Rover. [Sbwana Bay was where Waldeck also had rights for minerals called kesselger.] We have arrived at our camping site in between one and two o'clock. We have pitched our tents and arranged our water and all the necessary things to be done. I have just returned myself from a long walk along the beach which is about 200 yards from where we have pitched our camp through dense bush. This whole area, Charlie, is all bush which leads then on further out to rolling plains. In this area, we should find this kesselger. We have no maps to the location — well, that's my excuse anyway. We have found occasional natives . . . we showed them a bit of rock like kesselger but up to now none of them have been much help.'

Oseman, obviously enjoying the pioneering feeling, kept a daily diary on the tape for the guv'nor back home in south London. 'Today, we've been out trying to find the kesselger again. We found natives who knew where it was, but they were frightened to get in the Land Rover and show us. On one occasion, I nearly started a private war, because we drove into a village, I nearly ran over what they call their war sticks. Luckily Tom, who had been guiding us through some very thick bush, was sitting on the bonnet and saw them lying in the grass and shouted out stop. You can imagine, I really put the brakes on.'

But the novelty soon started to wear off: 'Today we're at Mkuse, that is the Ghost Mountain Inn. I am absolutely whacked. None of us feel too happy ourselves. It is very very hot and you can't stop sweating all the time. We unpacked the Land Rover into a garage there and Kruger, Peter Nicklaus [a German engineer who had joined the team] and myself proceeded to the perlite area.'

The next day, 17 February 1965, was much better. 'As you know, last night we spoke to you on the telephone in London. It seemed funny, so many miles away and hearing you so clear. Anyway, the good news is this. This morning, as we told you on the phone, we went back to the perlite. The idea was to meet a prospector who communicated with us by phone this morning. We got there about 7.45 and at eight o'clock on the dot the prospector arrived. We took him out to the Red Hill, to show him the part we wanted excavated. On our way back, Tom took a slightly different way. Instead of having to go all the way round this huge belt of bush we cut halfway through it. Suddenly we stopped, all leapt out, and found more perlite. This perlite stuff looks something like black stuff, Charlie, and by God, is there a load of it there. It stretches absolutely flat, and is easy to get at. But even more exciting was that Kruger screamed out, all excitedly: "This is where we'll find the diamonds." Immediately the prospector bloke came running up and started picking up bits of semi-precious stones. We found agates, opals and stuff like that. Opal itself is a precious stone, nearly on a par with diamonds, but they seemed very excited, all of them, and the gravel there is definitely diamondiferous. This prospector picked up a precious pearl. Kruger, being a bit slow, told him what it was. He immediately put it in his pocket. I felt like chopping his hand

184

off. Tom reckons that this pearl, as it was, was worth about £45. When I spoke to Kruger afterwards, it was decided just to treat the thing lightly and make out there would possibly be no more there. But I don't trust this man and I saw the look in his eyes when Kruger mentioned diamonds.'

When Charlie received this tape he was overjoyed. Oseman, the man he could trust, was describing Mkuse in a way that Charlie had never dreamt possible. There was even more perlite than the quantity which Waldeck had already been raving about. And now there were diamonds, opals and pearls almost lying all over the place.

But not everything was so optimistic. Major Nicholson, by now a director of Charlie's company, sounded a note of distinct caution. He had since Christmas, back in England, been studying the figures and looking particularly at the price structure of the perlite operation. On 13 January 1965, he had written to Charlie from his home in Cardington Road, Bedford, saying that having had a rough look at the various figures and costings for 'our project', he did not think it was a commercial proposition. The only real money to be made, he said, was with the expanders, the machines for heating the perlite to the temperature at which it exfoliates to many times its crude size. The Major suggested that he should accompany Charlie on his next trip and have more talks with Waldeck about this.

Charlie, in fact, had already been going into the question of the machines for expanding the perlite, which Major Nicholson had raised in his letter. Before Christmas, he had found that virtually the only company making the extremely expensive machines was one called Nikex, which was Hungarian. Hungary had its own plentiful supply of the perlite and was thus developing the necessary technology. In January 1965, Nikex had written to Anglo-American saying they would need a five-ton sample of the company's perlite in order to decide exactly what kind of machine they needed. Charlie called Major Nicholson and told him this. It was arranged that the Major would travel to South Africa, to develop some contacts and make an on-the-spot assessment.

Charlie also decided he would send out a man he knew called Jimmy Collins, to work and guard the mine at Mkuse. Collins was a large jovial Liverpool Irishman, who had for several years been resident in south London. Charlie had also in the past few weeks befriended an ex-Fleet Street journalist and executive called John Fisher.* He had left journalism to set up a public relations company, and had become much involved with clients wanting to float public companies. Even more important, it was his firm which had taken on the commission from relatives and friends of the Great Train Robbers to challenge their convictions and massive prison sentences. It was this work that had led to the announcement that the evidence of one of the vital witnesses, a Polish farm worker called Marris, would be re-examined. And it was because of this that Charlie had given the champagne party. The new hearing had failed to overturn Marris's evidence, but it was a good try as far as Charlie was concerned. Charlie had known several of the train robbers well. Some of them were from the same manor.

Charlie, through a train robber relative, contacted Fisher and asked him to come down to his house for a drink and a chat. Both men hit it off instantly. Fisher, hard-bitten as he may have been from his years in Fleet Street, was impressed with Charlie, like so many other respectable people before him. He thought here was a real grafter who was raising himself from the gutters and on his way to making his first million. He felt that he had a lot of public relations potential . . .

Charlie took him into his sitting room. He introduced Fisher to Jean and both men sat down at the bar in the corner of the room. Charlie produced maps and documents. He enthused about the possibilities. He told him of Nama-qualand, of Mkuse and of the distinct possibility of getting involved with diamonds. He explained how there were still many deals to negotiate, how he didn't fully understand company law and structures, but that he wanted to set up a public company. 'I'm going to make millions here,' he said.

* Pseudonym.

186

'If you are interested in taking part, then I'd like to have you involved.'

Fisher left saying he would think about it. He returned to his offices in Grosvenor Street. He hardly had time to turn things over in his mind before Charlie turned up at his offices. 'Have you made your mind up yet?' he asked. Charlie had already told Fisher about Waldeck and his connections with figures in the South African government. 'I've just had a tape from Waldeck – why don't you listen to it? You'll see what I mean about the scheme.'

Fisher had no idea that Charlie was a serious villain, but sensed that he was probably sailing close to the wind. So, too, he thought, were some of the top people he had met. He told Charlie he would help but not for money at this stage. He wanted to see how things developed, and find out more about what was going on. 'If it all works out, then perhaps we can talk about money.'

This greatly impressed Charlie, who had always had a fascination with straight people. He could see that Fisher wasn't on the make. Within days Charlie again turned up at Fisher's office. He told him that he had to go to a meeting about perlite with the top man from a large cement company at Stag Place in Victoria. He asked Fisher to come along and help him with the discussion.

Fisher agreed, but Charlie didn't really need him. He produced maps, articles from learned journals, and presented the man with a complete run-down on perlite. Fisher saw that the cement people were visibly impressed. He came away feeling convinced that Charlie would become a multimillionaire. Charlie asked Fisher if he wanted to become a director of the company. Having seen the reaction of the cement company, one of the most respected in its field, he could hardly say no. But he decided that he would still, for the time being, keep it on an expenses-only basis.

Up until that time, Charlie had used first the address of his scrapyard and then that of a London lawyer for Concordia. He told Fisher that he was looking for a good address. It was a godsend for Fisher who had more expensive Mayfair office space than he needed. Charlie jumped at Fisher's offer to rent an office in his premises at 65, Broadbent House in Grosvenor Street, just off Park Lane. He brought in the decorators and had some new wallpaper put up. He shipped in a desk and a table for board meetings. Charlie now had one of the best business addresses in London for his new and burgeoning enterprise. It seemed nothing could go wrong. How different it all was from the days of Jack Duval and the Common Market Merchants-related frauds.

The time for the trip to South Africa with the Major had now arrived. Charlie had hoped to be able to get himself and the others, including Nicholson, John Fisher and Jimmy Collins, across in a flight which had been chartered by the late Stanley Baker, the film actor.

Baker had come into the lives of the Richardsons through Eddie and his booming West End fruit machine business. Through the rich and famous friends he was getting to know he had been introduced to Baker. Eddie and Frank Fraser had got on pretty well with him. They weren't exactly from the same school, but Baker's tough Welsh Valley upbringing enabled them all to see eye to eye. Baker had taken them down to his home town and they had all had a riotous evening in his local miners' club. It was a pure coincidence that Baker had earlier met Aubrey through his millionaire pupil.

Eddie had taken to Soho like a duck to water. He loved its life and its secrets. Still with his interest in football, he, along with Baker and Frank Fraser, had taken an active interest in the Soho Ramblers, a very sociable team to be involved with. But Baker was now on his way out to South Africa to make the film that was later to be called *Sands of the Kalahari*. During one evening in Soho, he had told Eddie about the film and invited him to come out and see what they were up to. Eddie went with Baker, but it turned out there was not enough room on the plane for Charlie and his entourage. So it was decided that Major Nicholson and Jimmy Collins would fly out and that Charlie and Fisher would come a week or two later.

Charlie also now wanted to take with him Alf Berman,

the man to whom he had sold quantities of wholesale goods. Charlie was interested in Berman's money — of which there was plenty — and had convinced him, like many others, that there was a fortune to be made in South Africa. Very much in Charlie's mind was the cost of the necessary expanding machines for the perlite. He found out, to his horror, that they cost in the region of £33,000 each. Berman at this stage agreed to put in £26,000.

When Major Nicholson and Collins arrived in South Africa, they were met by Brian Oseman. Collins looked as fresh as a daisy but the Major was exhausted. He was left to rest for a couple of days. Such idleness was not for Collins, who had been looking forward immensely to his trip. He had been brought across to live up at Mkuse, where he could work and, perhaps most important, guard the diamonds and semi-precious stones which Waldeck had told Charlie about. For this purpose, Oseman had bought a second-hand caravan and a four-wheel-drive truck. The German called Peter Nicklaus had now also been taken on full-time, and the two were despatched up to the perlite deposits. Waldeck gave the expedition a .32 pistol for protection.

Oseman, meanwhile, organised a few meetings for the Major, with all kinds of important South Africans. Oseman took him to see the mine at Mkuse for a few days. He also took with him a drill to help with the perlite sampling. Oseman reported on what he had done in a letter to Charlie: 'I asked Jim to keep picking up stones hoping he may pick up a diamond. I am going down there on Thursday, to take them down a drill. I am also taking Herbert [the Major] with me to give him an idea of what the country is like down there.'

Oseman said that Waldeck had managed now to negotiate some rights to a deposit of kaolin just outside East London. But there were signs of friction developing between Oseman and Waldeck. 'I am afraid I have to keep pushing Tom. He really is under the cosh from his wife. She even tried to tell me what to do. I had to put my foot down and tell Tom to keep her out of the business. He told her off, she has been ill ever since. Herbert has nicknamed her Brass Face. I think

189

she is spending Tom's money before he gets it. Don't worry, I'll make double sure she doesn't spend yours.'

Although the Major was obviously enjoying himself, there were one or two little problems that Oseman had to sort out. When the Major met Ken Nicholson, he was shaken to hear that a lot of Charlie's people had travelled out on bent tickets. It was the first indication to the Major that anything was wrong with Charlie's venture. Oseman simply told the Major that the suggestion was rubbish. He explained that Ken Nicholson was sour because he had been eased away from the venture, and also that he had a drink problem. It seemed to satisfy the Bedford alderman.

One of Collins's first tasks was to prepare samples of perlite which Charlie wanted to send to the Hungarian expanding machine company, and to another German company which he had now found also manufactured the unwieldy machines. Collins loved it all. After a couple of days he wrote to Charlie in his eccentric style, telling him all that had happened. The letter was dated 1 March 1965.

'This is at the hurry up because we are 20 miles from the nearest post box. I am at the perlite mine getting the perlite ready for Germany and Hungary. We hired ten boys. They cost four shillings a day and their food which is nothing. You just buy a sack of meal. It's just like oats and a sack of sugar and thats all they get except on Saturday they get a TOO POUND TIN OF JAM. *THIS IS THE TRUTH*.

'Chas, you wouldn't believe it you have got to see this place to believe it. THE German KID and ME are here in the Mkuse. Its so big you carnt realise it. There is perlite all over the place and all kinds of coloured stone's some of them are opals, I am running around like a lunatic with A PICK & SHOVEL DIGGING FOR DIAMONDS. HONEST. DON'T FORGET TO COME. THERE IS A HOTEL WITH A SWIMING POOL 25 MILES away you could STAY THERE ... I AM WALKING AROUND LIKE Buffalo Bill, I HAVE A SHOOTER A RIFEL A KNIFE TALK ABOUT BILLY THE KID. HE'S GOT NOTHING ON ME.'

A few days later back in Johannesburg Collins sent

190

another of his colourful letters, complete with misspellings and unusual use of capital letters. He really loved it out in the bush.

'Hello Chas, JUST A LINE hopeing everything is OK. NOT much to say. they have found more perlite than you can dig up in a life Time. They havent sent the samples to Germany or Hungary yet. you know about the opals and diamonds. I will be there to morrow then I will Be able to Tell you more. CHAS, TW (Waldeck) is a NICE chap. But I dont think he has too much of an Idea. Honest, he lives in a different world than us, ITS hard to explain, if you was here just for a couple of days you no what you want done and you go all out to do IT. But they seem to waite for everything to come to them, or you carnt do it that way in SA. There is nothing wrong its just that they move slow nobody can do anything but Tom. he is the only one who no's anyone. So just come over for a couple of days dont stay LONG. Then you can get things going. or send someone who will be able to do so. Herbert held a board meeting YESTERDAY. I dont no too much about IT. ONLY that Herbert TRIED TO get things cracking. I couldnt be there Because I am NOT A MEMBER OF THE BOARD. I am going with Herbert, Brian to Toms tonight to a BARBACUE.'

13. On My Kid's Life

Charlie had been strenuously involved since the summer of 1964 with South Africa. But life carried on very much as normal in the rest of the Richardson world. His firm was now so well-oiled and organised, with the right trusted people in the right positions, that Charlie could let it almost run itself. Jean Goodman still controlled the scrapyard. Roy Hall, Reggie the Milkman, Johnnie Longman, Arthur Baron and a few others had remained the loyal working core of the organisation. The business, as ever, involved a mixture of scrap from dubious sources – in common with many other local scrapyards – and the more legitimate, large-scale Ministry of Works contracts.

The various long firms which Charlie was behind or financing came and went – as by definition they had to. Inter City and Georgie Green's Twelve Estates were now closed down. The arrival on the Addington Square scene of George Cornell and Brian Mottram had manifested itself into yet another long firm with Charlie's backing, this one called Saltus. It was based just round the corner in Caldew Street, and Green was moved in to carry on working there. He was soon joined by a small-time villain called Norman Bickers, a south London man who, among other things, had been shot in the head by a farmer who had caught him robbing his farm. Bickers, who had been a close pal of Ronald Biggs, one of the train robbers who was soon to make a dramatic escape from Wandsworth Prison, had not long been out of prison. He had been 'earning a living', as opposed to stealing, as a painter and decorator, and in this capacity had already worked in the Saltus premises, as well as at Peckford's and at Charlie's house. His new job, at the

192

counter of Saltus, involved handling all the usual long firm goods – shirts, fancy stuff, electrical equipment and so on.

Meanwhile Harry Waterman, the man who had met Charlie through Jack Duval, had been making himself busy for his new master. A wholesale chemist in Camden Town called Warren Stanley had got into financial difficulties, with debts in the region of £30,000. It was a well established business with a good name and plenty of trading contacts – an ideal one to take over. Waterman acquired the business – the man was glad to sell for a nominal price with its debts – and large quantities of pharmaceutical goods started being ordered in the usual long firm way. The man who sold the business had no idea, of course, what was going on. Charlie was pleased with Waterman and happy to take him along with him to the Astor Club and other places where he socialised – often at great expense. But some of Charlie's boys didn't particularly like smooth little Waterman. Cornell, the ex-East Ender who was now running Saltus, was just one of this number. During an evening in the Astor Club, he walked up to Waterman, who was sitting down having a meal. Cornell's serious drink problem was particularly apparent on the night in question. He picked up a spoon and jabbed it into Waterman's face. It was thrust with such force that it cut him badly.

The Astor Club was an expensive place to spend an evening. It laid on a good meal, and had a popular cabaret. It was nothing for £100 to be spent during an evening out – even at this time. Charlie and his friends were regular guests. He was known well to all the staff – he used to get up to capers such as walking up the main stairs on his hands. He had taken Waldeck there during his visit to London. But there were one or two incidents which caused disapproval. One night Charlie took a businessman friend along. He was told at the door that his father had been in the night before and half smashed the place up. He was refused entry. On the surface, at least, he accepted this with grace. He apologised, said he would make sure it didn't happen again, and went on to another place.

Eddie's fruit machine interests had developed rapidly into

a flourishing business. This, together with Revvon, the Deptford supermarket run by Eddie and his friend, had made Eddie a prosperous man. Throughout the late autumn and winter of 1964, as Charlie had been getting South Africa off the ground, Eddie had tried to become a patron of boxing. With a well-known figure in the sport he had attempted to set up professional boxing in the Republic of Ireland. He had made several trips there and had tried to interest Eamonn Andrews, the television personality and an ex-boxer himself, in becoming a figurehead. Andrews, however, refused, saying he had too many other commitments. He had also interested the *Daily Telegraph*'s boxing correspondent to join the venture. There were several meetings with Irish boxing representatives who keenly supported the idea, because Ireland had no existing professional body.

But there were several problems with the fruit machine business. The police had started nosing around after Eddie got into difficulties over one particular deal. Eddie, who saw first-hand how corrupt were the police in Soho, was damned if he was going to pay the law. As far as he was concerned, his business was strictly legitimate. There was no evidence of protection or any heavy-handed stuff. This had always been Eddie's approach. He played his cards much closer to his chest than Charlie. He was much less openly reckless. Anything that he was accused of, he would utterly and flatly deny. Invariably this was the right approach, for there would rarely be any evidence to support the accusation. If there was, then it was extremely unlikely that anybody would be foolish enough to tell the police or agree to go to court. But there were many problems associated with the fruit machines, mainly of territory. The success of his business had caused some resentment. On one occasion when there had been some trouble and Eddie had refused to pay the police, a senior detective got in touch with Charlie, who came and paid him some money to 'square things'. Eddie was livid with Charlie and they had one of their characteristically ferocious slanging matches.

'Your bloody machines are causing a lot of bother,'

bawled Charlie. 'You want to be careful, put some back handers around otherwise you'll get us all fuckin' nicked.'

And so life went on as it always had done. The violence that had characterised the Richardsons' world continued, as indeed it needed to if the gang was to retain its undisputed position. In Eddie's case, it was as much the threat of violence as the actual practice of it. Like some kind of south London Golden Eagle, Eddie rarely had to indulge these days: it was sufficient that Eddie was Eddie, and was associated with the people he was. Not for him the constant scrapping of the tin-pot villains who fought as readily as market sparrows. In Camberwell and its surrounding areas, the name Richardson was one to strike fear and submission into all and sundry. Violence was a constant factor running throughout the daily lives of the members of the gang, and the means by which Charlie maintained his powerful position at the top of the pecking order.

It was just a few days before Charlie left for South Africa with Fisher and Berman to join Major Nicholson that another round of beatings had taken place. This time Charlie was not involved, he just happened not to be there.

George Green and Norman Bickers had been working at the Saltus long firm for Cornell, Mottram and Charlie for some time. The money was good and they took to spending their loot in West End clubs and restaurants. On 4 March 1965, Green was at Saltus when Cornell arrived with Mottram having just seen a policeman. The detective, said Mottram, had helped them organise the robbery of a safe. He had told them where it was, what kind it was, and the best time to do the job. It had been carried out successfully, and Mottram and Cornell had been out to pay the detective his share.

Shortly after Cornell had returned, a bailiff had arrived demanding a cheque for £75 which Green had given to the Pinnochio Restaurant in Frith Street, Soho, where he had entertained several people to a lavish meal. He was a regular customer at the place, spending £20 to £30 a week. It was because he was so well known that the restaurant had readily accepted his cheque – one from Twelve Estates which had been closed down for some time. Cornell, when he ascertained what had happened, paid off the bill. But when the bailiff had gone, as the Old Bailey was to hear later, he turned on the diminutive Green and with the help of Mottram – a big, immensely strong man, just like Cornell – proceeded to beat him up.

Green had been sitting on the chair. Cornell bent down, picked up the chair, and tipped Green off like a bag of rubbish. Mottram and another man, HP Frank, watched as Cornell struck Green across the head with a large set of pliers. As Green lay on the floor, Cornell put the boot in. He picked up anything that came to hand and used it to hit Green. A glass tray shattered across the top of his head.

'You fucking berk. You must think we are little boys. We'll fucking well show you that we're not cunts.'

'Come on, George,' HP Frank said to Cornell. 'Turn it up. I can't stand too much of this cos of me heart.'

'Ah, fuck off,' said Cornell.

HP Frank was an ace when it came to the long firm routine, but he didn't like the violent side of things and he left.

Another round of kicking and punching was dished out on Green, who by this time was in a bad way.

'I'm going to see if Charlie's back,' said Cornell, picking up the 'phone. Jean Goodman answered. 'I've been giving this berk Green the treatment, and I'm getting tired.'

'What's it all about?' Jean asked.

'He thinks we're little boys. 'E's took a right liberty.'

'Please don't involve Charlie, he's got too much on his plate.'

'Well, send Roy round. Tell him to fetch some tea.'

Roy sauntered round from Peckford's carrying a mug of tea. 'What's this all about, then, George?' he asked.

'He thinks we're little boys, Roy. Give 'im a drop of tea.'

Hall calmly emptied the mug of tea over the injured Green. 'I dunno, George,' he said, 'thought *you* had better sense than that. You know what Charlie is. We'll just have to teach you a lesson, won't we.'

Green was made to sit with his back to the wall. He got

kicked in the stomach and chest.

'Let's break 'is fucking ankles,' Cornell said.

His shoes and socks were taken off. Cornell jumped repeatedly on his ankles. Green laid his feet and legs as flat as he could to try and save a broken bone.

Mottram, although a villain and a man of tremendous power, was not vicious or sadistic. 'Give it a blow, George,' he said, when he saw the agony Green was in.

'What d'you mean, "Give it a blow"? I ain't started yet. You ain't seen nothin' yet.'

Green immediately tried to take advantage of this first indication of a softening – in Mottram, at least.

'Give us a fag, for Christ's sake,' he said to Cornell, 'I feel bloody awful.'

Cornell took out the cigarette he had in his mouth.

'Here you are, George,' said Cornell, stubbing out the cigarette in the side of Green's face.

Another bout of savage beating followed. He was hit with an iron bar round the legs and stripped off. Cornell then heard Bickers arrive in the yard. He had been up to Waterloo to pick up a lorry. Green was bundled into the back of the little warehouse. He was unable to stand up. He was covered in blood, his head was bleeding badly.

'You whisper a dicky bird, you'll get it again,' Cornell told him.

Green heard Bickers knock at the door which had been locked. As soon as it was opened, he was punched full in the face. Green heard him scream out.

When Cornell accused him of the restaurant cheque, Bickers blurted out: 'It wasn't me, it wasn't me. On my kid's life, it wasn't nothing to do with me. It was George, he signed it, not me.'

It was a foolish move on Bickers's part. Not only had he grassed up his friend, he had taken an oath on his child. To thugs like Cornell, this was unforgivable.

'You cunt,' Mottram told Bickers. 'We've had 'im here all afternoon giving him the treatment and 'e hasn't come out with nothin', but you come out with it straight away.'

Bickers was pounded and beaten up. He was struck with

197

an iron bar across his head and legs, and kicked and punched all over by the three men, it was later stated in court.

Bickers had a bad beating, but not as bad as the one Green had had. Green was nevertheless able to drive home, and he dropped Bickers off on his way. That night Green turned up in the casualty unit of Kings College Hospital. Dr Howard Vaile, who treated him, found he had a fractured rib, cauliflower ears and superficial grazes. Green did not complain about his feet, and there were no signs of scalding – despite the tea which had been poured over him. Nor was any record made of his toes having been broken by pliers, as he was later to claim had happened.

To most people, these attacks were brutal. In terms of the south London code and sub-culture, they were not much out of the ordinary. Both men were villains anyway, both had had their share of fighting and violence. They had taken a liberty and deserved what they got. After the beatings followed another ritual south London practice. Both men were allowed to wash and were given new shirts, before a customary 'drink up' in the Army and Navy. 'It was just one of them things,' says Roy Hall today. 'They took a liberty. We got the hump. They got a whack.'

14. Death of a Prospector

News of the Green/Bickers beatings hardly caused Charlie a second thought. They were just another demonstration of the way his gang dealt with deviency through the use of violence. Charlie was much more preoccupied with his forthcoming trip to South Africa where he was eager to catch up with Major Nicholson who had been there for more than two weeks.

Five days after the beatings, on 9 March 1965, he left for South Africa with John Fisher, Alfred Berman and a geologist called Bill Hill. Hill had worked for Paul Getty, the millionaire oilman. His services had been acquired through an advertisement that Charlie had placed in the situations vacant column of *The Times*.

The group was met at the airport by Waldeck. They all then met in an hotel to review the latest position. Charlie flew down to Durban to check that some of the machinery he had sent over had arrived. It had, but the authorities would not release it until the purchase invoices had been produced. Since much of the plant was stolen, this wasn't all that easy. At Durban, the group was joined by Eddie, who had been having a whale of a time while waiting to drive up to the location of the *Sands of the Kalahari* film, and meet up with Stanley Baker. Eddie, whom Charlie always referred to as 'my kid brother' in this kind of company, was never in fact to get to the location. He borrowed a new car to try and drive there but it blew up. He and the others who were with him hired a plane from a farmer who acted as pilot. After some pretty hairy flying, they were forced down by bad weather and that was that.

Charlie meanwhile had decided that he would go up to Mkuse and the perlite mine with most of the members of his team. They arrived at the Ghost Mountain Inn, a modern, single-storey hotel named after the range of mountains in whose shadow it lay. It was about twenty-five miles from the perlite mine. After a good breakfast next morning, they travelled to the site. They were greeted by Jimmy Collins and Peter Nicklaus. There was a black mamba snake hanging on a tree outside the caravan. The German had shot it and the idea now was to attract the snake's mate, so that it could be killed too. Fisher was fascinated by the country: there were thousands of little yellow birds, lots of Fever Trees – apparently so-called because they are often associated with areas where there is malaria – and all kinds of snakes and insects. It was a good job that there was a plentiful supply of quinine and snake serum.

Collins was as brown as a berry and, although he claimed to have lost two stone, he still had a huge beer gut. He took Charlie and the others around the site, proudly showing them how they had organised the local Zulus. A hut had been built and the Zulu boys had already dug pits exposing the perlite. At one pit the boys were chanting in lovely African tones, not in their native language, but in English which Collins had taught them. The chorus line went: 'Egg and chips, egg and chips, egg and chips. . . .'

Charlie spent several days at the site. He and the others picked up some of the semi-precious stone which he had heard so much about. Charlie, Fisher, Waldeck and Major Nicholson then returned to Johannesburg. It was now clear to them all that they needed to get ahead with mining the perlite on a large scale, as quickly as possible. The question was how it should be done. Of all the various mineral interests he had at this time, it was the perlite that Charlie was keenest to push. The other things could wait for the time being. Waldeck had already suggested that it might be better to involve an outside company which was experienced in mining. The idea was again kicked around, and Fisher supported it keenly.

From their hotel room, Fisher rang up the Pretoria Portland Cement Company, one of the best mining companies in this field in South Africa. He asked to speak to the managing director. When he got through he told him all about the perlite find, and asked for a meeting. This was readily agreed. Charlie, Fisher and the Major then drew up a long letter outlining what they had in mind and what they wanted from the Pretoria company. They plucked a figure of 1 million rand (£500,000) out of the air. For this, the company could be offered a 49-per-cent share of the perlite at Mkuse. The letter was delivered by hand. Charlie and Fisher soon found themselves across the table with the managing director. He expressed strong interest. He decided that he would send his own geologist to the site and then meet to discuss the offer further.

With these negotiations now set in motion, Charlie decided to return to London with Jean Goodman and Major Nicholson. He persuaded Fisher to stay on for a few more weeks to help push ahead the Pretoria Portland Cement negotiations and to look after his other interests. Fisher, feeling more than ever that Charlie was on his way to fame and fortune, willingly agreed.

Major Nicholson had been of immense value to Charlie and Concordia not just with his advice and guidance, but in terms of the goodwill he had created. He had made many new, potentially useful contacts. His local newspaper, the *Bedfordshire Times*, reported his trip on 19 March 1965, a couple of days after his return.

Back in Bedford on Saturday after a business trip which entailed 3,000 miles of travel in South Africa was Alderman Herbert Nicholson of 29, Cardington Road. Looking bronzed and very fit, as appropriate to the Chairman of Bedford's Public Health Committee, Ald. Nicholson told our reporter: 'I have enjoyed my experiences, but it's good to get back to old Bedford. This town takes a lot of beating!'

Ald. Nicholson's business was on behalf of the Concordia Development (Namaqualand) Co. Limited of Mayfair, of which he is a director, and another firm. It concerned the mining of volcanic rock which expands considerably under heat and is important industrially.

Ald. Nicholson had a very friendly reception by officials and by other people he met on his travels in South Africa. He took a message from the Mayor of Bedford to the Mayor of Johannesburg . . .

Another dignitary who received Mr Nicholson was the Town Clerk of Johannesburg, Mr Brian Porter. Mr Porter was most helpful to Ald. Nicholson . . .

Much of Ald. Nicholson's time was spent in the wide open spaces and he lived for a week in the Bush under canvas, finding this a delightful experience. Monkeys, baboons and deer comprised most of the wild life he saw. He travelled in the car suited to the terrain.

South Africa has great opportunities for young people in Ald. Nicholson's view.

Shortly after Charlie himself got back to London, Waldeck sent another tape-recorded message reporting on the latest developments. The promise of the large quantities of perlite was living up to expectations. Nicklaus had exposed one bed of the material and found that it was well over seven feet deep – meaning that over the whole flat area there was a very substantial deposit. It would be easy to mine – virtually open cast mining. It was simply a question of clearing about a couple of feet of topsoil to expose the perlite and then slicing the stuff out of the gound. Waldeck said that he now expected that 30,000 tons a year could be mined easily from Mkuse, but he pressed for more information on the question of expanding machines. It was becoming clearer all the time that the money was to be made with expanded, rather than crude perlite.

But there were problems with Namaqualand, on the other side of the country. The deal between Charlie and Waldeck was still causing all kinds of difficulties with Waldeck's former partners. Waldeck told Charlie that Aubrey had been trying to buy up the other partners' shares. Each had had a quarter share of the first Waldeck company, and there was now a suggestion that the agreement between Charlie and Waldeck was not legally binding. 'We can expect the question of Namaqualand to rear its ugly head within the next few weeks,' Waldeck stated. 'I have indicated that we are prepared to discuss this in a gentlemanly manner, simply on a pure and business basis without getting all the domestic situations again opened up or without going into the various nefarious matters that were discussed last time.'

There had been nothing gentlemanly about the way Waldeck and Charlie had done their deal and cut out all the others. The discontent of Waldeck's former partners had been rumbling on for some time. When Ken Nicholson was eased out of Charlie's ventures at the end of 1964, he had seemed to join up with the increasing group of people who felt angered about the way they had been ditched in such a peremptory fashion.

Ten days later, Major Nicholson also addressed himself to this particular problem, saying he had written to the people concerned, telling them that he could serve no useful purpose in any discussions, ' . . . but I don't think you have heard the last of these two gentlemen by a long chalk,' he added ominously. He was indeed right. In the weeks to come, Aubrey was to go on to acquire the shares of Waldeck's former partners in the first Concordia. Each of the four men had had a 25 per cent share each. This meant that Aubrey now had 75 per cent of the interests of the initial company.

But Charlie was scheming in such a way that he hoped these interests would soon become null and void. The rights that Waldeck and his first three partners had had to the 4 million acres of Namaqualand had to be reclaimed each year. This was done by a process called repegging. Waldeck was the only one of the four men who knew about pegging. He spoke the local languages and himself had carried out the first pegging. His three former partners had no idea how to go about the vital repegging operation. And if the area was not repegged in time, then the rights that had been awarded would lapse. Charlie and Waldeck planned that this is just what would happen. Once the rights had lapsed – and thus Waldeck and his three partners would have lost all their claims – Waldeck would then re-acquire them through his government contact. These re-acquired rights would then belong only to Waldeck and Charlie, Waldeck's first three partners having completely lost any claims they had.

Increasingly, Charlie and Waldeck's ambitious plans were creating enemies. There was Aubrey, and his friend Gordon Winter. Then there were Waldeck's former partners, who, like Aubrey with whom they were now aligning, were angry and bitter about having been cut out by Charlie's deal with Waldeck. And there was the powerful businessman who had been associated with the first Waldeck group, and who had had the idea of smuggling out the diamonds in frozen fish. His idea – which had already occurred to Waldeck – was to arrange for discoverer's rights to be claimed on the diamonds. But Waldeck told the businessman that if he did this, he would inform his friend in the government and get any such rights declared null and void.

But there were fewer problems with the concessions at Meir, thanks to a little bribery and corruption. Waldeck explained to Charlie: 'When you were here last year the necessary funds were passed in the government direction in order to expedite the Meir situation – I will be calling on the particular government department when I visit them tomorrow for the lease, and I will try and expedite that little bit as well. Should we find that we are in difficulties there, and when funds become available at a later stage, we may be able to "grease the wheels" a little, to expedite the formal recognition.'

This graft was to continue for many months to come. The hand-outs included a present of a new car to one official. Even Jimmy Collins was involved with some surprisingly high-powered people. In another letter to Charlie he said: 'You have all the right people on your side as you can see I am now in Cape Town I have been to see the Minister of Mines and he will give you all the help he can . . .'

Waldeck also sent back another tape dealing with staff matters, and in particular with Brian Oseman. Although Waldeck had got on well with him in the beginning, there was now friction between the two men. 'Brian has been extremely useful in this country on his previous visits, but for reasons best known to himself, on his last return he has adopted an attitude which has not lent itself to good relations ... It is a matter which you must deal with. You are more aware of the full circumstances. I must place on record at this particular stage I think that the whole question of our consortium is very much over his head. . . I have asked him now to complete the office accommodation and the various small details which have been pending for some time.' Waldeck was also feeling some antagonism towards Jimmy Collins. And he wasn't all that sure about John Fisher whose developing friendship with Kruger annoyed him. The feeling was mutual, especially in the case of Collins.

'They are just not our kind of people,' Collins told Charlie in one of his letters.

But by and large the operation was progressing in a distinctly forward direction and Waldeck felt very excited and confident. He also thought the time had come for a grander house – in keeping with the position he now saw himself occupying. 'Rightly or wrongly,' he told Charlie on yet another of his tapes, 'people in this country attach a lot of importance to prestige and not so much to the individual. What I am referring to specifically is that my domestic accommodation or house that I am living in at the moment is not really suitable or conducive to the overall picture of our consortium. I have had, on many occasions, to re-direct people who wanted to see me, into hotels or in offices, which does not lend itself to our overall picture.' Waldeck had already agreed to buy a splendid house for £12,500 in a prosperous Johannesburg suburb called Melrose and now he wanted to borrow money from Charlie to clinch the deal.

While Waldeck was buying himself houses and running down most of Charlie's men, the various tasks that they were engaged in progressed well. Colin Riddoch – Waldeck had started to dislike even him – was able to bring Charlie up to date on the efforts to launch his cherished public company. In a memo dated 12 April 1965, Riddoch reviewed the position saying that a public company was an excellent way forward. Charlie had all the necessary ingredients: an asset of proven value and the backing of Pretoria Portland Cement, a major organisation of unquestionable repute. On top of this the perlite's earning potential could last for many years. He felt that if the perlite were to be put into a public company this would lay the foundation of a large fortune.

John Fisher, too, had been firing on all cylinders. The Pretoria Portland Cement negotiations were going well, and he was raising a lot of other interest. A Japanese company wanted to buy large quantities of perlite and there were other potential customers in the wings. However he had a setback when a car he was driving – a Vauxhall Viva belonging to Corris Waldeck – crashed into a lorry on the way back from Mkuse. Waldeck visited him in hospital, bearing flowers and a cheque for £10,000 for his new house, which he asked Fisher to sign. He explained that it had been sanctioned by Charlie. Fisher knew nothing about it and felt neither the time nor the place were appropriate for such a matter to be raised.

After several days in hospital, Fisher slowly started work again. He was approached one day by a prospector who told him that he had something to sell. The two men met up and got chatting. They got on well. Fisher told the man of Concordia's various rights.

'Rubbish!' the man told Fisher. 'You haven't got these rights any more than I have. All you've got to do is to go and peg the land and the rights are yours once you get it down with the Land Registry.'

Fisher was unaware of the plans that Charlie and Waldeck had to repeg Namaqualand. 'You must be joking,' he exclaimed.

'Look,' the man said, 'if you go with me tomorrow we can peg out a thousand miles of land. There is nothing to stop us.'

The ex-journalist didn't simply take the man's word for it. Next morning he went to the government department which dealt with mining rights. It indeed appeared to Fisher that Waldeck, and thus Charlie and Concordia, did not have some of the exclusive rights to the 4 million acres in Namaqualand. What rights existed were in the names of people Fisher had never heard of. Even worse, perhaps, was that there appeared to be some vagueness about the Kruger rights to the Mkuse perlite which Charlie and Waldeck had bought and put into the company called Lebombo. It appeared that Kruger had sold some of his rights to another unknown man. Fisher was very worried. He had never particularly liked Waldeck and now he was highly suspicious. He had already discovered that Kruger had got promising rights to anthracite. Kruger had mentioned this to Waldeck who for some reason had never told Charlie. In the hotel that night Fisher told Brian Oseman of his discoveries.

'I think Waldeck has got con-man written all over him,' Fisher said.

'I wouldn't tell Charlie that if I was you, mate. He'll bloody well kill you. He's spent all his money here, he'll go berserk.'

Fisher elaborated. Then Jimmy Collins joined the two men. He agreed with Oseman – that it would be dangerous to tell Charlie about his doubts. Both Oseman and Collins, south London buddies of Charlie, could see that Fisher was perplexed. They both liked him and recognised him for the straight man that he was. They took Fisher aside.

'Look,' Oseman said, 'you know Charlie is a right villain, don't you? He's not just a scrap dealer and all that. He's not going to thank you for telling him he's cocked it up here.'

That night, 15 April 1965, Fisher sent Charlie a telegram to his home address. 'Urgent you should be here soonest Stop many matters require your attention Stop everything going well but your presence essential Stop telephone me tonight any time at Kyalami Ranch number Johannesburg 7061202.'

When Charlie called, Fisher relayed his worst suspicions. He suggested that Charlie should not hand over the money for Waldeck's house until he had come over and had a look at the exact position himself. Charlie listened to Fisher quietly, hardly reacting at all.

'I'll come out in the next week or two. You pay Tom the money. Whatever you do, I don't want him upset. Don't say a word about it till I arrive.'

Fisher handed over the money. Waldeck was delighted and with Fisher met Charlie at the airport the following week. He had brought with him Paul Berman, the son of Alf Berman.

Eventually, Charlie and Fisher returned to the Kyalami Ranch on their own.

'So what's this all about?' Charlie asked.

Fisher related how he had discovered the doubts about the rights.

'Tom is a hundred per cent. You've got it wrong.'

This time Charlie showed his feelings. He was very cross — with Fisher. The two men parted that night on bad terms.

Next morning, Charlie was different. He couldn't have been more friendly. Fisher was keen that Charlie confront Waldeck. But Charlie didn't want to know. It didn't matter that the paperwork Fisher had seen in Pretoria raised doubts. Waldeck, after all, had the contacts in the government. Waldeck was the most important single person that Charlie needed. He had to keep in with him and keep him sweet.

Fisher could not accept Charlie's apparent lack of concern. He himself rang Waldeck and accused him point-blank of having kept secret the anthracite rights which Kruger had told him about. Waldeck was livid. Corris Waldeck remembered the row well. Her husband contacted Charlie and complained bitterly about what had happened. Charlie smoothed it all over, convincingly. 'He assured Tom that he had complete faith in him,' Mrs Waldeck said in a later statement.

Charlie stayed on in South Africa for some time and, as far as everybody could see, the operation was going ahead quite happily. He also started taking an increasing interest in Eddie Kruger, who seemed to have access to more mineral rights than had at first appeared. Even Fisher seemed, for the time being, to forget his doubts about Waldeck. On 26 April 1965, he wrote to a Mr Hellings, the director of Pretoria Portland Cement.

'Since your visit to the site on April 2 further exploratory work has continued. Our geologist Mr Hill informs us that he can now substantiate immediate reserves 6,000,000 tons plus. The possibility remains, as indicated in our very first memorandum, of even greater deposits. Mr Hill's current estimate can, of course, be confirmed by your own people.

'We agree that there is lack of evidence at this stage of tonnages of particular qualities of perlite. We are currently arranging the expansion of samples taken from all over the area surveyed but some time must elapse before this work is concluded.'

Fisher dealt firmly with doubts raised by Pretoria Portland about expandability of some of the perlite they had tested.

'We are surprised by your comments that a random sample did not expand satisfactorily. This is entirely at variance with our own research. Mkuse perlite has been expanded by Otavi of Germany (who, as you know, are desirious of ordering large tonnages); by Cullinan Refractories some time ago when our Mr. Kruger was first prospecting the area; by Expanded Perlite Ltd of London UK; and by the Hungarian Government Agency with whom we are discussing the supply of expansion equipment. Our information is that *all* perlite will expand satisfactorily given the correct expansion equipment.'

But then the problem of Aubrey cropped up again. In the early part of May, Charlie was sitting in the bar of the Alma Hotel having a drink when Aubrey came in. He walked up to Charlie.

'You bastard,' he shouted at him, oblivious of the other people around. Aubrey was in one of his reckless moods — what the millionaire would have considered 'artistic'.

'Don't be silly,' said Charlie, not wanting any trouble. 'Sit down and let me get you a drink.'

Aubrey told Charlie that he knew all about the perlite and Waldeck and Kruger.

'I don't know what you are talking about,' said Charlie, all innocence. 'I'm not interested in the mining any more, I'm just selling the machinery.'

'You must think I was born yesterday,' retorted the Welshman. 'I know all about what is going on at Ghost Mountain. You're a slimey bastard, you are, what a bloody way you've treated me.'

209

'Never,' said Charlie. 'I don't know what you're talking about.'

Aubrey sat back and took a sip of his drink. Charlie looked relieved that the man seemed to be calming down. Unseemly rows in smart hotels did little to enhance the respectable image he was building up. He kept his eyes fixed on the Welshman.

'Well, if you are not interested in mining any more, Charlie, presumably you're not interested in Namaqualand either,' said Aubrey. 'Would you get Waldeck to sell me his 25 per cent share?' he asked.

'I don't know,' said Charlie. 'I can't speak for Waldeck. I'll ask him, if you want. I don't know what he'll say, but I'll try him for you.'

What Aubrey didn't know was that Charlie and Waldeck only had to wait until August for the rights of the initial Waldeck venture to lapse. It was then that they planned to reclaim and repeg the rights solely in their names. In this way, the others would be legally, if not ethically, cut out for good. Charlie and Waldeck could then get their hands on the riches of Namaqualand.

Charlie told Waldeck about the incident. They agreed that the best thing to do was to play Aubrey along, pretending that there might be a good chance of his getting Waldeck's share of the Namaqualand rights. Charlie called Aubrey and told him that he had spoken to Waldeck. Aubrey again started occasionally seeing Charlie and some of his associates, especially Paul Berman, the eighteen-year-old ex-public schoolboy son of the flamboyant Alf Berman, who was by now a director of Concordia. Paul was working with Charlie and representing his father's interests.

Charlie decided to make another trip to Mkuse and see for himself how it was developing. He went with Jean Goodman, Fisher, Waldeck, Kruger and Paul Berman. They also took along with them an enthusiastic South African called Louis Wulff, who had a great interest in perlite.

Then an odd thing happened. Jimmy Collins and Peter Nicklaus were returning in the Land Rover from Sbwana Bay, looking at the kesselger, one of the many other minerals to which Charlie had the rights. They had with them Waldeck's brother Dan. On their way back they stopped at the Ghost Mountain Inn for a couple of beers before going back through to the perlite mine at Mkuse. When they finally arrived at Mkuse, Nicklaus told Collins to get the revolver from under the seat before they locked up. It was the .32 gun which Waldeck had given Brian Oseman who in turn had passed it on to Collins for protection. Collins had put his hand under the seat. But the revolver was not there any more. They started looking for it, and in the end roped in all the Zulu boys and others at the mine to help them. But it was never found.

According to Mrs Waldeck, it was around the time of this second trip to Mkuse that her husband started feeling that Richardson, Fisher and Kruger were forming themselves into 'a little clique'.

'After they had all done their little chores at Mkuse, we all went down to Durban,' she recalled. 'And suddenly, that first night in Durban, Richardson disappears, Fisher disappears and Kruger disappears. Tom gets a trifle annoyed about this, because he gets landed with Fisher's girlfriend, whom he can't stand, and Mrs Richardson, who he liked. Anyway, we had dinner together, Paul Berman had dinner with us too. The following morning, Tom was wondering what on earth is going on, the telephone rings, Tom picks it up and John Fisher directly and pointblank accuses him once again of having misled Richardson. . . . Anyway, Tom gets very angry, he puts the phone down on Fisher. He phones up Richardson and says: "Right, here and now we can terminate our agreement, I have had enough." Richardson smooths him all over, and says it's absolute nonsense, and says he knows it's nonsense, and of course he trusts Tom, he would trust Tom with his life. "On the life of my children," – this is a favourite expression of Richardson's – "On the life of my children, Tom, I'd trust you with my life, I'd trust you with anything I've got. I don't believe all this, it's a lot of nonsense on Fisher's part." So Tom said, "Fine, but know this. I'll have nothing more to do with Fisher. Nothing more at all. You remove him, I will not have any discussions with him." '

Everything suddenly appeared to be falling apart, just as the negotiations for a public company and the participation of Pretoria Portland Cement were reaching their critical climax. Waldeck started lashing out at virtually everybody involved in the enterprise. He demanded that Oseman finally be sacked. As far as he was concerned at least, this is what happened. He also had a flaming row with Jimmy Collins over his general behaviour. Collins packed his bags and went off to Lourenço Marques.

And as if this wasn't enough, Waldeck started falling out with Bill Hill, the Paul Getty geologist. Peter Nicklaus got so fed up with all the squabbling and insults that he himself decided to quit. In him, the venture lost a valuable field man, who knew what he was doing and who had the added attraction of having a Blasting Licence from the government.

Waldeck then started to fume with Charlie, who hadn't contacted him for several days. When he did, Waldeck again complained. 'What is all this nonsense about?' he demanded. 'Why is it that you feel, you and Fisher and Kruger, that you can't trust me?'

This time Charlie was less patient. 'Well, you know how we operate, you know we are just not like you South African people. We don't contact people as soon as we come into a place, we don't bother about things like that. When we are ready to say "hello" to a bloke, well, we phone him up and say "hello" to him. It doesn't matter that we have been gone for a couple of days. This is just our method of life, you mustn't take offence, you're too touchy.'

By this stage, Fisher had had more than enough. It seemed to him that the whole of the great Charlie South African exploit was suddenly turning sour. He decided that he would return to London and concentrate on his own business. There was no bitterness or recrimination, and Fisher did not break away from Charlie as such. He told him that he would still be there if he was needed in connection with any developments that had resulted from his work with Pretoria Portland.

*   *   *

212

But further serious problems were also developing. Unknown to Waldeck, John Bradbury had returned to South Africa. After he had been fired by Charlie five months before (after his affair with Corris Waldeck) Bradbury had got a job in South Africa as a driver in January 1965. He had then left for the Belgian Congo as a mercenary on 15 February. He had returned on 8 April from Leopoldville flush with money and the spoils of his wretched activities against the blacks.

It was inevitable that Bradbury, womaniser that he was, was soon having a torrid affair with a gloriously attractive model called Elsa Smith. Flash and boastful Bradbury had told the girl that he was none other than Charles Wilson, the escaped Great Train Robber. Like so many of Bradbury's fantasies, it was not perhaps without a vague basis in truth. During the preparation for the train robbery, the men concerned had worked out that it was essential for them to be able to uncouple the railway wagons as quickly as possible. According to a man who knew him, Bradbury had been sent up to a large railway yard in the North to learn exactly how to do the job. He was then brought back to London, where he taught the train robber concerned exactly how to execute the tricky task.

But Bradbury, who was one of those who later alleged that Charlie had brought some of the proceeds of the robbery into South Africa, had, during the course of his affair with Elsa, been regularly phoning his wife Sheila back in Peckham. He kept accusing her of having affairs, but he also told her how much he loved her and missed her. As if to prove it, he kept asking her to come out to South Africa. He was just a little bit too charming because in the end she agreed, thinking perhaps that he really meant it this time. Although she had been badly and cruelly treated by Bradbury, she put up with it like so many a wife of a south London villain. And they had had their moments together: sometimes he had been very tender. As Sheila sailed for South Africa, Bradbury hurriedly broke off his affair with his model friend on whom he had lavished luxuries. She was furious and hurt.

When his wife arrived they and a couple of Bradbury's friends rented a large modern house in Victory Park, a beautiful suburb on the outskirts of Johannesburg. It was an astonishing change of circumstances for Sheila, who had come from a little house in Peckham. For a few weeks she was delightfully happy. But one Sunday in May, she picked up the papers and across the top of the front page of the South Africa *Sunday Times* was splashed a huge story about Charles Wilson, the Great Train Robber, being in South Africa. The picture of 'Wilson' portrayed none other than her husband. The source of the story was the model Elsa, whom Bradbury had jilted and whose picture was also displayed in the paper.

Sheila Bradbury was not the only person who was furious. Waldeck, too, was understandably concerned about what effect this might have on the delicate negotiations with Pretoria Portland Cement, now reaching a critical stage. 'Very charming if Mr Hellings [the senior man from Pretoria Portland] should get to know about Mr John Bradbury, alias West, as having been associated with us somewhere along the line,' he commented with undisguised sarcasm. Charlie quickly rang Gordon Winter. 'Gordy, do me a favour,' he said, 'go and see Bradbury and knock him flat and knock the shit out of that story. It's causing me a lot of bother. See what you can do, Gordy, I'd be right grateful.'

Charlie also wanted Winter to help Bradbury sue the *Sunday Times* and Lionel Attwell, the reporter who had written the story. Winter was not prepared to do that – although he didn't tell Charlie this – but he was more than happy to knock the story down. He knew it wasn't true. Winter, in his journalistic capacity, interviewed Bradbury and took photographs of him with his ever-present camera. It had an extremely wide-angled lens, and was always hanging from his neck in readiness. The camera, operated by a silent remote mechanism hidden in his pocket, was mainly used for his BOSS work. People rarely realised they were being photographed – the camera could be pointing in quite a different direction from the person yet still get their picture.

214

On 23 May 1965, Gordon Winter added another story to his long list of scoops. Across the top of the front page of the *Sunday Express* ran the headline: 'Cockney settler says I am no rail robber.'

Just before Charlie returned to London, a party was held in the house of an eminent lawyer. It was a small gathering, with no more than twenty people present, all of them prosperous and well-dressed. Charlie looked particularly fetching in his 115-guinea hand-stitched suit. A fine buffet had been laid on for the guests who, as well as Charlie, included the government official with whom Waldeck had his special relationship. Waldeck himself was not present at the party, but Charlie was able to use the occasion to discuss several important matters. He cornered the government official and intently talked business.

A few days later, Charlie returned to London. He persuaded Eddie Kruger to go with him. Charlie was still after Kruger's other rights. Waldeck had tried to stop Kruger going when the matter had been discussed earlier. He told him that the London boys were after his shares. He was particularly concerned because during Charlie's visit he had seen Kruger drunk on a couple of occasions: Kruger had for many years been cured of a drink problem, but now it seemed to Waldeck that Charlie and his men had managed to get him drinking again.

Waldeck's general poor humour was not improved when he found out after Charlie's departure that all kinds of hotel and air ticket bills had not been settled. Worse still, neither his salary nor Bill Hill's was being paid. Waldeck sent Charlie an urgent cable asking for £3000. He also decided to send him a tape-recorded message, reviewing the overall situation. Diplomatically, he began his tape with news that would please Charlie. He told him that their latest mineral, bentontite, was looking more promising than ever. By converting the mineral to nitrate bentontite, it could be sold for £50 a ton. He had found interested customers and was in the process of drawing up legal contracts. He also reassured Charlie that the Meir rights had been confirmed by the Ministry of Mines, and that Portland Cement were as interested as ever in the perlite. But then Waldeck got to the point. 'I think the time is now ripe when you and I can lay our cards on the table in terms of our partnership. One has the right, and also the clarity of mind, to be able to discuss with one's partner the various aspects of things which are, in fact, not in order. I refer now, specifically to John Fisher. I have been told on numerous occasions, that you have a very peculiar way, but a very satisfactory way, of coming to the final conclusion, and the truth of matters, and in the spirit of that I have accepted most of the things that have occurred during the time that you were here; in that spirit as well, as long as Pretoria Portland Cement goes through — all these various activities — does it in fact matter? The answer is No, it does not matter. Because of that, I have stood the insults and filth from the Osemans, the Bradburys, the Nicholsons and including Herbert Nicholson as well ... I regret however to say Charlie that I have made up my mind — and I am determined about this — that in no further property in which I have any interest whatsoever will I be prepared for John Fisher to negotiate or to discuss or to be involved. I will not allow myself to be pushed around in his abrupt and ill-mannered manner ... I am not incapable of talking to people. I don't think that my appearance puts people off and I am as capable and as entitled to discuss matters in which I have a share in the presence of you and John Fisher.'

Charlie was not pleased with this latest outburst. He did not respond to it — nor to Waldeck's request for money. Still the machinery had not been released from the docks in Durban because no invoices had yet been sent and bills were piling up all over South Africa. Charlie turned his mind off, knowing that the Pretoria Portland Cement deal was going well. His next task was to get over to Hungary for a meeting with Nikex, the company which manufactured the vastly expensive equipment for expanding the perlite. He rang Fisher and asked him to come with him. Fisher knew well the importance of the expanding of perlite to the Pretoria Portland deal. So he agreed to go, feeling that he ought to finish off the business he had nearly brought to completion for Concordia. On 14 June 1965, he set off with Charlie,

Alfred Berman and Kruger. They took with them a sample of perlite. While stopping off at Zurich airport, Charlie bought the group expensive watches and lighters. It was always his style to shower presents on people.

In Budapest, they stayed at the Geleert Hotel, and were given red-carpet treatment by the Hungarians. The chief negotiator was an ex-football star. But there was little negotiation needed. Charlie had already made up his mind about the machines – they were desperately needed and were about the best available. Charlie, as usual doing nothing by half measures, ordered three. Alf Berman, who had been brought along because he had agreed to put up the £33,000 needed for one machine, nearly fell out of his chair. But Charlie took no notice. The Hungarians were delighted. They took the group in a government car on a long journey through miles of rolling plains, to see one of the machines working. It looked very good.

But just a few days before this trip, on Saturday night, 6 June 1965, Bradbury had taken his wife and a couple of friends out to a bar in the Rosebank Hotel. His wife Sheila, now long since divorced, remembers the evening well. They were all having an enjoyable evening, Bradbury seemed in a good mood. Then, later on in the evening, he got up. 'He said he was going to someone's house and that he had got to frighten someone. He said that he had to do a favour for someone and shoot through the window at Waldeck. He said that he wanted to scare him, because he had upset someone.'

As Bradbury left the hotel, the Waldecks had just gone to bed at their house bought with Charlie's money at 7, Arran Avenue, in the suburbs of Melrose. Tom Waldeck fell asleep; his wife carried on reading. She looked at her watch. It was quarter past midnight. She dashed to the lavatory, but then froze in her tracks. There was a terrible noise. It was as if some madman was knocking in the door with a hammer. There seemed to be groups of four distinct knocks. She rushed back into the bedroom, terrified.

'Tom, Tom, did you hear that?'

Waldeck was just waking. 'Yes,' he said, 'what on earth was it?'

He ordered his wife into bed. He got up, put the lights out and crept round the house. He came back to the bedroom. He picked up his revolver and checked that it was loaded. He put on a track suit and told his wife to stay in bed. He went to the back of the house and put Rex, his Alsation dog, on the leash. He crept out of the back door and fumbled right round the house. He could hear nothing, nor see anything. He came back into the house.

He went straight to see his wife, whose affair with Bradbury he had forgiven. They started to turn over in their minds what the dreadful knocking noises could have been. Corris made some tea, which they drank in bed. The only explanation that Waldeck could come up with was that it might have been some local kids playing stupid games. 'Ah, well,' he said, 'let's get some sleep.'

He turned the light out. Within seconds, the hard knocking noises started again. Bradbury had let off another round of ammunition and this time rushed away down the drive to the road.

Waldeck leapt out of bed, collected Rex and, this time, his big gun, the Triple Two. By the time he had got outside, Bradbury was in his car driving back to the Rosebank Hotel.

Neither of the Waldecks slept well the rest of that night. They woke late the next morning. When they did, one of their black servants boys rushed up: 'Master, did you see where they shot at the house last night?'

Waldeck realised for the first time what had caused the noise. He found spent bullets inside the lounge and study. Some of the windows had been pierced. Suddenly Corris, who was with him, turned cold. Their youngest son, Greg, was not yet up, and there hadn't been a sound from him – most unusual. They charged to his room. He was there sleeping. But above his head on the wall were two bullet marks. Had the child sat up, he would almost certainly have been struck in the head.

Waldeck, furious, called the police. They arrived and found the shells as well as cartridges. The weapon used had been an automatic. They asked him if he had any enemies. 'Could it be any of your business associates?' asked the captain of police.

Waldeck was certain it could not have been. 'It couldn't possibly be them, because if they harmed me, or if they killed me, if that was their purpose, they would gain nothing, they would lose. Everything they hold in this country they would lose. . . . They wouldn't be that stupid.'

Corris Waldeck remembered how Charlie had been keeping her husband short of money just recently. 'Are you sure it's not the London boys?' she asked.

'No,' said Waldeck, 'I am convinced it's not.'

She asked him whether he thought it might have been any of his previous partners. 'Don't you think they were fed up with your getting together with the London boys like this and making such a success?'

'Impossible!' said her husband. 'You're talking tripe. They wouldn't have the guts, anyway.'

In the next few days, Bradbury was to make further abortive attempts on the life of Thomas Waldeck. But not a shot was fired. It was small wonder, perhaps, in view of the events of 6 June, that Waldeck's life was insured for £25,000 . . .

Bradbury became increasingly distressed by the continuing pressure on him to murder Waldeck. He gained little comfort either when on 13 June he met an old friend from New Cross, Harry Prince, and discovered that he had been having an affair with his wife before she had come across to South Africa. Prince told him that he had come to take his sister-in-law back to London. In the meantime, he stayed with some other men from London at the Quirinal Hotel in Johannesburg.

Waldeck seems to have been unaware of the continued plans against his life. His main concern was still the lack of money from London. He was beginning to feel rather left out of things. He decided to go up to Namaqualand with a geologist, to follow up leads on the occurrance of potash. Waldeck spent a week in Namaqualand. He felt glad to be away from all the troubles. He was always happiest when

219

out in the bush, wandering around in his shorts prospecting for minerals. On Friday, 25 June, he returned to his house. He was very excited. 'Corris, the most wonderful thing,' he yelped as soon as he got in. 'We've found diamonds, but really we have found diamonds. Now I am going to catch these London boys.'

He sat down and told his wife all that had happened. He said that he would be able to get money from Charlie now and then use it to pay off all the debts that had built up in South Africa. He sent off a cable to Charlie: 'Found jars. Contact urgently, Tom.'

But Charlie was not there. Instead, Alf Berman rang him up. 'What do you mean, you've found jars?' Berman, surprisingly, did not understand that jars was slang for diamonds.

Waldeck was puzzled when Charlie had still not got in touch with him. On Monday, 28 June, he went down to the Map Department in Pretoria and saw his friend in the Department of Mines.

The next day was Tuesday, 29 June. It was to be the last in the life of Tom Waldeck. Just before seven in the evening he sat down with his wife and children for supper. The telephone rang and Waldeck went to answer it. After a few minutes Waldeck's wife called through.

'Hey, your supper's getting cold. Do you want me to put in the oven?'

'No, I'm coming right now.'

Waldeck came back through to the dining room. He sat down and had just filled his mouth with food when the doorbell rang. He complained about yet another interruption. He walked to the front door and opened it. Four shots rang out, one hitting the door, one the wall at the side of it. Waldeck fell to the ground, spurting blood. A bullet had penetrated his liver and ripped his spleen. Corris Waldeck screamed.

'MY GOD, my God, Tom, are you hurt?'

'Yes, horribly, police, get the police.'

A few seconds later, the poor man died, and a neighbour saw two men drive off in a blue Chevrolet.

220

Bradbury arrived back at his house, 3, Third Row, Victory Park. His wife remembers: 'Johnny looked terribly ill and he said, "Look, don't ask any questions. Is the stove alight? I want to burn some stuff." Then he said, "I should have shot a bloke and only wounded him but I think we have killed him." '

The gun that killed Waldeck was Gordon Winter's Beretta, one that he had lent earlier. That is a fact — one of the few that are undisputed. Winter got it back and he says today that he threw it into Germiston Lake outside Johannesburg.

Eleven months after the shooting, Bradbury was sentenced to death for the murder, later commuted to a life sentence. He claimed that he had only been driving the car to the scene, and that somebody else had done the shooting. He claimed that he didn't even leave the car. But that is not true: another undisputed fact is that Bradbury's footprints were found in the flower bed right outside the Waldecks' front door. To this day in South Africa, the file on Thomas Waldeck's murder is still open. . . .

15. A Nice Little Earner

At half past ten on 30 June 1965, the morning after the murder of Thomas Waldeck, Charlie received a telegram marked urgent from Corris Waldeck telling him that her husband had been shot dead. Charlie wrote a reply to Waldeck's widow on the back of her telegram to him: 'Dear Corris, Deeply shocked and sorry to hear tragic news. Making arrangements to fly out to you first available flight. Our heartfelt sympathy to you and your family. Chas, Jean and family.' In fact, Charlie was not to fly out in the way he promised. Instead, he sent out Eddie and his father the following day, 1 July. Charlie was never to see Corris Waldeck again, although he made numerous further trips to South Africa.

An hour and twenty minutes after getting her telegram, Charlie received another from South Africa, this time from Paul Berman. It was nearly seventeen hours after the shooting that the telegram was sent. Berman gave Charlie the news about Waldeck's 'terrible shooting accident' and asked for £500 with which to carry on business. Exactly a day later, Charlie was reading another telegram from Berman saying that he was coming home and Charlie meanwhile should not fly to South Africa.

Charlie's main preoccupation was to retain control of his interests in South Africa, which were all threatened by the death of Waldeck, in whose name, and through whom, Charlie had gained all his various concessions. Two days after the killing, Charlie wrote to his South African lawyers, Cliffe Dekker and Todd.

'Dear Mr Borgwardt, By now you have heard the tragic news concerning Mr Waldeck. My wife and I are stunned by this terrible news it seems unbelievable.

'By next week I shall be in Johannesburg with the Hungarian people. In my absence my father Mr C. F. Richardson, my brother Mr E. Richardson together with Mr Collins and Mr Kruger are in Johannesburg and will be in contact with you.

'The good work you have maintained all along I know will be continued by your good self.'

Charlie also wrote on the same day and in the same vein to Louis Wulff, the South African perlite expert, at the same time offering him the job of sales director. 'There doesn't seem to be anything we can say about this terrible business of Tom's death. Our thoughts and sympathies are with Corris and the children. We just can't believe that it could happen.'

But Charlie's efforts to keep a grip on South Africa soon encountered major difficulties. The shooting of Waldeck was widely publicised in South Africa, and although Charlie's name was not in any way connected to the killing, the police, in the course of their widespread investigations, interviewed all of Waldeck's former associates. These included many of Charlie's men.

The police were at a complete loss in the weeks following the murder as to who had done the killing and why. But Charlie's lawyers, Cliffe Dekker and Todd, seem to have been uneasy about several aspects of their client's South African interests. They were not people who engaged in anything remotely dubious. Having thoroughly examined the legal position and the effect of Waldeck's death, they told Charlie, he says, that he would have to liquidate all his interests that had come through Waldeck. These included the 4 million acres in Namaqualand, which Charlie and Waldeck had been planning to repeg in the expectation of foiling Richard Aubrey's moves to buy the rights from Waldeck's former partners. They also included the rights which Waldeck had acquired in the area called Meir, as well as many other assorted concessions for kaolin, bentonite, copper, coal and silver in other parts of the Republic.

The loss of these rights was not greatly important to Charlie. They were, after all, only *rights*. Nothing had been

223

done about developing them – that would require a great deal of money and organisation. The only area where development had taken place, of course, was in the perlite at Mkuse. All Charlie's money and efforts had been devoted to precisely this. And in the days after the Waldeck murder Charlie was clearly working on the assumption that the perlite was not in the slightest way affected by the murder. He was talking of bringing over the Hungarian experts and offering a job to Louis Wulff in the perlite operation. . . .

The main reason for his confidence with the continuing future of the perlite was his connection with the other South African in his life, Eddie Kruger, who had owned the original rights to the perlite at Mkuse. Earlier in the year, on 11 February 1965, Kruger had finally signed the agreement selling these rights to Waldeck, and hence to Charlie as well. These ceded rights had been put into the company called Lebombo, in which Charlie and Waldeck had $37\frac{1}{2}$ per cent each, and Kruger 25 per cent. Thus Charlie assumed that he could still retain his legal grip on the perlite through Kruger, whom he had been cultivating in the previous two months.

But there was another reason for his optimism. Charlie felt that simply by being Waldeck's partner he might be able to inherit Waldeck's interests. In the agreement that the two men had signed on 4 November 1964, Clause 15 stated: 'Upon the termination of the venture for any reason, the venture shall be liquidated and the parties, or their representatives, including the representatives of a deceased party, shall be appointed as liquidators. In such liquidation it should be competent for either party to acquire any of the assets of the former venture.'

Kruger was certainly keeping in close touch with Charlie in the days immediately following the murder. On 6 July 1965, he wrote complaining that the South African *Sunday Times* had mentioned his name and Mkuse perlite. He said, however, that the mention only appeared in the early edition and he understood that the police asked the newspaper to delete it. He had also been questioned by the police, but not yet made a statement. He reported that he had seen Corris

224

Waldeck that day and everything seemed OK, although he was still very upset. The main efforts were being directed towards finding out the financial position of the companies. He told Charlie that he was going to see Cliffe Dekker and Todd to ask them to make an urgent application to the court to obtain an 'interdict on Tom *Waldeck's personal a/c at the bank,* as also on Waldeck Holdings and Orange River Enterprises to prevent these going into *Waldeck's Estate.*'

Charlie was also being kept abreast of developments in South Africa by Jimmy Collins. He wrote to Charlie on the same day as Kruger, reporting that he had seen Corris Waldeck, who, he said, was very pleased with the telegram she had received and the condolences which had been passed on. But Collins added: 'So far everything points to Tom being a conman.'

It was all very trying and frustrating for Charlie. He was, most uncharacteristically, having to tread carefully through the minefield of delicate negotiations that were needed to retain his interests in the perlite. His men out in South Africa were trying to make the best of what in many ways was an utterly chaotic situation. Not only was there the problem of Waldeck's murder, there were all kinds of unpaid bills, the question of trying to keep alive the negotiations with Pretoria Portland Cement, and still the large quantity of machinery and plant lying at Durban docks, which the authorities would not release because of insufficient documentation.

But back in London, Charlie was able to be more like his natural self. On 8 July he was very pleased. Ronnie Biggs, one of the Great Train Robbers, managed with the help of outsiders to escape from Wandsworth Prison. When Charlie heard the news on the car radio, he positively beamed with happiness. It is claimed by some of his former associates that Charlie had good reason to be so pleased: the price of the train robber money that was apparently being ploughed into South Africa was precisely such an escape.

Charlie at this time was making great efforts to get the Hungarian expanding machines on their way to South Africa. But there were problems in obtaining permission for the two Hungarian experts, Mr Buji and Mr Kiss, to enter South Africa. The two gentlemen were world experts, and their knowledge was vitally necessary if the plants were to be erected and operated. The £33,000 price tag on the machines included their advice and know-how, and supervision on site.

In addition to these difficulties, Charlie still needed more money to pay for the machines. He had kept popping round to Alf Berman's, doing his best to persuade him to put up more money towards the cost of the expanding plant. Berman, having already invested about £31,000, appeared reluctant to invest anything more. This annoyed Charlie who, because he had supplied Berman with wholesale goods in the past, felt he had enabled him to make money and was owed a favour in return. Charlie did not accept Berman's lack of enthusiasm for further investment. One evening Charlie turned up yet again at Berman's Bermondsey warehouse in Jamaica Road and pressed him for money.

'I can't, I can't,' said the excitable Berman. 'Business is bad. Customers owe me all sorts of money.' He mentioned two debtors with whom, he knew, Charlie was acquainted, so as to make his reasons for refusal seem more authentic. 'I mean, Farraday owes me nearly six grand. And that Taggart* owes me and all.'

In fact, James Taggart did not owe Berman money. Another man, known in the wholesale trade as Tolla, owed the money. Tolla had been telling Berman that he could not pay yet because he himself was owed money by Taggart. But all this was mere detail for Charlie who, without Berman realising it, saw the perfect opportunity for helping Berman come to the right decision about further South African investment.

A few days after this exchange, on 15 July, at 6.30 pm, the unfortunate Taggart left his premises in Commercial Street in the East End and got into his American car to drive home to Hampstead. He had gone only a small distance when a car overtook him and pulled up in front of him in such a way

* Sometimes spelt 'Taggett'.

226

that he was forced to stop. Two men, whom Taggart had never seen before, got out of the car in front and swaggered towards him. They were Frank Fraser and a man called Tommy Clark. Clark was a petty Brixton villain with a nice prison record who, after being released from prison five weeks before, had come back to work for Charlie. Somewhat apprehensively, Taggart wound down his window.

'Charlie would like to have a word with you.'

'Charlie? Charlie who?'

Taggart looked up and saw Charlie emerging from the car that had pulled him up. Taggart knew Charlie a little, having sold him a few lengths of suit material through one of the firms that Bradbury had run for Charlie in Addington Square. He had also accompanied Charlie on a trip to Milan in 1963.

'Hello, Jimmy,' said Charlie, 'I'd like to discuss some business with you.'

There was no explanation for the dramatic way in which this impromptu meeting had been arranged.

'Yes, certainly, what's it about?'

'Well, before I go into that, would you mind dropping me at Alfie Berman's place? We can go through it then,' said Charlie, ever so politely.

Taggart, somewhat mystified, agreed. Without a further word being uttered, Clark got into the car in front, Fraser climbed into the back of Taggart's car, and Charlie sat in the front passenger seat. A few minutes later, Taggart pulled up in front of Berman's warehouse in Bermondsey. As he did, Clark arrived in the other car.

'I won't be a minute,' Charlie told Taggart. 'I'm just going to have a chat with Alf.'

Clark, meanwhile, got into the seat Charlie had vacated. After a short time, Taggart started asking what on earth was going on. He was a big strong man, an expert in judo, but he was beginning to feel apprehensive. Clark got out of the car, went into the warehouse, whispered to Charlie out of Berman's earshot, and then returned to the car.

'Charlie's going to be a while. He wants us to drive to the office and wait for him there.'

227

'Look,' Taggart said, 'Charles said he wanted to discuss business with me. If he does want to discuss business with me, now is the time. I was on my way home when you stopped me. I'm not going to hang round some old office just waiting for him.'

Taggart opened the door to get out. Fraser and Clark tried to stop him, unsuccessfully. Charlie suddenly appeared from the warehouse.

'What the bloody hell is going on?' Taggart demanded to know. 'And what the hell was that all about?' he shouted, indicating Charlie's two henchmen. 'What's this so-called business you said you wanted to talk to me about?'

Charlie paused. He realised that the moment had come to commence proceedings.

'You owe Tolla £900,' Charlie announced. That unpleasant leer appeared on his face.

'I don't care whether I owe him £900 or £9000, it's got bugger all to do with you.'

This was not the way to talk to Charlie, especially in front of Frank Fraser, always somewhat trigger-happy and twitchy. Before Taggart could say another word, he was attacked by Fraser and Clark. He was hit hard on the head with fists and a metal implement wielded by Fraser. He was dragged from the pavement and bundled into the car. Clark drove the car full speed to Charlie's Anglo-American premises just round the corner at 231, Rotherhithe New Road. Once in the yard, the gates were shut and Taggart was thrown into the sparsely furnished office, enduring another volley of punches and kicks to the head and body. He was then stripped completely by Fraser and Clark. Charlie sat at his desk, watching as Taggart was placed on a chair in the far corner of the room and again attacked and savagely beaten. He was kicked several times in his testicles.

Charlie picked up the phone. Taggart was just able to hear him make several calls. In some of them he was asking about the 'box'. But Charlie could not locate the electric torture contraption. He put down the phone and walked across to Taggart and started beating him, screaming that he was a police informer. Fraser, always eager to please,

228

picked up a wooden pole and smashed it across Taggart's head. He used it with such force that it eventually snapped in half, even though the pole was thicker than a broom handle. This malfunction didn't deter Mad Frankie, however. He merely carried on beating Taggart with the part remaining in his hand.

In between further sessions of beating, Taggart's clothes, car and briefcase were thoroughly searched and the papers were all assembled in the office. Charlie started leafing through them, particularly his bank statement.

Further attacks continued on Taggart until soon he was reduced to a terrible state. He could hardly see through his eyes because of the blood streaming over them from his wounded head. His naked body was marked and covered in blood. He had been hit with such force that blood was splattered all over the two corner walls. All seemed blurred and vague. Every part of his body had been kicked and punched with ferocious savagery, and there was a bad wound on the top of his head. Through this haze, on the very borders of consciousness, he heard one of the three ordering him to mop up the blood on the walls and floor. His underpants were thrust into his hand. Taggart groped like some half-dead animal round the lower walls and floor. He was then tied up with a long thick rope that was bound around him by Clark, as the court heard later.

It was into this scene that Alfie Berman then arrived. He had been asked by Charlie during one of his earlier telephone calls to bring round some beer and fish and chips. Charlie had already arranged with Berman, during his visit to the warehouse an hour before, that he would accompany him to Heathrow airport to pick up Eddie, who was arriving back from South Africa. That way, Charlie had reasoned, Berman would be able to get an up-to-date report on the South Africa situation. But much as Charlie enjoyed a little feast during the middle of one of his torture sessions, the arrival of Berman that particular night was for other reasons. The beating of Taggart was being laid on to show Berman what a useful friend he had in Charlie: a little trouble with a bad debt, then no problem; Charlie would sort it out, just like that. And Charlie, being devious, knew that Berman would get another message: it might be great to have Charlie as a friend, but deadly to go against him or to fall out with him as a result of not co-operating with his wishes. Charlie knew that Berman, like most basically decent men, would be horrified and frightened by the Taggart beating.

When Berman walked through the door into the office, he saw only Charlie and the other two around one of the three desks in the otherwise sparsely furnished room. He placed the two packets of fish and chips and the four half-pint bottles of light ale on the desk. But then, from the corner of his eye, he caught sight of a man slumped in the far corner of the room, covered in blood and cocooned in a mass of rope. He nearly jumped out of his skin.

'Oh, my god,' he wailed, 'oh my god.'

He looked at Charlie, and then looked again at the man. His head was swollen, his ears were swollen, his eyes were swollen, there were marks all over his body and there was blood smeared all over the walls behind him. Berman almost started crying.

'Oh my god . . . good god,' he choked. 'What's this man doing like this? How did this happen? What's the matter, oh my god, what's he doing like that?'

Charlie observed in silence, looking smug and pleased with himself. Berman glanced again at the damaged, groaning body in the corner.

'Oh no . . . oh no,' he cried, peering harder at the victim. 'Is that Jimmy Taggart . . . ? My god, it is Jimmy Taggart!'

'He took away a man's liberty,' Charlie calmly informed Berman. 'He's a fucking police informer.'

'But, but . . . but you . . . it doesn't matter what he's done, you can't treat a man like that,' said Berman, looking pitifully at Taggart. 'Let him go and put his clothes on. Let him have a wash and let him go home.'

Fraser shifted uneasily and looked at Charlie. As far as they were both concerned, the evening had only just started. Fraser was just checking that there was no sign of Charlie's relenting at such an early stage. He need not have worried.

'He's done some terrible things,' Charlie told Berman. 'He's not fit to live. He's an informer. You wait here a while, there's somebody else coming.'

Berman, excitable and flappable at the best of times, sat down in a daze almost as great as Taggart's. Charlie, Fraser and Clark casually started munching the fish and chips and swigging the beer out of the bottles. Berman felt too frightened to leave.

'Have some grub, Alf, and stop fucking worrying,' said Charlie.

It was this stage of the torture sessions that he loved greatly: the ritual informal meal-break which gave him that heightened and delicious sense of contrast – between his own state of complete control and that of the wretched impotence of the victim.

'Shouldn't Taggart have something to eat?' Berman asked meekly, hoping that this suggestion might somehow help.

'That bastard isn't fit to eat,' snarled one of the men, his mouth full of chips.

And far from helping, Berman's suggestion signalled the start of another session of beating. Fraser, having already broken the wooden pole over Taggart's head, this time used a metal instrument. Taggart, by this stage realising that his life was in danger, concentrated all his might into simply staying conscious. Berman started wailing. He had never before seen such a display of hatred.

The latest round of beatings spilled a lot more of Taggart's blood over the walls and floor. Charlie told Clark to chuck Taggart his underpants. 'Make the bastard clean his own mess up.'

Berman groaned and tried to take the underpants from Taggart. 'It's terrible. You can't do this, nobody gets treated like this.'

'For fuck's sake, shut up, Alf,' said Charlie, pleased at Berman's reaction. 'Let the cunt clean it himself. You just sit down and shut up. What's wrong with you, you lost your bottle or something?'

Taggart crawled around making futile efforts to clean the blood with his sodden underpants. Clark was then ordered

231

to tie him up again with the rope. It was wound round his neck, body and legs.

Charlie heard a car arriving outside. 'At long last,' he said.

During his earlier telephone calls Charlie had also rung Harry Waterman who was now one of his dogsbodies. Charlie had told Waterman at his Streatham home to go and tell that other great friend of Duval, Frank Prater, to come to the Anglo-American offices. Prater lived in Finsbury, north London, and Charlie had been unable to contact him himself on the phone.

Prater, it will be remembered, was Duval's great partner during the extraordinary frauds in 1962 involving Italian stockings, the Bank of Valletta and the air tickets fiddle. He had been sent to prison in 1963 after being convicted of conning the public through the casino syndicate. Just the month before, June 1965, he had been released and, through a mutual friend, had started working for Charlie at Anglo-American, in whose premises Taggart was now getting his beating. Because Prater was good with figures, banking and the books, Charlie wanted him to go through all Taggart's papers and work out how much money he could raise quickly. On top of that, Charlie also thought that Taggart had 'grassed' Prater to the police on the casino fraud for which he had been sentenced.

It was shortly before 9pm when Prater finally entered the office torture chamber. Like Berman before him, Prater did not at first see the naked battered body of Taggart, now lying in a pool of blood in the far corner of the room, his back towards the group of men. All he saw were the remains of the fish and chips on one desk, and Charlie sitting an another going through a bundle of papers and cheque books.

'Hello, Frank,' said Charlie. 'We've got someone here I think you know.'

'Who?' said the happy-go-lucky Prater.

Charlie gestured towards the corner where Taggart's savaged body lay like a lump of butcher's meat. 'It's your friend Jimmy Taggart.'

A look of horror spread across Prater's face. He had never

before in his whole life seen a single human being in such a dreadful state of humiliation. He moved closer towards him, cautiously. Prater gasped. Taggart's head had swollen to almost twice its normal size.

'We want you to talk to him,' said Charlie. 'Find out how much money the bastard's got.'

Taggart, still forcing himself to remain conscious, was aware that Prater had arrived. He knew he was not a man of violence and felt some comfort by what he sensed was Prater's horror. He hoped that Prater's arrival might end his ordeal.

For about the first time in his life, Prater was speechless. The man who had defied the Mafia gunmen in the Bank of Valletta with Jack Duval couldn't think what to do.

'Well, my god, you'd better untie him first if you want me to talk to him. How can anybody hold a bloody discussion in *that* state?' Prater was realising that the only thing to do was to play along with Charlie, then gradually try and extricate himself and Taggart.

Clark, on a nod of the head from Charlie, went across to Taggart and untied the rope that was all around him. He sat him on the chair in the corner, still stark naked. Prater, now seeing a full frontal view, was even more shocked, especially by the size of Taggart's head. Prater could see from the general tone of the arguments that were taking place, and particularly from Fraser's manner, that there was no sign of the violence ending. When Taggart agreed that he owed the man called Tolla money, Fraser said menacingly: 'You're not thinking right. You're not thinking right.'

But Prater then sat down and started going through all of Taggart's papers. He fairly soon had worked out that there was about £1200 available from his current personal account and from his business account at a company called Paul and Paul.

'Yes, he's all right for about £1200,' he informed Charlie, matter-of-fact. 'Don't worry, you can definitely get hold of the money,' Prater added, anticipating Charlie's next question.

Prater went across to Taggart. He suggested that he

should pay the money over. It would be a way of extricating himself from the terrible situation he was in. Taggart agreed that he would write two cheques in the name of Berman for the money he owed to the man called Tolla. This appeared to satisfy Charlie, but Fraser was not keen.

'How can you be sure?' he asked Charlie. 'If we let this bastard go he'll nick the lot of us.'

But Charlie seemed content that the money would be paid over. He didn't want to delay the argument anyway, because he had to get down to the airport to pick up Eddie whose plane was due in at 10.20pm. He left the building with Berman. 'I'll be back later,' he told Clark and Fraser.

Prater went across to talk to the wretched Taggart, to try and comfort him. He looked more closely at his body. The wounds were appalling. His whole body was red from the chafing of the heavy rope in which he had been repeatedly tied up and then untied. There was one particularly bad wound on his head. The blood was congealing around it, but some was still trickling out down over his face. But the other two men were only worried about whether Taggart would go to the police.

'What will you say if anybody sees you like that?' asked Clark.

'I'll tell them I was in a car accident, say that it was a bad smash . . .'

'Yes, well, you mention a fucking word about this, we'll fucking well kill you next time,' said Fraser. 'You understand? Next time we won't just play around with you, we'll really fucking hurt you.'

But Clark was softening. 'Are you sure that you can get home all right like that?'

'Yes, don't worry. I'll take it easy. It'll be OK . . .'

'Perhaps we should let him go now,' Clark suggested to Fraser. 'He'll be all right, I think, I don't reckon 'e will cause no problems.'

But Fraser wouldn't have any of it. 'We'll wait until Chas gets back. I don't trust the cunt at all.'

Clark took Taggart outside the office. He poured buckets of water over Taggart to try and wash the blood away. Such was the degradation that Taggart had been through, this further indignity hardly mattered. He staggered to his car and picked up a new shirt which was part of a batch used as samples. He went back upstairs and was helped to dress, minus underwear which was all now revoltingly congealed with blood. The group settled down to wait for Charlie's return. Prater talked quietly to Taggart in the corner, still trying to comfort him. He arranged that after they had been released from Charlie's custody, he would drive home Taggart's big American car. Prater suggested that Taggart could follow him in his Mini, which would be easier to drive. Taggart agreed and told Prater that they would have to stop to get some petrol because he had almost run out.

Eventually Charlie returned with Eddie, fresh from his trip to console Corris Waldeck in South Africa. Berman had come back into the yard from the airport, but had decided to drive straight back home. He had already had more than enough.

Next day, after Taggart had been helped home by Prater, Berman called him on the telephone. He told him how sorry he was about what had happened, and was concerned that he go to a doctor. But Taggart paid over the money to Berman, who had already explained that none of it was for him. Taggart knew that if he did not pay up, there would almost certainly be a repetition.

He was even too frightened to go to a doctor in case it led to the police being called in. He lay in bed for five days until eventually a friend called Bennett fixed him up with a doctor called Micalef in the East End. The appointment was made only after assurances of secrecy. The doctor came to the friend's house. What he saw there horrified him, even though he was an experienced doctor, and even though it was five days after the beating. Both Taggart's eyes were a solid mass of bright, bright red. His ears and head were still swollen and his face was disfigured. There was massive bruising all over his body and face, and his genitals were black and swollen. There were still marks all over him from where the rope had been bound round his raw and naked body.

Dr Micalef suspected that Taggart had a fractured skull. He urged him to go to hospital straight away. Taggart refused point-blank. 'He looked grotesque,' Dr Micalef recalled later. 'I am sure there was a fractured skull or fractured nose ... He had been subject to a high degree of violence ... apart from the head and face injuries, the patient was covered in bruises, huge bruises all over his body, arms, legs and the inside of his thighs ... there were huge effusions of blood underneath the skin.'

Such were the dreadful consequences of what Charlie describes urbanely as 'a couple of right-handers, a couple of whacks'. His excursions in South Africa into high finance and surface respectability had done nothing to change him from what he primarily was: a gang leader who, through the ruthless application of violence, presided over a vast network of criminal activity. His power in the London underworld was greater than ever before. The Richardson name commanded new levels of fear in men as the network of the organisation spread further and wider.

One of the most important places where the Richardson tentacles reached was the Soho clubland in which the fruit-machine interests were booming under Eddie's and Frank Fraser's control. This whole area provided Charlie with a marvellous source of information and gossip about what was going on in the underworld.

And it was through this Soho grapevine that Charlie found out in the summer of 1965 about a huge fiddle that had been going on at the Heathrow airport car parks for over three years. The information came via a man called Alexander Herman. Charlie liked what he heard very much indeed: the attendants had altered the time clocks which marked the parking tickets, so that vehicles were shown to have been in the park for less time than in reality. The motorists, of course, were charged the full price. The attendants pocketed the difference. In this way the men at the airport had been making in excess of £1000 a week, or £50,000 a year, or half the amount that the car parks were taking altogether. It was a perfect racket for Charlie to move in on. The muscle of his gang could be used, if necessary, to coax the men into giving him a share – for 'protection'. And Charlie was not an unreasonable man: he thought he would help himself to half of the proceeds.

He sent Eddie and Frank Fraser down to see the men to organise the deal. But the men, not surprisingly, were reluctant to give up half their loot just like that.

Even if Charlie had been prepared to forego the £500 a week – which he certainly wasn't – he could not allow a refusal like this to pass. Word would otherwise soon get around that somebody had defied the Richardsons. There was no room in this world for compromise or negotiation or loss of face. If Charlie ordered it – that was that. It had to be done. The day it didn't would mark the beginning of the end for the Richardson gang.

As a result, one of the Heathrow men was kidnapped and locked up in the cellar room of the offices of Atlantic Machines, the Richardsons' fruit machine company. After spending more than a day in the hole, he was taken to a room upstairs where Charlie was sitting at a desk. Frank Fraser was there, and another member of his family. So too were some of Charlie's other men, including Tommy Clark. Charlie questioned him in detail about the fraud, who was involved and how exactly it was done. The man talked freely, realising that there was nothing else for it. The alternative was certainly a savage beating, or worse. He agreed that Charlie could have £500 a week – 'for protection'.

Despite this co-operation, Charlie suddenly ordered the man to take his clothes off. He made him remove every stitch. The man felt such a fool standing there stark naked in front of Charlie and his men. They all sniggered at him. Then Frank Fraser's relative was ordered into action. He set about the man with a wet knotted towel. He hit him only a dozen times at most, and it wasn't a savage beating. He was neither cut nor knocked unconscious. But, above all, he was humiliated.

A man who witnessed the scene drove back afterwards with Charlie to the Anglo-American yard.

'What was that all about?' he asked.

'Well, it's 500 quid a week.'

'But you had the £500 without even asking the guy to take his trousers off. He agreed to everything.'

'Well,' said Charlie impassively, 'you've got to teach them a lesson, they got to realise that you are the guv'nor.'

For the remaining year of the Richardson's reign, the gang was to take its £500 a week from the Heathrow car park men. At first Eddie and Frank Fraser used to travel down to a cafe near the airport once a week to collect the money in Eddie's green Bentley car. But soon they got bored and ordered that the money be sent to them at a Soho address. It was what they called a nice little earner.

16. The BOSS Affair

But these violent events were all a matter of domestic routine. What Charlie was really interested in was his foreign affairs and cracking ahead with the perlite. He needed somehow to sew up Waldeck's rights and then form a new company with Eddie Kruger to develop the perlite, with the help of Pretoria Portland Cement which was still interested.

Charlie felt he needed a fresh face out in South Africa, a respectable, knowledgeable man to help him achieve all this. In recent months Major Herbert Nicholson had faded somewhat, and anyway he was not exactly a new face. Charlie approached a man called Victor Doel who had worked for an airline concern for which Charlie had earlier in his life scrapped old planes. He was one of those men whom Charlie had met when he was in his early twenties and expanding his scrap business. Doel, an accountant by training, had fascinated him, and he had talked with him on any occasion he could, trying to pick his brains and learn about the business world. Doel had found Charlie quite impressive and resourceful. Like so many others, he had absolutely no inkling of Charlie's real nature.

At first Doel was not too interested in the perlite proposition that Charlie put to him. But Charlie, as always, persisted. He produced documents and agreements as well as geologists' and other experts' reports to prove to Doel how wonderful perlite was, and what massive potential existed at the Mkuse mine. Charlie naturally simplified matters considerably, and conveniently left out crucial and awkward details.

Charlie wanted Doel to emigrate to South Africa and try and sort out all the problems associated with Waldeck's death, pick up the Pretoria Portland Cement negotiations, and then become managing director of the new perlite company. To assist his arguments with Doel, he brought along Alfie Berman who, despite the Taggart beating and despite other worries he had about Charlie's South African concern, still keenly supported the perlite operation: he was trying to protect the £30,000 he had already invested. Berman offered Doel £5000 as a consultancy fee just to drop everything and go out to South Africa for two or three weeks. The idea was that if Doel was impressed by what he saw, then he could work full-time for Charlie in South Africa. It was an offer that Doel found hard to resist. And on 9 August 1965, Berman and Victor Doel caught the plane to South Africa.

They met up with Jimmy Collins and Eddie Kruger at the Quirinal Hotel. By this time, Charlie had already discovered from Collins that he would not be able to inherit Tom Waldeck's perlite and other shares. Collins had been regularly visiting Cliffe Dekker and Todd and just a few days before the Berman/Doel visit had written to Charlie in his inimitable style: 'Just a quick line To let you no what is happening. I have just left Borgwart ... Mrs Waldeck wants £50,000 POUNDS for TOMS SHARES, which they reckon she's entitled too on ADVICE giVEN BY A Q.C. I mean she is entitled TO The SHARES, NOT THE MONEY.'

Doel, with professional skill and flair, started addressing himself to this problem of Waldeck's shares, and to discussions with Eddie Kruger for his perlite rights. He contacted Pretoria Portland Cement and explained to them what the position was, saying that he hoped it could all soon be sorted out.

But as Doel started getting a grip on the situation, Charlie faced some niggling problems back at the London end of the operation. The volume of free air travel that Charlie and his merry men had been enjoying back and forward to South Africa was starting to cause difficulties. A company called the German Travel Bureau was threatening to get Anglo-American, in whose name the tickets had been purchased, wound up unless the debt was settled immediately.

Another firm, Robson Travel, was also pressing hard for £2777 that was owed. A complex fiddle had been worked out, involving both Concordia and Anglo-American buying on credit from the firm, which had no idea that the two companies were connected. By the time they realised, it was too late. An employee of the firm later destroyed the Anglo-American file after receiving money from Charlie.

There were all kinds of other unpaid bills – to contractors, the Post Office for the telex machine, and many others. The main response to this seems to have been to try and set up new frauds and fiddles on other firms. For example, Charlie wanted a new caravan out in South Africa. If he had paid the full price for purchase and shipping, it would have cost him nearly £1200. The way Charlie managed matters it cost him £125. One of the gang went down to a firm called Anthony Bruton Caravans in Coulsdon, Surrey. A model costing £500 was ordered on 23 August, and a hire purchase arrangement agreed. A guarantor was put forward, a £125 deposit was paid, and the caravan was towed away. On 9 September 1965, Anglo-American wrote to Trans Lloyd Overseas Ltd. 'Dear Sir, Would you please arrange shipping for our caravan marked Aaclund No 7 to Durban on SS Tentallen Castle as per our verbal instruction.' A few days later the instruction was carried out and an invoice sent to Anglo-American for £606.1s.6d. It was never paid. Nor were the remainder of the HP payments to Anthony Bruton Caravans. A few months later, two Scotland Yard officers were to find the caravan out in the wilds of remotest Mkuse.

It was hardly surprising that some of the company figureheads, such as the late Sir Noel Dryden, started to worry. As some of the stranger goings on became apparent to Sir Noel through the almost perpetual alcoholic haze he lived in, he took protective measures. 'As neither you nor I have any idea what is going on in regard to Anglo-American Engineering Corporation,' he wrote to the office manager, 'I shall be glad if you will put this letter on record.

'We have no information on policy, expenditure or trading, and appointments made to clarify these matters are broken. Under the circumstances I cannot hold myself responsible for any actions taken by the company.'

Not long before this, John Fisher had also resigned. By August 1965, he realised Charlie was doing more than sailing close to the wind. The Waldeck killing worried him. He handed in his resignation on 27 August, choosing his words carefully to avoid inviting Charlie's wrath.

'Dear Chas, I am hoping to take up an important post shortly with a leading international company. Part of the condition of the employment is that I shall have no outside business interests and I would therefore like you to accept this as my formal resignation from the Board of Directors of Concordia Developments (Namaqualand) Ltd.

'Whilst I am writing my I remind you that you have promised the due rent on your Grosvenor Street office by mid next week and also a decision as to whether or not you wish to retain them. Should you decide to keep them I will let you have the name of the solicitors who will be handling rents on behalf of the new leaseholder.

'In passing, as of the end of next week, they have informed me they will definitely repossess if due rents are not paid.'

This didn't bother Charlie. A few weeks later he was to take an office just round the corner at 139, Park Lane. It was a perfect front.

Meanwhile, Berman and Doel had been busy in South Africa. Doel had quickly impressed himself on the scene. He discovered things which puzzled and confused him but nevertheless pushed on in the areas which were clearer. His main priorities were to make sure Charlie got Waldeck's shares, and particularly his perlite interests, and to set up the new company for exploiting the perlite with Eddie Kruger, the vital link with the Mkuse rights.

When Charlie had found out that Cliffe Dekker and Todd insisted he would have to purchase Waldeck's rights from his widow, who was the sole beneficiary, he changed solicitors.

His new firm was called Lubbers, Spitz, Block and Carel. Victor Doel had established a good relationship with a man there called Mr Rubenstein, and negotiations for Corris Waldeck's shares were started with her lawyers.

With his affairs thus being straightened out by the competent hands of Victor Doel, Charlie decided himself to come out to South Africa. Seven weeks after the death of Waldeck, he took off from Heathrow with Tommy Clark. They were met at General Smuts airport by Alf Berman who, much to Clark's amusement, was wearing a flashy, bright yellow suit.

Doel had established for himself that there was a wonderful potential in the perlite. Charlie and Berman discussed matters with him, and finally persuaded him to become managing director of the new company they were planning to set up. But Doel dictated many conditions and safeguards. By the time an agreement had been signed, he was guaranteed £15,000 to buy a house of his choice, 6 per cent of the shares of the new company and a salary of £5000 a year, plus a car. Because of the total uprooting that the move would involve for himself, his wife and his four children, he wanted all kinds of other assurances.

Doel seems to have been worth every penny. By the middle of September 1965, he had supervised the purchase of the Waldeck shares and, through Charlie's new solicitors, had organised the setting up of the new company, which was called South African Perlite Mines and Industries Propreity Ltd (SAPI). He had also more than kept alive the interest of Pretoria Portland Cement and, drawing on other earlier work done by people like John Fisher, had developed negotiations with several other companies who wanted to buy Charlie's perlite.

The actual agreement between Charlie and Corris Waldeck for all of her late husband's shares was signed on 23 September 1965. For £50,000, to be paid in stages, Charlie bought all the various interests which he had shared with Waldeck before his terrible death. These included Waldeck's shares in the four joint companies that had been set up: Lebombo Mineral Developments, Orange River

243

Enterprises, Waldeck Holdings and Concordia Developments (Propreity) Ltd. As a result of the deal he also got all the Kruger rights to the perlite that Waldeck had acquired on 11 February 1965, various rights to kaolin in East London, South Africa, rights to a bentonite deposit in the Orange Free State, and rights that might exist to mineral deposits in the Meir district. But the key part of this agreement was, of course, the Kruger perlite rights.

It was an expensive deal for Charlie, especially since he had to pay all Mrs Waldeck's legal costs and allow her to keep the house which he had brought for his former partner.

The day after this agreement was signed, the new perlite company, SAPI, was formally set up and registered. Largely as a result of the services of Victor Doel, the whole perlite venture had been rationalised, simplified and put on what seemed to be a sound footing. Charlie would have 75 per cent of the shares of the new company, Kruger 25 per cent, in return for his various rights to the Mkuse perlite. All the other companies, saving Lebombo, would become dormant, and all future development of the perlite would be carried out by SAPI, which became a wholly owned subsidiary of Lebombo.

And what great plans there were for the future. SAPI, now the exclusive owner of the perlite rights in Mkuse, hoped to sell 50 per cent of its shares to Pretoria Portland Cement for £250,000. This money would be used for the development of the mine. It was expected that with the expanding machines from Hungary in place, 100,000 short tons of expanded perlite could be produced each year, which could be sold at £42 a ton. There was also a demand for the crude perlite. It was estimated that the mine could produce 65,000 tons a year of the crude, at £15 a ton. The total estimated net trading profit of the new company on these figures would be £2,900,000 a year.

All this was not just wishful thinking. The detailed economic survey of the company, which had been organised by Victor Doel, had included a thorough scrutiny of every cost and other factor. Negotiations had taken place with South African railways, and a cost per ton for transport agreed. Firm orders had also now been achieved. The Kobe company of Japan wanted large quantities of the perlite as a substitute for slagwool for insulation at oxygen plants. Several other companies such as Thermal Insulation Supplies and Contractors were also very interested.

For the more distant future, the plans were even greater. 'It is the intention of the Board', said a brochure on the new company, 'to establish and register a subsidiary company of South African Perlite in Ireland, export the crude perlite ore from Durban to Ireland and install two or three plants ordered from Nikex Hungarian Trading Company in Ireland to expand the perlite for the United Kingdom and European markets.'

And, last of all, it was hoped to realise Charlie's long cherished ambition going public through the stock exchanges and floating at least 50 per cent of the share-holding in a public issue.

Charlie had now been involved in South Africa for just over a year. It had taken desperate effort by Charlie, much of it legitimate, to get the operation moving. There had been squabbling and in-fighting. There had been bungling, deception, hope, despair, scandal and even murder. But now, at last, the perlite was ready to go in what seemed a very big way.

It was during Charlie's August-September visit that another important development occurred. Many months had passed since Charlie had last seen Jean La Grange, the seductively attractive wife of Gordon Winter, whom he had met on his very first visit to South Africa. He had fallen head-over-heels for her, but had been become so preoccupied with his work that she had gradually faded from his thoughts.

But around this period he met her again by chance, and soon he and Jean were having a passionate affair. The meeting probably took place at a Johannesburg night club called the Mikardo, a favourite haunt of Charlie and his men, which was underneath the building where Jean was living with her mother. A birthday party had been held there on 14 September for Tommy Clark. Alfie Berman, who enjoyed a reputation as a playboy and big spender, insisted that he collect the not inconsiderable bill. Nobody had argued with him.

Whatever the exact date and circumstances of the re-meeting with Jean La Grange – Charlie thinks it took place earlier in the year – they were both soon consumed by each other. It was possibly the only really good relationship that Charlie ever enjoyed with a woman. When they met, Jean was working as a fashion model. She told Charlie that her marriage to Gordon Winter was over, that they had separated. Gordon Winter was himself aware of what was happening, however.

'Charlie phoned me and said: "Gordy, Jean and I are friends. Any aggravation to you? Do you want to re-marry? Do you want to get her back?"

'I said: "No ways, Charlie. I don't want any re-marriage."

' "I just thought I would ask out of courtesy. She said she doesn't want to know and you don't want to know her. You are getting a divorce and I don't want to tread on any toes, don't want to break up a marriage."

'I said: "Well, Charlie, million per cent. I hope you are ecstatically happy."

'He said: "So glad about that, mate, you've done me such a big favour, thanks. Nice to be straight with each other, isn't it." '

Shortly after their affair began, Charlie took Jean on a holiday to Nice. The exact date is, again, unclear, but Harry Waterman remembers the holiday because he was taken along as a general dogsbody. 'I can speak French and he took me along to get things fixed up for him,' Waterman recalls. 'She was very nice and we stayed at the Hotel Negressco. I couldn't get them out of bed to go to dinner. They were stuck in that room for five days. I think they were very fond of each other.'

Charlie was utterly and completely in love. He was fascinated by Jean. She had beautiful long dark hair, which Charlie loved to see hanging half way down her back. She spent hours making herself up, but she never looked overdone. She had glorious dark playful eyes, and often put

246

on a little girl act. Yet she was intelligent and articulate and could be the perfect, sophisticated partner. She teased Charlie, yet admired him and looked up to him.

But Charlie had no idea that she worked for South African intelligence. Neither had he any notion that Gordon Winter was an important agent for Republican Intelligence. And it was this connection that was soon to cause a problem.

Charlie was waiting for Jean at her flat one evening, expecting her home from work. When she arrived, she was obviously worried about something. He pestered her about what was wrong. Finally she told him that she had been to see 'her uncle'. According to Jean, he was none other than General van den Bergh, the head of South African intelligence. Jean told Charlie that he was concerned about her living with Charlie. He had said Charlie was a villain with a record, and that he wanted her to marry a nice Afrikaaner boy. She told Charlie that she had defended him strongly to van den Bergh. 'He says he wants to meet you and have a chat. I think it best you do.'

Next day, Jean took Charlie to a government building in Pretoria where he was introduced to General van den Bergh himself. It was all very polite and civil. Van den Bergh told him that he gathered Charlie was trying to develop a big business out in South Africa, and said that he knew some important and influential people.

'Yes,' said Charlie, 'it could really be marvellous and bring a lot of money in for your country. I really think it's a great place here.'

Charlie was at his impressive best, well-dressed and putting on his charming forceful businessman act. The conversation turned to some of the recent unrest in South Africa, and to South Africa's enemies. Charlie agreed: it was all terrible.

'Yes,' said van den Bergh, 'I understand that you yourself have met Nelson Mandela's wife.'

Charlie was taken aback. He had indeed met Winnie Mandela through Gordon Winter a year ago. But how did van den Bergh know this? (It took Charlie some time to realise that Gordon Winter must have passed the information on and that he was himself a BOSS agent now and at the time of the Waldeck murder.)

The conversation between the two men developed and became more relaxed. General van den Bergh was a diplomatic type of person when he wanted to be and could couch a threat in the most friendly and charming manner.

'Charles, terrible things could happen to you and we really must protect you against any possibility that one of our officers should unwittingly stumble on something that could hurt you and I wouldn't be able to clamp it down . . . We really must think in terms of absolutely cementing your position, Charles . . .'

Charlie was fully aware of the threat that was being made, but he was encouraged by the whole tone of the proceedings.

'Well, what can I do? I'd be only too pleased to help. I'll do anything you want for South Africa . . . '

The conversation swung back again to South Africa's enemies, particularly those who were based in London: bodies such as Anti-Apartheid, Christian Action, black African organisations and Amnesty International. The anti-South Africa movement was approaching its height in Britain. Powerful and influential people such as Harold Wilson and Barbara Castle had thrown their weight behind the movement. South Africa's golden image was being badly tarnished and van den Bergh and the government were desperate to stop it getting any worse.

'You see what they are trying to do to our country!' van den Bergh stated. 'All commies and long-haired weirdos.'

'Yes,' said Charlie enthusiastically. 'Yes. All bloody riff-raff.' Despite his own extraordinary deviency, he had never had any tolerance of blacks or folk-singing types, or of anybody who seemed to depart from the norm.

'It would really help us if we could get . . . if you could help us obtain . . . information about some of these people.'

'How? How?'

'Well, the more we can find out about them, the more we will be able to stop them damaging our country . . . the trouble is, we have to be careful . . . '

And so the conversation proceeded. Eventually, a deal was done. Charlie was recruited to work for South African intelligence — since 1968 universally known as BOSS. The general wanted Charlie to rob the various London offices of anti-apartheid organisations, to steal anything and everything he could, and to send the material back to South Africa. Charlie agreed eagerly. He even started making suggestions of his own. Van den Bergh also discussed other ways in which Charlie could help South Africa: in particular, he wanted to know if Charlie could get hold of arms, which were in short supply.

Their arrangement was excellent for both men. For van den Bergh it could not have been better: Charlie was a top villain for whom such robberies would be a doddle. He had on his firm all kinds of skilled burglars. If Charlie or his men were caught, who would believe it if he claimed he was working for BOSS? It was much better to use a top villain like Charlie than BOSS's own agents. If they were caught in the act it could only be highly embarrassing. It was a perfect way for BOSS to get masses of vitally important information about its enemies without the risk of discovery. And the BOSS interest in these London organisations could not have been greater.

The arrangement was equally valuable to Charlie. He already keenly understood the benefit of having unofficial arrangements with the police. For him now to be tied in with the top police in South Africa was wonderfully advantageous, especially in the wake of the Waldeck killing. He felt that he could almost have *carte blanche*, that he would enjoy undreamt-of protection and unofficial assistance.

As soon as he returned to London, Charlie set to work for BOSS, making inquiries through the underworld grapevine about getting hold of arms. He eventually spoke to an ex-boxing champion who had a business associate called 'Bob'. Both men were connected with an arms company based in West London. They put Charlie on to a German arms dealer who told him that he could supply Bloodhound missiles and Centurian tank spares.

On 28 September 1965, a telegram was sent from

249

Charlie's Concordia offices to an address in Johannesburg: 'Spares and Bloodhounds possible, information pending . . . Letter follows immediately.'

Three weeks later, the recipient wrote to Charlie at 65, Grosvenor Street, London W1. The letter was headed: 'Re: Tank Spares: Bloodhounds: Aircraft Manufacturing Plant.' It stated:

Dear Sirs,

On Mr J. Collins' return to South Africa, he discussed with us the above. Firstly:-

1. *Tank Spares*:-

We are told by Mr Collins that all tank spares are available in Hamburg, Germany. Before our Mr C. flies over to London, it would be appreciated if you could please send us urgently, a comprehensive list of what is available in Hamburg. We are prepared to establish a letter of credit for the tank spares, therefore please expedite this information at your earliest convenience.

2. *Bloodhounds*:-

We were told by Mr Collins that there are available two types of Bloodhounds, these specifications are also required urgently as our Government are starting to negotiate with France and Italy at the present moment.

3. *Complete Aircraft Manufacturing Plant*:-

Mr Collins also informed us of the above that is available for a quick sale at £40,000, could we please have full details of all Plant equipment, the cost of production of the 5 aircrafts in final completion and brochure on the Prospector aircraft. We feel we might be able to place the above plant etc with one of our associates here in South Africa, to make this possible full data from you is required . . .

Charlie gave all the further details to a BOSS agent in London, known to him as 'John', who had been assigned to handle him. 'John' then asked Charlie to see if he could obtain the blueprints of a missile being made at the British Aircraft Corporation factory at Weybridge. Charlie had a look at the factory, but decided it was too risky.

He also inspected the premises of Christian Action in

Amen Court, just round the corner from St Paul's Cathedral. BOSS was extremely keen to get hold of the private papers of Canon John Collins, the eminent church-man who had founded and headed the body which was one of the most effective opponents of South Africa's apartheid policies. But again, Charlie decided it was too risky. However, BOSS did not have to wait much longer for information about Christian Action. Soon they came to know everything about the organisation through another source.

At the time of Charlie's recruitment, General van den Bergh had information about a plot to assassinate Dr Hastings Banda, then Prime Minister of Malawi. Dr Banda, a strange, Glasgow-educated man, was the only black leader in Africa to have dealings with the South Africans. He was an important friend and ally indeed. General van den Bergh, knowing that London gunmen were going to be used for the assassination, asked Charlie to try and use his influence to stop it. Charlie, through his superb information network in the underworld, was able to find out who had agreed to do the killing. Charlie persuaded them to drop their plan. With the Richardson gang at the heights of power, few would dare to cross Charlie, and anyway, there was money for them if they agreed. Dr Banda survived and went on to declare himself President of Malawi for life, operating one of the weirdest and most puritanical regimes ever seen in Africa.

As Charlie went about his business back in London in late September and October of 1965, he had never been in a more confident frame of mind. At home, he occupied a most powerful place in the underworld. And in South Africa, not only did his business ambitions seem about to be fulfilled but he had what he thought was the protection of working for BOSS. This, more than anything else, he felt, would guarantee that he could operate safely in South Africa for as long as he wanted. But as on past occasions when Charlie had felt in these confident moods, it proved to be a sign of impending danger. . . .

Sure enough, on 8 October 1965, disaster struck, without

Charlie even realising it.

He had heard about some kind of bank being opened up in Wigmore Street. Charlie thought it sounded interesting. He summoned Frank Fraser and Frank Prater and they drove up to Wigmore Street to check it out. By one of those strange quirks of fortune, they spotted Jimmy Taggart, the man who had received such an appalling beating three months before, coming out of the bank they were interested in.

The first Taggart knew about the close proximity of two of his earlier torturers was a shout from behind him as he walked along Wigmore Street. He was with a friend called Farrow, and they both turned round. Taggart, to his horror, saw Frank Fraser.

'I want to have a word with you,' Fraser informed him, without any civility or explanation.

Taggart was terrified. 'I've got absolutely nothing to say to you whatever,' he told Fraser. He quickened his pace and hissed to his friend to keep on walking, to ignore Fraser.

Wigmore Street, in the heart of the West End just behind Oxford Street, was crowded on a busy afternoon. The unpleasant Fraser style that had shown itself in Taggart's earlier kidnapping in Bermondsey was restrained by the number of people milling around. Instead, he followed alongside Taggart.

'I'm warning you, you bastard, unless you fucking-well stop right now and talk, you'll get the same as before.'

Eventually, Taggart stopped. He had seen two uniformed policemen about fifty yards away walking towards them. He decided he would tell Fraser to clear off. But then Charlie appeared in front of him, as if out of thin air. He put out his hand to Taggart, wanting to shake hands. Taggart was having none of it.

'Come on, Jimmy,' said Charlie. 'Let bygones be bygones. It was all a bad mistake. I know it was over the top . . . it was just one of those things. I'm sorry, OK? Let's talk, shall we?'

Taggart saw a cab coming down the street towards him. He hailed it, urgently. The two policemen were now only a

252

few yards away and still approaching. The cab pulled up. He opened the door.

'Get in! Get in!' he told his friend desperately.

Charlie and Fraser were left standing on the pavement, furious. But there was nothing they could do.

That night, Jimmy Taggart hardly slept. He felt haunted by the latest attentions of Charlie. He didn't know what it had been about, or why they should want to see him again. He had decided after his first beating never to let his path cross again with the Richardsons.

Next day, it was a fine early autumn morning. Taggart got into his car and did what not a single one of Charlie's previous victims had dared do. He went to see the police. Not any old copper: Taggart went to a man called Gerald McArthur. Then Assistant Chief Constable of Hertfordshire, he was about the only copper whom Taggart felt he could trust.

It was a terrible indictment of the London detective squads that a man like Taggart had to go to an outside force. Other victims such as Bunny Bridges and Lucien Harris had been too terrified to go to the London police. They feared, from the corruption they had seen at first-hand or heard about from reliable sources, that Charlie would be told by a corrupt detective that somebody had 'grassed' him.

The consequences would have been terrible. It was an equally appalling state of affairs that the Flying Squad, which had been set up in 1929 especially to deal with the very type of major crime that Charlie was involved in, had been unable to do anything about him.

But as Assistant Chief Constable Gerald McArthur sat in his Welwyn office quietly listening to Taggart's shocking allegations, it was the beginning of the end for the Richardson gang.

17. With a Little Help . . .

Gerald McArthur quickly realised how vital complete secrecy would be. The very circumstances of Taggart's visit indeed dictated it. Ahead lay one of the most difficult operations: the seeds of destruction that were sown by Taggart's allegations were to take nearly two years before they bore fruit. The only immediate result of the chance Wigmore Street meeting between Taggart and Charlie was that Frank Prater decided to quit. He felt after only three months' work at Anglo-American that the whole Richardson scene was too heavy for him. He was soon to find himself in trouble and talking to Gerald McArthur. . . .

But Charlie was walking on air. He was utterly unaware of the McArthur development. The South African venture was going better than ever before. Of course, there were the niggling little problems that were always associated with Charlie's activities. Victor Doel cabled Charlie about the quantities of heavy plant that had now been lying on Durban docks for nearly a year. There was still no sign of the necessary paperwork. Cliffe, Dekker and Todd, his first solicitors, were also threatening legal action over Charlie's £1200 unsettled account.

But the only thing that mattered now was SAPI, and getting Pretoria Portland Cement to invest money in the Mkuse mine. And during the month of October 1965 Victor Doel in South Africa had been engaged in protracted negotiations with the company.

Discussions progressed so well that Charlie decided to travel out to see Pretoria Portland. Jean La Grange was also on his mind. He had spoken to her on the telephone, and written several letters. It irritated Charlie that he had to be careful about Jean Goodman who, as ever, was running his scrapyards. On 19 October, he cabled Jean La Grange at her address at 15, Chatham Court, Bok Street in Johannesburg. 'Arriving Wednesday sorry regarding delay. Will explain fully when I see you.'

For most of his life Charlie had been relentlessly active. He was always looking for new schemes to pursue, new deals to pull off. It didn't matter whether he had £1 in his pocket, or a million. He had always been hyperactive. But with Jean it was different. He was happy to give up work to be with her. When he made his latest trip, he spent many hours in her company. He still found time, however, on 29 October, for a meeting with Pretoria Portland Cement. The company had sent drilling teams down to the mine, and although they were making only slow progress, Pretoria Portland was becoming increasingly interested.

Charlie, with his hopes flying high, returned to London. He had only been back a couple of days when he received a cable from Doel, telling him that a decision was almost certain to be made by Pretoria Portland very soon. Charlie waited impatiently for further news while Doel put the finishing touches to SAPI's re-application for the rights to the Mkuse perlite – a procedure made necessary because the deal involving the cession of Kruger's rights had not been notorially attested. The discussions that had taken place about the application had seemed to go well, especially with the help of Gerald Rubenstein from Charlie's new firm of South African lawyers. And on 8 November 1965, SAPI received a letter from the Office of the Mining Commissioner endorsing their prospecting lease, Number BP 22, and giving the company the right to remove 100,000 tons of perlite a year, subject to a royalty of twenty cents a ton, payable to the government.

It was a good sign, but better things were to come. By the late afternoon of the same day, Victor Doel was at the Pretoria Portland Cement telex machine, bursting in his excitement to get a message through to Charlie. Several thousand miles away in London it was 5.15pm. The machine in Charlie's office jumped to life and chattered away like the Saturday afternoon television football results.

255

Pretoria agreed participation 50 per cent Stop terms payable five installments Stop first payment on signing agreement Stop agreement conditional quantity quality erection of pilot plant B and Kiss available in Johannesburg to expand Stop payment of 1st installment not repeat not dependent on conditions above Stop SA Perlite must agree transfer in trust repeat in trust 50 per cent mining rights to Pretoria as security Stop Pretoria also agree to deposit 25,000 rand working capital and pay all costs for immediate mining and transport of perlite Stop no lines to London can you phone 58-6162 Stop reply telex Stop Doel

The Doel message was soon confirmed by another from Bob Hellings himself at Pretoria Portland Cement. Charlie, when overjoyed at good news, was never the kind to jump up and down with excitement. A quiet smile was all that usually sufficed. He was very pleased by the news, but his reaction was cool.

A period of strenuous activity followed in the next few days, sorting out details of the proposed deal. And then, on 18 November 1965, Charlie's moment came. Pretoria Portland Cement wrote to him and Victor Doel at SAPI's offices in Loveday Street, Johannesburg, making a formal offer of £250,000 for 50 per cent of the company's shares, subject to certain conditions. Pretoria Portland agreed to make £12,500 immediately available. Charlie was excited and pleased that the offer had been made. But he started to feel that the deal was worth a lot more. He told a businessman friend that he thought he should have been offered £2 million. There was always more than an element of fantasy in Charlie's assessment of any given situation.

Charlie's solicitors replied six days later, dealing as best they could with the twelve conditions that Pretoria Portland had laid down. These included SAPI's being able to prove that the perlite mine had a minimum reserve of 26,000,000 short tons of the material; that all Corris Waldeck's interests inherited from her husband were extinct; and that the pilot

8. Charlie on the run in Toronto, 1960.

9. Charles Richardson and his two eldest sons in 33a, Addington Square.

10. Jack Duval.

11. John Bradbury.

12. The photograph of Lucien Harris taken by a Customs undercover agent soon after Harris's beating in June 1964.

13. Best of friends: Gordon Winter with General H. J. van den Bergh, holding Winter's son, at van den Bergh's Pretoria farm in 1979.

14. Aspiring to great heights in South Africa, 1964.

15. Jean La Grange, who took Charlie to BOSS.

16. Major Nicholson (right).

17. Charlie with Roy Hall, 1980.

expansion plant from Hungary was available for testing the perlite.

The most pressing problem for Charlie in the days after the offer had been made was indeed the installation of the expansion equipment and getting visas for Mr Buji and Mr Kiss, so that they could come to South Africa and supervise all technical matters. Charlie had agreed five months previously to buy one pilot plant and two full-sized sets of expansion equipment. The various discussions and negotiations between Charlie and Nikex had, during the past few months, been bedevilled by language and immigration problems. After the agreement by Charlie in June 1965 to buy the machines, Nikex had again asked for a five-ton sample of perlite so that they could carry out tests to establish exactly which was the best possible system for the South African perlite. The sample had eventually been sent off. But it disappeared en route during August and, having eventually been traced to Trieste, arrived in Budapest very much later than planned. But the results were excellent and the contract for two machines, plus the pilot plant, had been finally completed on 22 October 1965.

Just over a month later, on 30 November, the pilot plant arrived from Hungary at Durban. It was destined for a suburb of Johannesburg called Wynberg, where a site had been acquired for its installation and operation. All that seemed now to stand between Charlie and his millions was the arrival of the vitally necessary experts, Messrs Buji and Kiss. Charlie claims that he managed to get over the visa problems involved with a little help from his friends inside BOSS, who, he says, allowed him to bring in Mr Buji on a false passport. Whatever the actual mechanics, Buji arrived in London in early December. By the start of the New Year, he was in South Africa, ready to supervise the erection of the pilot plant. It was not often that people from communist bloc countries had such access to South Africa.

Charlie was, in many ways, elated at the way his vast — although shambolic — efforts over the past sixteen months in South Africa were now culminating. But just as his venture appeared to be going well, he seems to have become dissatisfied. Although Victor Doel had done marvellous work, Charlie began to feel niggardly. It was almost as if he was jealous of some of Doel's success. He felt that he was perhaps losing some of his direct control and authority. Such a state of affairs was quite unsatisfactory. Charlie always had to have total and utter control. Doel had been out in South Africa for four months, operating virtually as a one-man company, yet Charlie started to think that Doel was wasting money and not doing his job properly.

As well as this, Charlie had recently been cultivating a businessman called Stanley Woods, one of the biggest metal mill dealers in London. Charlie, like dozens of other scrap metal merchants, sold much of his material to Woods, who then sold it to the steel mills and foundries. Woods was yet another in the long line of respectable people whom Charlie had managed to impress. For several years, when the need arose, Woods had lent Charlie and other trusted scrap merchants money with which to buy in metals. It was a variation on the system that Charlie used with the totters. But with so much of his time and money being spent in South Africa, Charlie had run up a large debt with Woods. When he realised that Charlie owed nearly £40,000, Woods ordered the debt to be cleared at once.

'He came to see me personally about this,' Woods remembers. 'He wanted to put up as collateral some property, I think it was a night club in the south London area. When my secretary investigated it, it was already mortgaged, so therefore a second mortgage wouldn't have been a lot of good.

'He had a project going in South Africa; he was mining out there, exfoliating perlite. He came up with the suggestion that it was very, very good and he brought me various letters with various international names on the letterheadings. He also had a couple of very old Establishment South Africans involved, all very respectable-sounding people. What he wanted to do was instead of paying us back the £40,000 he owed, he wanted to pay us in shares. He was going to sell out and he was asking a very large sum of money, and that correspondence that he got on him looked as

258

though it could well be. In that light I advanced him some extra money and he gave me some of his shares.'

Woods was only the latest of that group of people whom Charlie had managed to persuade to do things for him and who were eventually to come badly unstuck. In the end Woods was to lose, he estimates, over £100,000 as a result of being interested by Charlie in the perlite.

But in November of 1965 Woods felt the prospects looked fine. He had advanced several more large sums of money in exchange for Charlie's shares. And by this stage, he had put in so much money that when Charlie asked him to become directly involved, the day after the Pretoria Portland Cement offer on 18 November, he could only agree. Charlie wanted Woods to become his partner – with half his shares in the perlite company – in return for more capital. Woods sent out two of his men, Fred Pace and Alf Durrell, to report on the position in South Africa. Durrell, now dead, was an ex-Flying Squad detective. He was a loyal and hard-working employee of Stan Woods, who needed such people to make sure that his company did not unwittingly buy stolen metal.

'They had a look round and they came back with a very favourable assessment. At the same time they thought it was very viable,' Woods says.

In further discussions with Charlie, it was agreed that Woods would become even more involved, by helping to finance the development of the perlite. But he wanted, understandably, to make sure he had much more direct control now that he was considering putting in a lot more money; he wanted to nominate his own managing director, and to buy out the many other people who had been given shares by Charlie. Woods already had the impression that some of the venture bordered on the chaotic. Charlie had started paying people such as Jimmy Collins, and a geologist who was doing work, in shares instead of money.

Charlie instructed his solicitors in South Africa to arrange an agreement between himself and Woods and to help him buy out the others, including Victor Doel. Despite this consummate ingratitude, Doel helped to start arranging the deal. He agreed to resign as managing director of Lebombo in

259

favour of Mr Woods's nominee, and to work in close harmony with him and to give him all the assistance he could. Although Doel was, remarkably, still prepared to help Charlie, he nevertheless felt bitter about the peremptory way in which he was being demoted. Previously he had kept his feelings to himself. But now, in a letter to Charlie on 21 December, he gave vent. 'Personally, I cannot feel that here is a fair and reasonable solution,' he said, adding that in the five months he had worked for Charlie in South Africa he had given up everything to toil on his own as a mixture of managing director, company secretary, chief accountant, sales manager and negotiator. He complained bitterly that Charlie had shown little trust in him, and that he had had to discover for himself some of the more important facts which Charlie had omitted to mention. The general circumstances, he said, had been chaotic.

Charlie had already intimated to Doel that he reckoned he had misspent £7000. This was so often Charlie's way: when he did anything that was unfair, he would almost always manage to justify it to himself, even if it meant totally distorting the facts. It had been exactly the same with Benny Wajcenberg, for instance, nearly three years before. Charlie had owed the Pole commission, yet accused him of owing the money.

Doel, like Wajcenberg, tried to show that far from owing money, it was he who was owed. He explained how in the absence of funds from Charlie, he himself had had to pay a solicitor's bill with the new lawyers for £1000. He had also paid out of his own pocket other bills amounting to £2500 owed by Lebombo. He said he was owed £1500 in salary and had not received the promised provision for his children. All the money that Charlie had promised had never materialised, he complained. He had only just managed to stave off action in the courts from Cliffe Dekker and Todd, Charlie's original South African solicitors, to collect the £1200 they were owed.

Charlie shrugged all this off. With Stanley Woods now firmly behind him, he was in the best position he had ever experienced. It seemed to him that the perlite was now ready

260

to go. As well as the Woods backing, there was the Pretoria Portland Cement offer, and the first expanding machine had arrived. The necessary Hungarian perlite expert would be able to get into South Africa thanks to BOSS which was, in Charlie's mind, fast replacing the earlier 'arrangement' that Waldeck had had with the government friend.

Life was never again to be so good for Charlie; soon the ungainly edifice that he had constructed on the shaky foundations of his unusual deals was to start tottering and then to come crashing down all around him.

But in December of 1965, the Camberwell gang leader was in a confident mood. He had hoped to go out to Johannesburg to spend Christmas with Jean La Grange. That had to be put off. On 21 December, he sent her an urgent telegram. 'Dearest Jean. Impossible to phone. Have tried for days. Be with you 28th. Will try phone Tuesday. Love you always. Charles.'

Charlie was particularly generous with his Christmas presents that year. He popped around to Alfie Berman's and gave him a £300 gold watch. Berman feigned gratitude, but he wasn't that impressed. 'It's only my bloody money anyway,' he thought to himself. Indeed, the watch was to be about the only return he had on the sum of nearly £60,000 that he had invested in South Africa.

Charlie was bored at home that Christmas. He was eager to get ahead with the perlite, and was thinking about Jean La Grange. He saw a completely new life opening up for him. It was a picture born out of fantasy: he would be a rich respectable businessman; and he saw Jean La Grange at his side. He cabled her again: 'Dearest Jean. Miss you so much. Loneliest Christmas I ever spent. Only days now. Love you always. Charles.'

But Christmas in a year's time was to be even lonelier. While the Pretoria Portland Cement negotiations had been coming to a head, John Bradbury had arrived back in South Africa. Immediately after the Waldeck killing, Bradbury and Harry Prince had been questioned over a period of weeks by the police. Their investigations got nowhere, however, and

261

both men were told they could go. Bradbury started drinking heavily. He told his wife that they had shot Rex, the Waldeck's dog. The long-suffering Sheila started getting beatings again from her husband. 'In the end we had to run from South Africa,' she recalls.

They crossed the border into Rhodesia where Bradbury got involved in various fights at hotels. They moved to Zambia but, without work, he soon ran out of money. In December 1965, he was deported back to South Africa by the Zambian authorities because he was destitute. Sheila Bradbury, by now utterly fed up, decided to return to England with the children. Bradbury said he would remain for a little while and try to earn some money.

But far from getting work, Bradbury had been spending his time in bars, shooting off his mouth. One night, he accepted a drink from a pleasant, well-dressed man. His name was Dr Gideon van Gass. They talked about this and that. Bradbury thought the man was a right mug. What he didn't know was that van Gass was an insurance investigator, assigned to look at the strange circumstances surrounding the death of Tom Waldeck whose life had been insured for £25,000 not long before the killing. Bradbury thought this friendly stranger would be good for a few drinks.

A couple of days later, the men met again. Bradbury accepted the drinks which van Gass offered him. His tongue started loosening, and he bragged about his various exploits, off-loading on the patient Dr van Gass some of the more weird concoctions of his strange imagination. The conversation was steered to the subject of 'that dreadful killing of the mining prospector'. It wasn't long before Bradbury told the man that he had been involved, and that he had had an affair with Corris Waldeck. Van Gass did nothing. He bought Bradbury another drink and changed the subject. He asked if he could see him the following night at the Hillbrow Hotel. Bradbury readily agreed, thinking another night of free drinks was on the way.

When the meeting took place on 7 January 1966, van Gass got Bradbury on to the subject of the Waldeck murder again. As the evening progressed and he had more and more to drink, he talked even more freely than the night before. He had been forced to get involved in the killing, he confided. He had said more than enough to satisfy the inquisitive Dr Gideon van Gass by the time five detectives pounced on him. They were members of an elite, tough squad of police. One of their more effective methods of getting people to talk was to start crushing their testicles with nut-crackers. It was a technique that had never been known to fail.

18. Useful at Government Level

Sheila Bradbury had been out at sea for three days. She had caught the *Windsor Castle* on 4 January 1966 from Cape Town on her way back to England, on a ticket paid for by the British Embassy. Bradbury had cried like a little boy as he stood on the dockside watching them walk up the gangway.

The ship's bursar told her that she was wanted on the ship-to-shore telephone. It was a Colonel St John Pattle. He said that he was a policeman and that her husband had been arrested for the murder of Thomas Waldeck. Sheila told him she didn't believe it, but in her heart of hearts she knew that it was the case. She refused Colonel Pattle's request that she get off the ship at Las Palmas and return to South Africa.

But the Colonel, who had made a great name for himself as an ace fighter pilot during the Second World War, could do without the help of Sheila Bradbury. Her husband, now in deep trouble, was singing like a bird. He smothered the police with stories of Charlie Richardson and the Great Train Robbers. He talked so fast that the police couldn't take it all in at first. Bradbury was desperate to save his own neck. He started saying that he had been forced to do the killing, completely against his will. It was only because Charlie Richardson was such a violent, brutal man that he had agreed to do it, he was to allege in a South African court later.

When Bradbury was arrested, Gordon Winter was also detained. His borrowed gun had, after all, been used for the killing. Winter had long since told General van den Bergh about some of the circumstances surrounding the Waldeck killing. Due to his BOSS connection, Winter found himself locked away in a comfortable cell in the Fort Prison under the 180-day detention law, until now only used for political prisoners. Winter became the first man in South Africa ever to be held under this law on non-political grounds.

Bradbury was hauled up before the Magistrates' Court in Johannesburg on 10 January 1966, three days after his dramatic arrest, and granted a formal remand in custody.

The police by this time had begun to fathom out exactly what Bradbury was telling them. It was an incredible story, in which more and more details emerged about Charlie Richardson and the life of his gang back in south London. The South African police quickly realised that the London businessman behind some recent big mining deals was a very big villain.

Suddenly, and for the first time, Charlie was directly connected to the murder of Thomas Waldeck. And not just in police circles. On 16 January 1966, only nine days after the arrest of Bradbury, the *News of the World* ran a story under the dramatic headline: 'Murder Inc.'. The story was filed from a special correspondent in Johannesburg.

> Three London men are wanted by detectives investigating the murder of a wealthy Johannesburg diamond prospector and businessman, who was shot down on the doorstep of his home by a man wearing a tasselled fisherman's cap.
>
> Police believe the shooting was carried out by a 'Murder Incorporated' organisation based in London.
>
> South African detectives have worked closely with Scotland Yard which has supplied them with photographs, full descriptions and dossiers giving all details of the wanted men.

The article then named Thomas Waldeck and reported:

> This week 34-year-old British-born Lawrence 'Jimmy' Bradbury appeared in court here for remand before preparatory examination of an allegation that he was involved in the murder.
>
> The actual details will only become known when the examination is held. Under South African law no actual

265

charge is framed against a person appearing at a pre-paratory examination until he is sent for trial.

Charlie, although his name was not mentioned, was furious. The timing could not have been worse. He instructed a London solicitor called Raymond Davis to start libel proceedings. That, too, was to turn out to be a bad mistake. Raymond Davis's letter to the *News of the World* stated that he represented a Mr Charles Richardson who was chairman of a company called Concordia. One of the paper's top reporters, a man called Peter Earle, was deputed to start looking into the whole affair. It was the beginning of what was to become fantastic rivalry between the *News of the World* and Roy East of the *People* to see who could reveal more about the terrible Richardson gang.

The ripple of alarm that ran through various places in Johannesburg during this period in January 1966 was soon to become a tidal wave. Bradbury was making so many allegations about Charlie to Colonel Pattle that soon the police chief was on his way to London to talk to Scotland Yard. He arrived on 21 January 1966. The link between a murder and mining interests in South Africa, a major south London villain and gang boss had been made. The two police forces were able to exchange all kinds of information which each, for different reasons, found extremely valuable.

Meanwhile, in his own separate operation, Assistant Chief Constable Gerald McArthur had been plugging away with Jimmy Taggart, who had by now told him everything he knew or had heard about in connection with the Richardson gang. There had also been a further development. In December 1965, Frank Fraser had had an argument with a man called Christopher Glinski in offices at Vauxhall Bridge Road. Fraser had threatened Glinski and hit him over the head with an umbrella. Glinski, who also knew people like Duval and Prater, was soon talking to Gerald McArthur.

McArthur by now realised the full extent of what he was up against. He knew that most of Charlie's victims, and others who could give information about his widespread criminal activities, would be too terrified even to talk to him, let alone go to a court of law and give evidence. He drew around him a group of twenty hand-picked detectives whom he could trust never to leak anything about the secret operation that he was mounting against the Richardsons. The slightest leak would have been disastrous. He knew that if Charlie found out, then he would either terrify people or pay them not to give evidence against him.

In Johannesburg, Bradbury again appeared in court. He was again remanded in prison, until 26 April when he was to be tried by the Supreme Court. Colonel Pattle and his men started getting down to the nitty-gritty of preparing their case.

As usual, Charlie's troubles never came alone. There was so much pressure on his Anglo-American company from creditors that it had to be wound up. This, together with news in London of the Bradbury arrest, alarmed Major Herbert Nicholson, who decided to resign from Concordia. It was another six months before he contacted Charlie again.

But the most difficult problem for Charlie was without doubt the effect of the Bradbury arrest on the operation in South Africa. People had started realising that Bradbury was the man who the previous year had been alleged to be Charles Wilson, the escaped Great Train Robber. In an attempt to distance Bradbury from himself and the perlite concern, he juggled his shares and interests between his two companies, Lebombo and SAPI.

But Pretoria Portland Cement, being part of a powerful group of companies, had its own contacts in high places in South Africa. As they gained a clearer picture of just who Charlie was, or seemed to be, and what he had been up to in both South Africa and London, they decided to drop him like a hot brick. They had also examined the perlite 'prospecting area' and gained a more complete picture of the general set-up at Mkuse and of some of the other problems associated with Charlie's venture.

Their hand-delivered letter to Charlie on 18 February 1966 was a terrible blow. It minced no words. The perlite, they said, occurred only spasmodically, and its recovery would prove costly. The reserves approached only a fraction

267

of the claimed 26,000,000 tons. As far as Pretoria Portland was concerned, everything else was wrong, too. They doubted that the perlite could command anything like the price Charlie had stated. The pilot expanding plant was incomplete and inadequate, needing redesign. There was no reliable information about demand for perlite, and little chance of recovering outlay. 'Our assessment of the whole proposed venture is that neither the exploitation of crude perlite nor the production of an expanded perlite from pilot plant stage to full commercial production is an economic proposition. We record that we shall not negotiate further and that we now withdraw completely from the proposed venture.'

Charlie was stunned by the letter. He felt convinced that the reasons given for withdrawal were not really true. Pretoria Portland had been involved now for nearly a year and knew exactly what was involved, he thought.

All his hopes for the perlite now rested on Stanley Woods. No agreement had yet been signed between Woods and Charlie but Woods was so involved through all the personal loans he had made that he had no choice but try and help salvage the perlite. Like Victor Doel, who was still plodding away in South Africa for Charlie, Woods was unaware of the connections between Bradbury and Charlie, and of the significance of several other events. He had again sent out his two men, Alf Durrell and Fred Pace, and early in the year had made his own first visit to South Africa. By this time, Charlie had cleared an airstrip at Mkuse, and had organised other developments: a bridge had been built over a river running through the area of the mine, and accommodation had been arranged for the Zulu workers. Woods recalls: 'We flew down to the mine and we saw all the digging going on and it seemed a hive of industry. We stayed there a while and were shown around by Eddie Kruger, I think it was, and he seemed to be quite competent.'

But Woods soon found there were many problems. The bridge over the river had been washed away and needed rebuilding. The mass of machinery that had been sent to Durban by Charlie well over a year before was still lying there, with huge customs charges to be paid. 'Not only that, you had the background of the murder out there, and this clouded the issue.' He concluded, too, that the government was using delaying tactics on the question of granting further permission, now needed if the mining operation were to continue. Nevertheless Woods, a much more conventional and solid businessman than Charlie ever could be, still felt there was a terrific potential if only the mess were sorted out. He helped pay off the customs charges on the machinery and tried to deal with some of the problems connected with the pilot plant.

By the time Stanley Woods first visited South Africa, Charlie had at least overcome the problem of getting the Hungarian experts. On 18 January, a formal contract had been signed between Victor Doel and Buji in Johannesburg. For £625 a month Buji was made technical manager of the company, with responsibility for running and operating the expansion plant; a £2500 bonus was promised should the company produce up to 1,000,000 tons of perlite a year. Any inventions he made in the course of his work had to be handed over to SAPI. Charlie also had to pay money to the Hungarian company for Buji's services.

When Buji arrived in South Africa, he got down to his job enthusiastically. With the support of Victor Doel, he arranged for the topsoil over an area of 120 square yards of the mine to be bulldozed away. This revealed a thick deposit of light green perlite which excited the Hungarian scientist. The Zulu boys, brought in with their picks and shovels, stockpiled 200 tons of the stuff ready for the expanding machine. Buji also blasted a pit to a depth of twenty-five feet. He was delighted by the fine perlite exposed. He told Victor Doel that they would easily be able to remove 50,000 tons of good quality perlite from the small area on which they had worked.

Doel, despite the fact that all his letters to Charlie were being ignored, still plugged away faithfully. He finalised a deal with South African railways to transport the perlite from a railway station site which had been obtained at a place called Moshlinga. He planned to build a loading ramp as quickly as possible. By the end of February 1966 Doel had also organised a three-quarter-acre stockpiling site in Johannesburg and a larger site in Durban. He continued paying out money to buy the extra bits and pieces that were needed for the expanding machines, and clinched three sizeable orders for perlite from major companies.

Doel tried to save the Pretoria Portland Cement deal, but without success. He told Charlie that he thought they had pulled out only because of the 'continuous damaging press reports'. However he was able to tell Charlie on 2 March 1966 that five other large concerns were interested in a possible involvement. The idea he was working on was to try and get two or three of these big companies to buy jointly 50 per cent of the perlite shares. Doel also reported that although the machinery from Durban had finally been released, apart from a couple of machines, most of it was useless, fit only to be scrapped. Worse still, the police were now nosing around the sites in Durban and at the mine where the machinery was stored.

'Needless to say, an enormous amount of work has been necessary to arrive at this state of affairs, and the details would fill a book. . . .' Despite the terrible frustrations and despair, no effort had been spared, he told Charlie, to bring the perlite to success. Woods's money had already saved the venture from collapse, and it was now up to Charlie to dissociate himself completely from the perlite and to allow the people in South Africa to get on with the job. If only Charlie had listened. . . .

Charlie's reaction to these valiant efforts in such trying circumstances was to consider sacking Doel on the spot. But then he remembered that Doel had insisted on all kinds of safeguards in his contract with Charlie which had eventually been signed the previous October. So he decided to instruct Brian Rees, his solicitor and landlord at Park Lane, to seek advice on whether he would be liable if he dismissed Doel. His grounds were, incredibly, that Doel had misspent £7000 and that he had neglected his duties as managing director by not paying for the docks charges on the plant which had been stuck at Durban for nine months

270

by the time Victor Doel had first been persuaded to go out to South Africa in August 1965.

The legal advice made it clear to Charlie that there was no way he could get away with the sacking of Doel. He was livid. He saw it as yet another example of how 'bent' the legal system was. Anybody who didn't agree with his own distorted assessments was always 'bent'.

But Charlie, by the time he had received this legal opinion, had other things on his mind. Following the collapse of the Pretoria Portland Cement negotiations, Charlie had flown out to South Africa. Using a false passport, he had been able, as always, to walk through immigration without being checked. This time he had come over solely to try and recruit the help of BOSS with his deteriorating fortunes. Jean La Grange organised for him another meeting with General van den Bergh. The head of BOSS told Charlie what they wanted. It was nothing less than a series of raids on the London-based offices of various anti-South Africa organisations. Charlie was told to remove as much material as he could and send it back to Jean La Grange. The General said they were particularly interested in complete lists of members of the various target organisations.

Charlie returned to London. He was labouring under the delusion that the more dirty-work he did for BOSS, the safer would be his interests in South Africa. In particular, he felt that BOSS would be able to help with the terrible dangers stemming from the Bradbury arrest.

Charlie wasted no time. On 3 March 1966, after earlier surveillance had been carried out, he drove up to Charlotte Street. He parked his car not far from the headquarters of the Anti-Apartheid movement, on the upper floors of a Georgian terrace in a bustling part of the West End. Charlie entered the building and walked into the lavatory which, as he knew, was on the first-floor landing. He locked the door, hoping that no one would need to come in. Although the office closing time seemed to vary, he knew the front door was usually locked by 7pm. He had been there a short while when he heard two people wandering down the

271

stairs chatting. As they left the building he heard one of them say: 'Make sure the door is shut properly.'

Charlie sat tight, listening hard for any sign of life inside the building. Then he made his way to the office and proceeded to pick up anything he thought looked interesting. He remembered that BOSS was particularly interested in the indices of members and their addresses, and of who was who in the movement. These he found in a top-floor office, shoving them in his sack. Charlie took a considerable quantity of other material. What it all was he didn't quite know. He drove back to Peckford's and locked it up.

The next day, he tried to sort the material into different lots. Most of it he couldn't fathom, and he found it hard to understand why BOSS was so interested. Little did he know to what great uses South African intelligence could put this information.

On 5 March, two days after the robbery, Charlie sent a telegram to Jean La Grange at 810, Windsor Gardens, Bok Street, Johannesburg. The telegram was marked urgent. It was sent from London at 12.20: 'Papers despatched as promised which you felt would be useful at government level. Flight number 227, arriving Sunday 1405, parcel number 4130284. Another collection awaits despatch if this first batch is proven useful. Ticket in David's hands. Love you always. Charlie.'

19. Gang Bang at Mr Smith's

BOSS was indeed pleased with the information contained in the first batch. Charlie was asked to bring the rest of the material himself, and to have further discussions. He set off for South Africa feeling confident that all this work for BOSS would help him get over the problems associated with Bradbury, and cherishing the prospect of seeing Jean again. But, by the time he got back to London, only a few days later, disaster had struck in a very big way. And this time it was to do with his younger brother Eddie.

For nearly two years now, Eddie had been very successfully running the fruit machine business with the help of Frank Fraser and others. He still had his profitable wholesaling business at Deptford and was enjoying his life immensely. He was, of course, still very much involved with Charlie, but he felt that the various arrangements that existed gave him a sufficient degree of independence. There were still heated arguments between the two brothers, but when the chips were down they always stuck loyally by each other. Eddie, who had shied away from people like Jack Duval earlier on, had not been much interested, either, in Charlie's South African venture. His main area of activity was in the thriving business of putting gaming machines into various clubs in the West End and up and down the country.

But the very success of this fruit machine business was, inevitably, to be the cause of some difficulties, mainly of territory. With Eddie's machines went both written and unwritten protection. Alby Woods, a haulage contractor who had invested in the machine company, was always amazed at the effect the presence of Eddie's machines had on the general order in any given club: 'People wouldn't start any trouble in these clubs, because they knew that

Frank and Eddie had machines in there. They never had hardly any trouble with their machines. They didn't have to go round and bash people up.' But, unfortunately for Charlie, and everybody else, this wasn't invariably the case. As the business had expanded on this kind of reputation, so too had the friction and resentment of other people increased.

Since an earlier meeting of the Richardsons with the Krays and others in the Kings Head pub, an uneasy truce had existed between the big London gangs. It had been agreed that they would each leave the other alone as long as each remained on his own ground. But this pact was beginning to look a little frayed around the edges. Hours before Charlie had burgled the Anti-Apartheid offices, one of the men who worked for Eddie's fruit machine company, Jimmy Andrews, had been shot and badly injured in the legs over in the East End, on Friday evening, 4 March. Word went round that this had been organised by the Krays. There was a distinct feeling of tension in the air. Ronnie, the more dominant of the Kray twins, was reported to be in a wildly dangerous mood and looking for someone to murder.

It was against this background that Eddie's fruit machine company actively engaged in expanding its already large interests. The same man who owned the Horseshoe club in Southport, where Eddie and Frank had escaped conviction after an ugly fight, had recently opened a club in Catford in south London. Its name was Mr Smith and the Witchdoctor. It was a smart club with a good bar, a dance floor, gaming tables and a dining area where guests could buy a good meal. Business had boomed from the start, but there was one slight problem. Some local men had appointed themselves 'minders' of the club. An unofficial arrangement had somehow evolved in which they dealt with any troublemakers in return for free drinks. The club had quickly become their main watering hole. The management, which was doing its best to run a well-ordered establishment, was unhappy about this.

Eddie was approached and asked if he could do something to help. It was the kind of request that Eddie often received.

274

Indeed, he traded on it: in return for restoring order, he would get his own highly lucrative fruit machines installed, or be paid 'protection' money.

As it happened, Eddie was well aware of the men who had appointed themselves guardians of the Mr Smith club. They were a group led by brothers called Haward, men whom Eddie and friends knew reasonably well, but who were certainly not 'on the firm' – not, as they say in south London, 'regular drinking partners'. And only a few weeks before, Billy Haward had been approached by Frank Fraser and by Johnnie Longman – the man who had for some time been running the Sales Associates shops for Charlie – about going into partnership in one of the Hawards' clubs.

Phil Wilson, the man who ran the bingo hall and who had been conned along with Charlie by Jack Duval in the Common Market Merchants escapade, remembers the occasion well. 'I was friends with the Richardsons and I was friends with the Hawards. I have known them for years, since I was a little boy. Flash Harry [Haward] was inside at the time and his brother got him a club at Lewisham Way. One day the Richardsons come around, it was Johnnie Longman and Frankie Fraser, and he was talking to Bill at the table. After they had gone, Bill said to me: "They wanted me to go into partnership with them in the club I got for Harry." I said, "Well how can you go into partnership with them when you had brought the club?" "That's right," said Haward, "that's what I told them." '

Wilson says the discussion between Haward, Longman and Fraser had been amicable. But such appearances didn't mean a thing. This rebuff from a group which the Richardsons regarded as distinctly in League Division Two, plus the more official request for help, provided an excellent opportunity for expansion into the Mr Smith club.

Eddie and some of his men paid their first visit to the club. 'There was a little mob in that corner, and a little mob in this corner,' says Phil Wilson, who had taken a group of his lady workers down to Mr Smith for a special treat. 'I thought to myself, it won't be long before there's trouble here.'

275

And how right he was. A couple of days later, on Monday, 7 March 1966, Eddie and Frank Fraser arrived at the club in the late afternoon for a meeting with two representatives of the company which owned it. According to evidence given in court later, both these men discussed with Eddie the question of club security, and problems such as finding suitable doormen. 'I wanted to get hold of some employees with good local knowledge who would keep better order than I thought was being kept,' one of the management team recalled.

As far as Eddie was concerned, the deal was now on. He was free to move in to protect and assist the running of the club.

Another member of the management remembers Eddie returning later on in the same afternoon and saying, 'Those two men for your door you asked me to get for you . . . well, I think I've found them. I'll bring one down tonight to see if he is suitable.'

To Eddie, the takeover that he planned was routine and legal. All it would require was a suitable team of his men to confront the Haward group and let them know that the Richardsons were now minding the club. There was no reason why there should be any violence at all.

However, the Haward gang may have been Second Division in the Richardsons' eyes; they were nevertheless as tough as they come. They had different ideas. They wanted to keep their club. Word went out that a showdown was on for that night.

Staff at the club felt the atmosphere changing as the evening wore on. Eddie chatted to the barmaid – the same girl who had previously dispensed free drinks to the Haward mob. When he had finished, Billy Haward called her across to chat with him. Eddie and his men – Frank Fraser, Harry Rawlins, Billy Stayton and Ronnie Jeffrey – mixed easily enough with Haward and his men, Dickie Hart, Henry Botton, Eddie Gardner and others. As yet there had been no incidents to test which of the two gangs would sort it out, and thus claim the rights to the club.

But by 11pm the atmosphere was thick with apprehension. 'After the cabaret I noticed a number of strange faces that I did not know,' said one of the staff. 'My wife worked there. I wanted to make sure she was out of the place and I took her home.'

Then a telephone call came through to the club. The receptionist answered. It was somebody asking for Billy Haward. This answering service was one of his perks. As he took the call, the receptionist heard him asking the caller to come around. The man seemed reluctant. 'We'll be all right, don't worry,' Haward said.

As he leaned back, the receptionist noticed something under his jacket. 'I saw a gun. It was strapped on his shoulder, inside his jacket.'

It was in fact a sawn-off double-barrel .410 shotgun, barely the size of a pistol. But others of Haward's friends were also armed that night. One of them had a .45 automatic.

Another associate of Eddie, Jimmy Moody, arrived, apparently by coincidence. Tension increased and ordinary guests started to leave. The members of the two rival groups mingled with each other in what, on the surface, seemed a reasonably friendly manner. Strange ritualistic displays were being performed. A kind of territory-marking was taking place.

Staff at the club felt some relief when at about 2am both groups of men got together on the slightly raised area of the club where guests could buy meals. They pulled three tables together and the entire group of about sixteen men chatted and drank amongst themselves. But appearances were again deceptive. Some of the men were getting very twitchy. The manager told some members of staff to go home early, as virtually all the other customers had already left. Voices around the dining tables started to get louder. Everybody knew the showdown was close at hand.

It was a little before 3am when Eddie chose his moment.

'Right, drink up. That's your lot.'

Silence fell around the table, cluttered with empty glasses and swimming in spilt liquor.

'Well, now, that's a shame, Eddie,' said Haward. 'We was

just getting the flavour.'

His friends laughed. The barmaid who had been sitting on a table on the balcony scurried off to see the manager. Eddie paused. He looked at Haward.

'Drink it up,' he said calmly. 'I'm running this place now.'

'You're what?' asked Haward. 'I thought the management was!'

The barmaid came back timidly on to the far end of the raised dining area.

'Get into the kitchen,' ordered one of Haward's men called Dickie Hart. He was the man with the .45.

'No, let her stay here,' said Haward. 'There's nothing here to bother us.'

She sat alone at her table.

'Who do you fuckin' well think you are?' a big blond man called Peter Hennessy suddenly bawled, half drunk, at Eddie. He was one of Haward's men. 'I'll take you any day, you half-baked fuckin' ponse.'

Frank Fraser shifted. Harry Rawlins looked expectantly at Eddie, one of his best friends.

'The only drinks from now on are those that I pour,' Eddie said, much more determined now than before.

'Ah fuck you, you cunt, I'm going to help myself.'

Hennessy went for the bottle. Eddie grabbed his glass and smashed it against the edge of the table.

'On the floor! On the floor!' he screamed at Hennessy, dragging him down the two stairs to the dance floor.

Dickie Hart stood up and fired his gun. All the other men jumped up. Tables were upturned and a terrible fight began. Eddie carried on hammering Hennessy. More shots went off. All the staff rushed out of the door into Rushey Green at the front of the club. Harry Rawlins crashed to the ground with severe gunshot wounds on his left arm.

Eddie joined the general melée. Tables were smashed. Haward staggered, and collapsed to the ground with a massive wound inflicted by a rod struck on the top of his head. There was blood splattered all over the walls, and pools of it on the floor.

Then Dickie Hart lost his gun. He rushed outside to

Farley Road through the back entrance. Frank Fraser and others pursued. More shots followed, waking residents in the road. Many sprang to their windows and saw men in lounge suits fighting it out viciously on the pavement. Dozens of 999 calls were made.

Ronnie Jeffrey arrived outside through the back entrance. There was somebody groaning on the pavement, with others fighting around him. 'Turn it up,' he screamed, starting to go.

Somebody called out at him. He turned round and was blasted in the groin with a shotgun.

Henry Botton arrived at the back-entrance scene. He saw Dickie Hart and Frank Fraser lying close together on the pavement. Other men were kicking the body of Hart.

'You're fucking mad, Frank!' he yelled at Fraser.

A local resident thought he saw a man smash a bottle in the face of one of the men lying on the pavement.

The deadly brawl continued for several more minutes on the pavement outside the back of the club in the quiet residential road.

By the time it was over, Frank Fraser lay groaning face down in a front garden of a nearby house with a bullet in his leg that had shattered his thigh bone. Eddie Richardson had been peppered with shotgun pellets in his thigh and his backside. And Dickie Hart, a local thief and friend of Billy Haward, lay dying in a puddle of blood at the back entrance. His face was badly smashed and a bullet, which had entered his back, lay near his heart. A glass jemmy had also been stuffed down the front of his trousers.

As the police and ambulances arrived, a resident was trying to administer first aid to Hart, whom he had at first confused for a sack.

Billy Haward had escaped, later to turn up at a friend's house, where his savage head wound was roughly and amateurishly stitched together.

Eddie and his mate Harry Rawlins had also got away just in time. They had been rescued by Jimmy Moody who had bundled them both into his Jaguar before screaming off at high speed. Rawlins had lost a lot of blood and was in a bad way, although Eddie's injuries were not serious.

As Chief Superintendent John Cummins, head of the Catford police, was being dragged out of bed to be told of the incident, Moody was pulling up outside the front gate of Dulwich Hospital. Eddie, Moody and another man helped Rawlins and laid him over a child's cot in casualty. The duty night porter looked on in amazement and then called the duty sister. She was less taken aback at the sight of the blood-drenched man.

'Good Morning,' she said, surveying the scene before her and instantly assuming command. 'Give me a hand to lift him on to the bed.'

This done, Moody and the other man present rushed out, screeching off into the night in the Jaguar. Seeing that Rawlins was in no condition to be asked questions, the sister asked Eddie his name. He said nothing.

'Please, what is your name?' she asked, firmly.

'Smith,' said Eddie.

'Now that doesn't sound very convincing, does it?'

Eddie looked on as the sister also tended Rawlins.

'OK, it's George Ward, George Ward is my name.'

'Is this your friend?' asked the sister.

'Yes.'

'And what is his name?'

'Er, that won't be necessary. Just forget it.'

Shortly afterwards the hospital authorities were telling the police about a man called George Ward who had been dumped at their hospital with leg wounds and who had with him a seriously injured friend, whose name he would not give.

Chief Superintendent John Cummins was driven at high speed through slumbering south London towards the hospital. He entered the cubicles where doctors were treating both men. A sardonic flicker of recognition spread across his face.

'Well, well, well,' said the detective, 'if it isn't Eddie Richardson. And how did you get this little lot?'

Another deadly blow had been struck against the Richardson gang.

*   *   *

Charlie was sharing a bed with Jean La Grange in Windsor Gardens, Johannesburg. He was sleeping well, having earlier been congratulated by General van den Bergh on his Anti-Apartheid robbery, and told what an honourable profession spying was. Charlie felt really confident that things were going to be all right.

When he was told the news about Eddie and the affray early on the morning of 8 March, a shiver of apprehension ran down his spine. It was all he needed. 'On learning of my brother's injuries and possible charges, I returned to the UK to visit him in hospital and to do my utmost to see he did not get convicted and sent to prison.'

By the time Charlie arrived back in London, the situation had worsened. The Mr Smith Affray received massive publicity and attracted hordes of police. Even more were to be on the scene two days after the fight, including Detective Chief Superintendent Tommy Butler, the legendary detective who convicted the train robbers.

On Wednesday, 9 March, two days after the affray, George Cornell, the tough East Ender who was now working with the Richardson crowd, called up Alby Woods, the friend of Frank Fraser who was now in Lewisham Hospital. Cornell, who had also been known as Myers in the East End, wanted Alby Woods to give him a lift to Stepney to visit Jimmy Andrews, who had been shot in the legs a few days earlier on the orders of the Krays. Cornell had been disqualified from driving, so Woods agreed. He knew Jimmy Andrews anyway and thought it would be nice to see him.

As they came out of the hospital, Cornell asked Woods if he wanted to have a drink. Woods agreed, but said it would have to be quick. They went to a well-known East End pub nearby called the Blind Beggar. Woods recalls: 'As we are walking across the pavement a young fellow came across and said "Hello" to George. I didn't know him at the time. He came in and had a drink and the three of us went into the saloon bar.'

The bar was deserted apart from one old boy who was sitting in the corner. The 'young fellow' had a couple of light ales and took his leave. A couple of other people whom Woods didn't know but who were acquainted with Cornell came and went. Cornell was sitting at a barstool at the corner of the bar, Woods was standing next to him, his back to the entrance.

'Let's make a move,' said Woods, needing to get home.

'Let's just have one more drink and call it a day,' said Cornell. 'Same again please, love,' he said to the barmaid.

Woods became aware that something had caught Cornell's eye.

'Well, look who's walked in,' said Cornell, his voice sneering with contempt.

Woods looked over his shoulder and saw two men wearing raincoats. One of the men was Ronnie Kray. He was armed and in a murderous mood. Cornell was one of the few men in the world who showed neither fear nor respect for the Kray gang. Recently he had called Ronnie a fat poof in front of other people, referring to what everyone knew was his weakness for young boys.

Kray and his partner walked towards the corner where Cornell was sitting. They stopped only a couple of feet away. Ronnie pulled a pistol out of his pocket. He lifted it and took aim at Cornell's forehead.

Alby Woods threw a glance at Cornell.

'He was smiling at them, looking straight at them,' Woods remembers. 'As I looked back again, the bullet came across my face and I ducked. I don't know whether the first bullet hit him or not. But when I ducked, so the gun went off again and George came down beside me.

'They were pumping bullets all around us and then they ran out of the pub. The barmaid was screaming. I looked at him and there was blood all coming out of him. They hit him in the head and the face. They hit him the first time, but he didn't go down the first time, he came down the second time. He was moaning, he still wasn't out. He was taken to hospital straight away; it is opposite the Blind Beggar. That was that.'

Alby Woods went into hiding. When he was finally picked up by the police and asked to pick out Ronnie Kray from an

ID parade, he said he couldn't recognise anybody who had been there that night. It probably saved his life.

The killing of George Cornell sent shockwaves through Scotland Yard and the underworld alike, coming as it did so soon after the affray at Mr Smith. Next morning, the *Evening Standard* reported:

> Scotland Yard this afternoon confirmed the connection between the murder of Richard Hart in Catford and the murder of George Cornell at the Blind Beggar public house, Stepney.
>
> Scotland Yard said in a statement: 'As there is undoubtedly a connection between the murder of Richard Hart and George Cornell, Commander Ernest Millen has decided to depute Detective Chief Superintendent Thomas Butler of the Flying Squad to co-ordinate the two inquiries by Detective Superintendents John Cummins and James Axon.'

Powerful forces were stirring in the pub headquarters of the London gangs. The Krays had for long had designs on the West End, but had been restrained by the presence of Eddie and his powerful alliances with people like Albert Dimes. Now Eddie and Frank Fraser were lying in hospitals and almost certain to be charged, and George Cornell, one of the Richardsons' most powerful henchmen, had been liquidated. And the Krays knew that Charlie was having one or two problems himself.

According to Alby Woods, there had been little trouble between the Richardsons and the Krays before all this. 'The Krays respected them and didn't come nowhere near,' he says. 'When Eddie and Frank was about they never came in the West End. Whether they fancied themselves, I don't know. But as soon as that happened at Mr Smith's and Frank and Eddie all got done, all of a sudden I should imagine that they want George out of the way. You see, when Frank and Eddie got done, the Krays had a licence to go into the West End and take over.... They wanted Cornell out of the way, no doubt about it. As soon as they got him out of the way they could do what they liked and they did. They went into the West End.'

The execution of Cornell brought a quick but hollow gesture of retaliation; Roy Hall, the loyal little hard-working man whom Charlie had taken on as a schoolboy, was a good mate of Cornell. He took Cornell's widow, Olive, out for a few drinks to console her. They had much to drink and she demanded to know why nobody had avenged her husband's death. Roy got hold of a pistol and drove to Vallance Road in the East End, where the Kray twins lived with their mother. In the early hours of the morning, he shot out the windows of their little house, while 'the boys', as they were called by their adoring mother, took their beauty sleep inside.

Affairs could hardly have been worse for Charlie as he arrived back from South Africa, still desperately trying to save his mining interests. But chickens were coming in to roost elsewhere. On 13 March, just under a week after the Cornell killing, Jack Duval made his first statement to the police.

Having fled the country after cleaning out Charlie and Phil Wilson at the Common Market Merchants long firm, Duval had returned early in 1966 and with a couple of friends settled in Leeds, where he carried on the only trade he knew, frauds and long firms. But in the course of his flitting all over Europe in recent years, he had committed many passport offences by using false names, some of them those of Charlie's men. The police had at last caught up with him and on 25 March Duval was sentenced to a year in prison for the passport offences. The sentence was lighter than he might have received had he not been talking thirteen to the dozen with Gerald McArthur, the Assistant Chief Constable of Hertfordshire.

The by now grimly determined McArthur was building up a full head of steam. On the very day that Duval made his first statement, Jimmy Taggart – the man who had first alerted 'Mac' – also named Tommy Clark in a signed statement as one of the men who had taken part in his ferocious beating on 15 July the previous year. The day after this, on 14 March 1966, at midnight, the inevitable happened. Eddie, along with others including Billy Haward, Harry Rawlins and Jimmy Moody, was charged with the Mr Smith affray. 'I am completely innocent as will no doubt be established,' Eddie told Detective Chief Superintendent Butler and Chief Superintendent Cummins. 'No doubt' was a phrase Eddie often used in this situation.

Charlie, increasingly worried about the forthcoming Bradbury trial in South Africa, activated the whole of his gang. They were put into action against all the potential witnesses. He wanted everyone who might be able to give evidence seen and either terrified or paid to play it right down. Amazingly, Eddie got bail. It wasn't to last for long, though.

Charlie was now under extraordinary pressure. His whole world was collapsing around him. The Krays were poised to march into the West End; Eddie and Frank were in real trouble; South Africa was extremely precarious; and, unknown to Charlie, more and more people with information about his savage violence were talking readily to Gerald McArthur, often in the hope of getting lighter sentences for their own crimes.

With arrangements in full swing for the 'nobbling' of the case against Eddie and Frank and the others now in hand, Charlie turned again to his work for BOSS. He set about the task with determination, feeling that the more he pleased BOSS, the greater were his hopes of retaining his interests in South Africa.

BOSS had been particularly interested in the activities of an organisation called ZAPU, the Zimbabwe African People's Union. It was one of the most influential groups representing blacks who were fighting against oppression. Their offices at Kings Cross presented no problem for Charlie. It was simply a matter of forcing a lock on the door and helping himself to documents. The offices were plundered on 18 March. Charlie sent his customary telegram to Jean La Grange: 'Jean three parcels number 4137275 and one parcel number 4137277 on flight BOAC 121 arriving

Joburg noon Sunday. Love, Charles.'

But there were greater problems with another body that interested BOSS, Amnesty International. This organisation had done great work fighting for some of the more appalling cases of individual South Africans persecuted by the government for their political beliefs. Early one evening, Charlie sized up their offices, then situated in a quiet alley called Craven Court just off Fleet Street. He saw large locks on the doors and realised that breaking in would be difficult. Amnesty, because of the world in which it dealt, knew only too well of the dirty tricks that intelligence agents got up to for their countries. The windows were also secured very well. Charlie wandered round into the next road, Fetter Lane, which ran parallel with Craven Court. There was a large building with a 'To Let' sign outside. From what Charlie could see, its rear would border on the back of Amnesty International's offices. Next day he rang the estate agents. He gave a false name, saying he was a businessman possibly interested in the lease, and asked if he could send somebody around to pick up the keys for him.

It was as Charlie had hoped: the back of the building to be let looked right on to the Amnesty building. And on the top floor the window was virtually opposite another in the back of the Amnesty building. He realised that a short plank would span the gap, enabling him to enter through Amnesty's top-floor window. Charlie left the building and drove to Gamages, the department store then in Holborn. There, he had copies cut of the keys, returning the originals to the estate agents.

Later that night, he used the duplicate key to get into the building and climbed into the Amnesty building as planned. He took everything he could see vaguely relating to South Africa, putting it all into plastic sacks he had brought along. He took notebooks, letter-headings, files and lists of members and their addresses. He passed the sacks through one of the ground-floor windows that led on to Craven Court where some rubbish was waiting to be collected, let himself out and quickly put two of the sacks into his van. But then he was noticed by a couple of people, who stared at

286

him. Charlie decided to drive off straight away and return in the early morning to pick up the other sacks.

When he returned he found to his horror that the other sacks and all the rubbish had gone. The dustbin men had just been past on an early morning central London shift. He felt bitterly angry at his bad luck. But he sent off what he had. On 30 March, two days after the robbery, there was the usual telegram to Jean: 'Jean one parcel number 4341224 on BOAC flight BA III. Arrives Thursday noon. Two letters inside parcel. Love Charles.'

Charlie was contacted a couple of days later. BOSS wanted to know where the rest of the papers were. They could tell that Charlie hadn't sent everything.

The three robberies that Charlie carried out for BOSS during March 1966 went unpublicised at the time. Nobody saw any particular significance or pattern to the events. But eight months later, on 20 November 1966, the *Sunday Telegraph* reported the thefts. More surprising, perhaps, the break-ins also got coverage in South Africa's *Rand Daily Mail*. It was stated in an article on 24 November:

> There have been four mysterious raids on the offices of anti-apartheid organisations in London this year, the London *Sunday Telegraph* reports.
>
> The raids took place in this order:
> * On March 3: Anti-Apartheid movement office raided and notebooks files and address cards stolen.
> * March 18: Zimbabwe African People's Union offices raided and subscription lists and all written material and photographs since 1962 taken.
> * March 20: The then publishers of *Zimbabwe Review* were raided and 2000 copies of the review were slashed. The only things stolen were letters connected with the Zimbabwe African People's Union.
> * March 28: Offices of Amnesty International raided and files, cheques, address cards and a parcel addressed to ZAPU stolen.

It is not clear whether Charlie was responsible for the raid on the *Zimbabwe Review*.

The *Sunday Telegraph* article stated: 'Secret agents are working in London for the Smith regime and the South African police, and are almost certainly responsible for a series of raids which were disclosed last week on the offices of Anti-Apartheid and African freedom movements in London.' It added: 'By stealing documents and address lists, the agents have placed in jeopardy the freedom of clandestine supporters of anti-apartheid and of full democracy who are now living in South Africa and Rhodesia.'

The same 20 November article also reported a smear campaign designed to discourage British supporters of African freedom movements. Letters were sent to such supporters on headed notepaper of ZAPU, which, of course, Charlie had raided on 18 March that year. The letters, purporting to come from ZAPU itself, must have had a bad effect on British sympathisers. They talked of hanging racists in Africa and of the need to increase terror tactics. It was to this kind of use that BOSS was putting the fruits of Charlie's labours. . . .

20. The Press Hounds

It was perhaps a sign of a kind of madness in Charlie that he placed so much confidence in the help that BOSS could give him. It never apparently occurred to him that he was merely being used to do South Africa's dirty work in London. Charlie always assumed that everybody wanted to do him a favour. It never crossed his mind that BOSS, if necessary, would drop him like a hot coal, safe in the knowledge that nobody would believe him if he decided to open his mouth.

It was an even greater insanity at this period, with his empire of crime being so assaulted on all sides, and with a desperate shortage of money to finance the massive undertakings he was already involved in, that Charlie should have tried to open up a major new operation.

During the month of March, Charlie had heard about large new deposits of perlite in the Greek Island of Lesbos. A Greek prospector called Papaconstantinou had a mining lease which he wanted to sell. Charlie had written to the man on 18 March, the same day that he carried out the ZAPU robbery, asking him for 'details of Mining already taken place to date, Geological report of Deposition Lesbos and Core Drilling report if available re quantity and analysis of Perlite expansion results.'

In the early part of April Charlie then travelled with an Athens lawyer and Jimmy Collins, who had been called back from South Africa, to inspect the island and to meet Mr Papaconstantinou. He liked what he saw and told him that he thought it was worth £50,000. He left Jimmy Collins in Greece and instructed the lawyer. He seems to have made quite an impression on the lawyer, just as he had on countless other upright citizens in the past. The lawyer wrote to Charlie on 17 April: 'I will always have the best memories

289

from you and this trip. Let's hope that the pains you took will not be in vain.'

But time was to run out on Charlie. Had he been able to proceed with the development of Greece, it would have been Mkuse all over again. The prospector had three partners who held 60 per cent of the shares and who seemed disgruntled. There was a dispute about whether the deposit was a quarry or a mine. This was important. If the deposit was a quarry, then the title to it lay with the owners of the land; thus they would have to be cut into the action. Although the Ministry of Industry thought it was a mine – and this was in Charlie's favour – the courts in Athens had ruled that it was a quarry. But as Charlie was engaging in this quite extraordinary distraction, the problems with all his other activities were just about to breach the dam.

When the *News of the World* had published its article about a 'Murder Incorporated' group being behind the killing of Waldeck four months before, Charlie had instructed solicitor Raymond Davis to sue for libel. On 3 April, this move backfired terribly. For the first time in public, Charlie's *name* was directly linked to the killing. Peter Earle, the *News of the World* reporter despatched to make further inquiries into the matter, had been working overtime. And on 3 April 1966, he was to get his chance to publish under the headline: 'The *News of the World* and a writ that was dismissed'.

On February 5, we received a letter from a firm of solicitors, Raymond Davis and Co., of Russia Row, Cheapside, London. This stated that they were acting on behalf of a firm called Concordia Developments (Namaqualand) Ltd, and its Chairman, Mr Charles Richardson.

The solicitors stated that their 'clients complain that a series of articles has recently appeared in the English and South African newspapers which have caused our clients to be identified quite erroneously in the public mind with the name Murder Inc. and that your article constitutes, therefore, a gross and most damaging libel upon them. In accordance with our client's instructions, we have today

290

issued proceedings claiming damages for libel, and an injunction against you, and we shall be glad to know on whom we may effect service of the writ.'

Then came the crunch:

> At no time had the *News of the World* mentioned Concordia Developments or the name Charlie Richardson in connection with its story from Johannesburg.

At the time of the first *News of the World* story, Charlie had acted with extravagant dumb innocence. He demanded that the *News of the World* be sued to the hilt, to show the world what a terrible wrong he had suffered. But Charlie's brave words came to nothing, as Peter Earle's 3 April story continued to reveal:

> Raymond Davis was immediately referred to the *News of the World* solicitors and on Feb. 14 they received a writ.
>
> During the next three weeks, however, no statement of claim was received substantiating the writ for libel. Without this, no further proceedings are permitted by the rules of the High Court.
>
> Accordingly on March 8 a summons asking for the action to be dismissed was issued by our solicitors. This summons was heard in the High Court chambers by Master Ritchie on March 16 and he made the following order:
>
> 'That this action be dismissed with costs to be taxed and paid to the defendants (the *News of the World*) by the plaintiffs for want of prosecution unless the statement of claim be served within 14 days.'
>
> Failure to comply with this order meant that the action started by Mr Richardson and the company Concordia Developments would be dismissed by default.
>
> The deadline for complying with the order of the court expired at four o'clock on Wednesday afternoon.
>
> Since that time, as both parties are free of legal entanglement, I have made strenuous efforts to contact

Mr Charles Richardson, who lives in Acland Crescent, Camberwell, London, and has an office in Park Lane.

For Mr Richardson might be in a position to throw light on some of the background of one of the most intriguing murder mysteries of our time. . . .

When I asked for him at his home I was assured by a relative that he was at one of two hotels in Johannesburg. But when I telephoned there, I was unable to establish contact with him.

(It seems extraordinary that, as the relative claimed, Charlie was in South Africa at this time, with all the publicity in the English papers, and with the Bradbury trial due in a couple of weeks.)

But the *News of the World* story was nothing compared to what else was printed in the newspapers in the following weeks.

On Thursday 7 April, four days after Charlie had been named in the *News of the World*, Eddie and the others involved in the shoot-out at Mr Smith appeared at Greenwich Magistrates' Court, charged with causing an affray. 'Scenes in Mister Smith's Club at Catford were like a Wild West Film, Greenwich Court heard today,' proclaimed the *Evening Standard* that night. Eddie Richardson was named in court as the leader of one gang, Billy Haward as the leader of the other. Despite the nature of the allegations made in the court, Eddie still kept his bail.

All kinds of connections were now being made in public between disparate parts of the Richardson empire. The Bradbury trial was even previewed in the English papers, shortly after the first affray hearing. The *News of the World*, for example, reported:

A lonely man from South East London will appear in court in connection with a murder in South Africa next week.

He is John Bradbury, also known as John West, and he was detained after a South African mine owner was shot dead in cold blood.

Bradbury became lonelier when one of his best friends, George Cornell, was shot dead and several of his former associates were wounded by gunmen.

This is one of several curious links between the 'gang killings' in London and the murder last June in Johannesburg of gun-carrying Thomas Waldeck – a mining man involved in a fabulously rich mineral strike on South Africa's Ghost Mountain.

Another link is provided by two brothers named Richardson. Both are large shareholders in a scrap metal company in South East London.

One is Charles William (Charlie) Richardson of Acland Crescent, Camberwell. The other is Edward George (Eddie) Richardson of Sidcup Road, Eltham.

Charlie Richardson was a business partner of Thomas Waldeck, the man shot in South Africa.

Eddie Richardson was one of the men wounded by shotgun pellets outside a Catford gambling club called Mr Smith. . . .

John Bradbury knew both the Richardsons, as people do when they come from the same area. They went to the same school.

When the Bradbury trial finally began on 26 April it wasn't just the popular press that covered his sensational allegations. *The Times* headline announced: 'Murder Trial told of torture by London Gangsters: Accused man feared reprisals.' Its report then stated: 'Bradbury told the court that a London gang leader used to hold mock trials, using a stolen judge's robes – with sentences ranging from death downwards. At one such trial, a man who had crossed the gang leaders in the protection racket was tried, sentenced, and nailed to the floor by his knees, he said.'

Gordon Winter, in the same *Times* report, was quoted as saying that if he had not been held in 'protective custody', undoubtedly he would have been killed by London gangsters. 'Mr Winter told today of his association with Richard Aubrey, a Londoner who, he said, told him a large amount of money was coming into South Africa. The witness added

293

that he had suspicions that the money had some connection with Britain's Great Train Robbery. Mr Winter said he lent Aubrey his pistol the night before Waldeck was killed.'

The Times did not reveal that the gang leader who had allegedly forced Bradbury to kill Waldeck was Charles Richardson. Neither did the *Daily Express*, which referred to Charlie as 'X':

> Startling allegations of London gangland thuggery were made in Johannesburg today by Lawrence 'Johnny' Bradbury, who is accused of killing a South African gold prospector.
>
> Bradbury said he was ordered by a London gang leader to murder 34-year-old Thomas Waldeck.
>
> But he denied doing the shooting. He said that he simply drove another member of the gang to Waldeck's house. . . .
>
> Bradbury described how 'X', the gangland chief, held mock trials of double-crossers in London.

The South African newspapers were less coy about naming Charlie. However, the London *Daily Mail* was able to report the allegations of Waldeck's widow, in which she named Charlie:

> She spoke of a Charles Richardson, a man called Simmons or Symonds (later identified as Harry Prince) and [another man].
>
> Mrs Waldeck said she learned after the shooting that the men she mentioned were 'hoodlums'.
>
> Mr Hannon (Bradbury's counsel): 'And at the top of the pile was Richardson?'
>
> Mrs Waldeck: 'Yes.'

The *Mail* report went on:

> In court today, Dr Gideon Van Gass, an insurance assessor, said Bradbury had told him that a man named Harry Prince was responsible for the shooting.

Dr Van Gass said that Bradbury claimed he was forced to drive a car to the scene of the shooting. He did so because he feared reprisals by the London gang against his family.

The extraordinary volume of publicity both in London and in South Africa was to be another devastating blow against Charlie. It didn't do Eddie much good either. The day after the Bradbury trial started, he lost his bail. It was to be another ten years before he walked as a free man, despite the efforts Charlie was still to make in an attempt to save him from conviction.

On the fourth day of Bradbury's trial, Bradbury appeared in the dock with both wrists bandaged. On the evening of 29 April 1966, he had slashed them in a suicide attempt in the Fort Prison. Bradbury had only the day before alleged that Charlie and Eddie had punished him by slashing his wrists in the early days of the gang. According to his wife Sheila today, this was nonsense. She had just broken off her engagement to him: 'I got a call from a hospital and they said he had slashed his wrists in the Walworth Road, which I think he blamed Eddie for. They just wanted me to pacify him until he was back to normal . . . they told me that he was definitely mental.' (She still, however, married him.)

With everything at stake, Charlie took desperate measures. He had again changed his solicitors in South Africa, this time to a firm called Messrs Sidney S. Hoffman and Fevrier. Stanley Woods acquired the services of Mr Rubenstein from Charlie's previous firm, to assist him with his steadily greater efforts to rescue some of his investments.

With publicity from the Bradbury trial at its height in London and Johannesburg, on 29 April Charlie's solicitor in London, Raymond Davis, telephoned the new solicitors and instructed them to brief a lawyer to represent Charlie at the trial. That afternoon he wrote confirming his instructions, and offering his opinion that the evidence given in court, together with the published newspaper reports, seemed to implicate Charlie in criminal activities, including the murder of Thomas Waldeck. 'We should be grateful if you would communicate with the South African newspapers in appropriate terms to prevent further publications of a similar nature.'

This letter, together with a long detailed statement by Charlie giving his side of events, was personally delivered to the Hoffman and Fevrier offices in Johannesburg by none other than Jean La Grange, who had flown to London earlier in the month to see Charlie. Shortly after the letter had been delivered, Advocate Joubert appeared in court on behalf of Charlie. It was too late for him to make a major impact. The evidence had been completed when the court rose on the previous Friday. But he did his bit: 'I wish to address your Lordship very briefly on the purpose of my prsence here today,' he said with due dignity.

'In doing so I am mindful of the fact that I have no *locus standi* in these proceedings. We have, however, received instructions from a London firm of attorneys to hold a watching brief for a Mr Charles Richardson, whose name has been mentioned during the course of this trial, and against whom allegations of a very serious nature have been made.

'The allegations levelled against him could possibly seriously embarrass him in the future. I am mindful, too, of the fact that I am not permitted to comment, by virtue of the *sub judice* rule, on the veracity or otherwise of any statements made to this court under oath during this trial and involving Mr Richardson.

'The instructions were given us for the specific purpose of determining what legal steps should be taken to determine this very issue. The complexity of the situation is, therefore, self-evident, and I beg the court's leave to be permitted to remain here ... until the determination of these proceedings.'

The 'determination of these proceedings' happened shortly after Mr Joubert sat down. Mr Justice Snyman and his two assessors did not accept Bradbury's defence that he had been forced to become involved in the killing as a driver because he was terrified of Charlie. They didn't even accept that he had only been the driver. Bradbury was sentenced to be hung by his neck until dead. Mr Snyman ruled that Bradbury could have done something to save himself and Waldeck if, as he claimed, he really didn't want to be involved with the murder.

The verdict received mass coverage in the South African papers that night. But alongside these reports was given the statement made by Advocate Joubert. Charlie was encouraged somewhat by this. He decided that his South African lawyers should be instructed immediately to proceed at full speed with libel proceedings. Like the same earlier move against the *News of the World*, it was to do little to help. Charlie was trying everything, desperately, to try and stop the endless flow of bad publicity. He went to see a powerful businessman friend of his, who, apart from being an ex-Conservative MP, knew about publishing and newspapers. The man, unable to contact Charlie by phone, had written to Jean Goodman on 30 April, at the height of the Bradbury trial, stating:

'I have yet again been approached by the Press over Charlie. *Why the Hell* they think I know anything about him, God knows, as I have patiently explained each time. I was introduced to him by two well-known baronets, with impeccable references from Price Waterhouse and had nothing but kindness and honesty from him, giving him, at the same time advice on his businesses. . . .

'*However*, when I warded off the *People* this morning, they put up one idea which, rightly handled, might get things under control. They want a statement from, or interview with Charlie. This must obviously be very carefully arranged, with all safeguards and with an undertaking they will publish all the text without comment. (And it will of course have been approved by his solicitor beforehand.)

'Although this would be regarded as a scoop, it might be the way of redressing the balance of the appalling publicity and innuendoes at the moment — and take the attack right into the enemies' camp.'

Charlie was not amused by the suggestion that the *People* should be used to do this job. Roy East had already in the

297

past written about a vicious gang scouring Europe in search of Jack Duval. And just as Charlie read this letter, the *People* produced another story about the amazing antics of the same, unnamed gang:

Locked away in the offices of the *People* this morning is the dossier of Six Frightened Men. Six stories of brutish violence that bring fresh, fearsome evidence of the extent to which 'Crime Incorporated' is flourishing in Britain.

Six men who tell of beatings, stabbings and torture at the hands of London gang bosses, six more reasons why the *People* repeats its demand: SMASH THE GANGS! SET UP A SPECIAL CRIME COMMISSION NOW!

The need for such a tribunal, before which suspects could be forced to give evidence, becomes all the more urgent after the past week's astonishing allegations in a South African court that a man was murdered on the orders of a gang in London.

Colonel St John Pattle, of Johannesburg CID, told the court that after inquiries in London he was convinced there · was an organisation 'specialising in blackmail, murder and extortion'.

Why doesn't Scotland Yard move in and smash the organisation which is blackening our name all over the world?

Having posed the question, the *People* then answered it:

First, they are hamstrung by rules of evidence, designed to protect the innocent.

So far, also, they have been unable to break the rule of fear which the gangs have set up, not only over the crooks they control, but over innocent citizens who have accidentally become involved with them.

Two of the six frightened men the *People* referred to were Jack Duval and Jimmy Taggart. The other four were not named. But whoever they were, Charlie's victims were rarely simply 'innocent citizens' going about their lawful business.

298

This further onslaught against Charlie by the *People* meant, for obvious reasons, that he could not turn to them in the hope that they would publish a sympathetic interview, as his businessman friend had suggested. He turned instead to South Africa, where in many ways he had most to lose. With the help of Jean La Grange, who was doing so much to try and help Charlie that it annoyed his lawyers, a story was arranged with the *Rand Daily Mail*, one of South Africa's most liberal publications. On 6 May, three days after the *People*'s latest mauling, the *Rand Daily Mail* carried a banner headline right across the top of its front page: 'WALDECK – BY RICHARDSON'. There were further sub-headings: '*Mail* man talks to mystery man in Bradbury murder trial', and ' "Tom and I were good friends . . . his death cost me a great deal" '. The report was by Des Blow, who has taken a keen interest in the Richardson story ever since:

Charles Richardson, 32, whose name was mentioned in the Bradbury trial, told me yesterday that he intended to come to South Africa in the future 'to clear my name'.

'But business or pressure of business is keeping me in London now,' he said. 'I am managing director of six companies in England and cannot afford to be picked up in South Africa for 180 days.'

It was a lovely assumption on Charlie's part that he would be treated only as Gordon Winter had been and placed in detention rather than arrested on the spot by the very determined Colonel Pattle. It was a nice little touch, too, that he mentioned in passing his position as managing director of six English companies; what a marvellous picture it conjured up. Des Blow's interview with Charlie continued:

Mr Richardson, who had previously refused to speak to the press – either overseas or in South Africa – broke his silence yesterday for the first time since Bradbury's arrest.

He had earlier offered to pay my air fare to London for

299

the interview, which eventually took place in an hour-long telephone call to London.

Mr Richardson said he had lost a great deal by the death of Thomas Waldeck.

'Tom and I were 50 per cent partners in all our mining ventures,' he said, 'but many of the concessions lapsed after his death because they were not notarially attested.'

Speaking in a Cockney accent, he said, 'I had no reason to wish Tom Waldeck dead.

'We were good friends. Shortly before his death I lent him £10,000 without security so he could buy his luxury home in Melrose.

'When Mrs Waldeck cabled me of her husband's murder, I immediately sent her £1000 from my own personal savings to tide her over any immediate difficulties. Does that sound like a man guilty of murder?'

What Charlie omitted to mention was that at this very time he was defaulting on payments of the £50,000 which, three months after the murder, he had agreed to give Mrs Waldeck for all of her late husband's rights. But the article continued:

He (Charlie) said he would have liked to have asked Mrs Waldeck during the trial whether she had ever been badly treated by him.

'Tom brought no money into our partnership. I put money into enterprises for both of us. The partnership has cost me more than £200,000 . . . only two days before his death Tom telephoned my London office to say that he had discovered diamonds in Namaqualand. His death robbed us of this find as the prospecting rights were in his name and they died with him.'

Charlie denied that he knew Harry Prince: ' "And I only knew Richard Aubrey slightly. He went about saying I was his partner, but this is not true." '

300

21. Well Overdue

While Charlie had been suffering the continuing salvos of publicity, many other events had been taking place behind the scenes, away from the front pages. He was still doing his best to frustrate and interfere with the pending trial of his brother Eddie over Mr Smith. But most pressing and urgent of all, he had been re-grouping his forces in the hope that he could still save the perlite.

Several major new problems were caused by the Bradbury allegations. The South African government and the Ministry of Mines pulled right back, not wanting in any way to be connected to the shocking claims that were being made public by the day. This couldn't have come at a worse time: Charlie's prospecting rights to the perlite were just about due for their annual renewal. Had it not been for Bradbury *et al.*, renewal would almost certainly have been a formality. Now the South African government was delaying, waiting to see how the situation developed before giving even an indication as to whether or not it would renew the precious rights.

By the beginning of May 1966, when Bradbury was sentenced, Charlie had sewn up the backing and finance of Stan Woods. On 6 April 1966, both men had signed a Heads of Agreement – a kind of agreement in principle. The document stated that Stanley Woods would acquire 50 per cent of Charlie's perlite interests for £245,000. Charlie was unhappy about letting so much go, but he had no choice. He had also, in return, had to sign a document which safeguarded the interests of Mr Woods, who had already invested tens of thousands of pounds. If ever Charlie sold out to anybody, he would first have to pay back £50,000 to Woods. On top of that, Woods had a lien over 50,000 tons of the perlite as a further security.

But Charlie's problems by this stage involved far more

than simply raising the necessary finance. Even he was starting to realise that he would have to distance himself more publicly from the perlite venture if it were to succeed. He resigned from both Lebombo and SAPI, backdating his resignation to 20 January 1966. Victor Doel put his finger on the problem very nicely in a letter to Fred Pace, one of Stanley Woods's representatives, on 7 April, the day after the Heads of Agreement had been signed between Charlie and Woods. Having complained that his contract with Charlie had been violated at the slightest whim, he said that it was essential that South African participation of some kind was invited and that Charlie be persuaded to move completely out of Lebombo and SAPI publicly. 'This is not an assumption, calamity howling, or intimidation, but based on reliable sources of information coupled with my own knowledge gained at first hand in my recent negotiations and discussions, commercially and politically, some of which I am unable to divulge.'

Similar sentiments had been conveyed to Charlie by Jean La Grange, although in a more friendly way. From this period onwards, she was to travel between London and Johannesburg with breathtaking frequency in an untiring effort to help Charlie save the perlite. On a couple of occasions she made the twenty-hour round trip twice in the same week. Charlie, as much in love with her as ever, took a first-floor flat at 7, Pembroke Mews in Kensington for her to live in and share with him. He was now talking about marrying Jean La Grange. He formally divorced Margaret, his first wife, on 18 May 1966, on the grounds that she had deserted him. He hadn't worked out what to do about Jean Goodman, his common law wife who was still working in his scrapyard. But for the time being he gave Jean La Grange shares in his Johannesburg companies.

An even more important addition to his new team was the man called Major Theodore Marks, a most eminent and respectable South African who was friendly with the Minister of Mines and many other of South Africa's most powerful citizens. Charlie wanted Jean and the Major between them to represent the bulk of his interests in South

Africa. They would give him a respectable front, but at the same time allow him to maintain direct control. He also brought back Colin Riddoch, who in the early part of 1965 had investigated the possibilities of floating a public company, and deployed a man called Dave Stedman, who had been working at Anglo-American. By the time Bradbury had been sentenced to death on 2 May 1966, this new salvage team had been formed.

Jean La Grange, who had helped to organise the *Rand Daily Mail* story, now busied herself with other newspapers, doing her best to put Charlie's side of the story across. Charlie's new South African solicitors, Hoffman and Fevrier, proceeded with the libel action against the prosecution witnesses in the Waldeck murder trial. They told Charlie's London lawyer that they would have to buy a transcript of the Bradbury trial for £60 and that they would have to seek the expert legal opinion of Eric Morris, senior counsel, and of Eugene Joubert. They wanted to know exactly why Charlie felt the witnesses had been motivated by malice. There was also another difficulty: the solicitors felt because Charlie 'has the fear that he may be detained if he should visit South Africa', any proposed action would be that much more difficult.

Charlie hit back strongly, convincing himself more than ever in his own mind that he had been wronged. He consulted Raymond Davis, ordering him to tell Hoffman to sue, among others, Mrs Waldeck, to whom he still owed money. Davis relayed the latest instructions to Hoffman in a letter on 12 May. But the early promise of an aggressive action simply did not materialise. By 8 June, nearly a month later, Hoffman and Fevrier – who by this time had had their eyes opened by several other aspects of Charlie's problems – wrote to Raymond Davis saying they were dropping the case. They displayed thinly veiled contempt for a mass of papers which Charlie had sent across to them via Jean La Grange on yet another of her trips, saying they had no idea how the documents could be of any use.

During May, while the action was petering out – at the cost of £210 to Charlie – several other interesting events had been developing. On Friday the thirteenth, Jean La Grange arrived back in Johannesburg from her latest trip to London, with several of Charlie's new team. She rang up Mr Hoffman at his home that evening and told him that she wanted an urgent meeting to discuss the renewal of the perlite rights.

Charlie had now convinced himself that he could, through the services of Major Marks, not only get the rights renewed but also renege on his recent agreement to sell so much to Stanley Woods. Woods at this stage had been pushing ahead as best he could. He was working – understandably – on the assumption that having signed an outline agreement with Charlie, he had his full backing and support. He did not realise that Charlie was now mounting some kind of rearguard action.

The meeting demanded by Jean La Grange took place on the following night, Saturday 14 May, and lasted two hours. Present were Mr Hoffman, Jean La Grange, Colin Riddoch, Dave Stedman and Major Marks. Hoffman reported in a letter to Raymond Davis three days later that 'Major Marks was personally acquainted with the Secretary for Mines and the Minister for Mines' and that Marks was going to do his best to persuade them to renew the rights.

During this meeting, Mr Hoffman was told about the involvement of Stanley Woods and Victor Doel in Charlie's perlite. It was the first he had heard about them, and he listened wide-eyed. He was so worried and puzzled that he immediately cabled London and demanded proof that Jean and the Major were indeed empowered to act on behalf of Charlie. Raymond Davis cabled back immediately confirming that they were, and asked Mr Hoffman to give them every assistance.

Jean La Grange then asked Hoffman to contact Gerald Rubenstein, Charlie's previous lawyer, as quickly as he could to get from him a copy of the agreement that he had supervised between Charlie and Corris Waldeck. The agreement had been signed on 23 September 1965 selling all Mrs Waldeck's inherited rights to Charlie. Hoffman was able to do this only with some difficulty but when he had succeeded,

304

Jean La Grange again came to see him. She asked whether the document was legally binding. Mr Hoffman was shocked. He said of course it was. He could not understand why the question had been asked.

Major Marks, meanwhile, started trying to use his influence to secure the renewal of the threatened prospecting rights. He was confident that he could. Not only did he know the mining minister, he had also been associated in the past with Pretoria Portland Cement. He was sure he could assist in finding a company to buy 50 per cent of Charlie's interests. On Monday, 16 May, Major Marks had a meeting with the Secretary for Mines. Discussions seem to have gone well. When the meeting was over, the Major telephoned Mr Hoffman who reported the conversation back to London.

But by this stage Hoffman and Fevrier were clearly beginning to feel uneasy about aspects of their newest client. On the same day that the firm reported the Marks meeting with the Secretary for Mines Mr Hoffman sent a private and confidential letter to Raymond Davis, noting that Charlie had hired no less than six firms of lawyers in London and Johannesburg in connection with South Africa, and that payments were still outstanding to most of them. Hoffman demanded a £500 down-payment.

The news about Major Marks's meeting pleased Charlie greatly. He started to act as if hardly anything was wrong. He was further encouraged about his prospects after another meeting, on 22 May, with the former Conservative MP who had suggested giving the *People* an interview. Charlie had told the man all about his problems, simplifying as usual. The man, feeling genuinely sorry, told him he must hit back in an aggressive style. He felt so strongly about Charlie's plight that the following day he sent a letter to Raymond Davis, setting out his advice:

'I had a long talk with Charles yesterday, both about Africa and his public image. . . . I advised him that he must hit back at once to stop the flood. . . . My feelings are very simple. I am sure that the best way *now* to both consolidate his businesses *and* to project the right image *and* to sort out the complicated African affair satisfactorily, is for an investment holding trust, to take over all his interests with a very strong and very large board (suggestions attached) with Charles carrying control of most or all of the shares, and with a small management Board (including yourself or an accountant) – then the whole thing can be launched on a quite different basis from the present controversy which (a) he will win and (b) will quickly die . . . today's newspapers are tomorrow's fish-and-chip papers!'

The man went on to list the possible people who would sit on the board that he was proposing. The names included one earl, one member of the Saudi Arabian royal family, two lords, one lord's son, one knight and one JP. 'These are not only potentially very profitable, but also of immense prestige value and final seal of the Establishment – which Charles needs – and I am sure we can and could work something out.' He did, however, add that the list was not necessarily definite – 'because although they are all associates and colleagues of mine, I have not yet approached them on this participation matter.'

This was a dangerous letter. It induced in Charlie's already deluded mind an even greater state of fantasy, in which he seemed to close off all the stark reality that was staring him in the face. He consulted further with Raymond Davis. His instructions to him reflected the advice to adopt an aggressive line. He was in that half-crazed state of mind, incredibly thrusting and active, forcing on and on, utterly disconnected from reality. He stood over Raymond Davis as he dictated a six-page letter to Hoffman and Fevrier with Charlie's latest instructions. The letter said that Charlie would not permit 50 per cent participation for less than £250,000; that he wanted Victor Doel sacked; and he wanted to pull out of his deal with Stanley Woods, and drop him just like that.

But Charlie's state of delusion about the real position in South Africa was even greater than this. The very essence of the salvage operation was that Major Marks would sit on the board as somebody completely acceptable to the South African government. It was the only hope there was. But Charlie had other ideas. 'Mr Richardson', the letter continued, 'has no intention of permitting a government

306

nominee to hold his shares and it does not, in fact, seem necessary that this should be done in order for the Mining Lease to be renewed.'

He also demanded that Hoffman and Fevrier saw to it that Major Marks, Jean La Grange, Colin Riddoch and Dave Stedman acted unanimously as a group. He wanted them each to give Hoffman written instructions on every matter. 'He cannot see that this will hamper progress in any way but at least it will ensure that Mr Richardson is fully in the picture as to progress as well as your goodselves,' the Raymond Davis letter stated. There could be no better indication of the paranoid world of fantasy that Charlie was now living in. Encouraged by his businessman friend's attitude, and by the success he was having elsewhere with some of the Mr Smith witnesses, he had completely lost grasp of what was really going on, and suspected everybody in South Africa.

The letter, as usual, was taken across to South Africa by Jean La Grange. She was fast becoming the most expensive postal service of all time. When it was received by Mr Hoffman, he blew his top. He could barely believe this latest development in the increasingly strange affairs of Charles Richardson. He immediately sent a telegram to Raymond Davis, bitterly attacking Charlie's lack of realism and saying that the venture was in jeopardy unless the lease was renewed and Stanley Woods continued to finance the perlite.

Raymond Davis clearly got the message. He called in Charlie and reasoned with him, gently trying to tell him a few home truths. He cabled Mr Hoffman, giving him the power to act in the way he saw fit. Charlie's latest frenzy of fantasy was burning itself out. . . .

It was on the very day that Charlie's wildly unrealistic instructions were received that Major Marks had gone again to the Ministry of Mines. He, like Hoffman and everybody else, was working on the assumption that they were all working as one, and in the circumstances, they were making surprisingly good progress. This further meeting on 1 June with the top people in the Ministry had gone well. But the Department was adamant that renewal of the Prospecting Lease would only be granted if Charlie no longer stood as a director of either the

307

Lebombo Company or SAPI and if his shares were transferred into the name of an acceptable nominee.

For a time Charlie's attitude changed, as a result of the angry Hoffman cable. This meant that Stanley Woods was now able to work towards saving the perlite in closer conjunction with Major Marks and Hoffman and Fevrier. There was reasonable progress. On 6 June 1966, Mr Rubenstein, Stanley Woods's lawyer, spoke to Mr Nel, the Secretary for Mines, who was reasonably confident that the Minister would renew the Lease, if all Charlie's shares were transferred to a government nominee such as Major Marks and if somebody like the Secretary for Finance or the Government Mining Engineer could be given a place on the perlite company boards.

As the days of June slipped away, the basis for a possible salvage seemed to emerge. But still the legacy of Charlie's strange way of operating continued to cause problems. Mr Hoffman complained that he was still in default with his payments to Mrs Waldeck and that £1200 was owed to Nikex for the services of Mr Buji. There was a risk that he would be recalled unless this was paid, and this might be a fatal blow. On top of this Stanley Woods was not prepared to put in any more money until Charlie signed an acceptable deal.

While all these desperate – and high-powered – efforts were taking place, Charlie, back home in London, had been tearing around frantically trying to foil the forthcoming trial of his brother. He and his men had seen many of the possible witnesses. Money had been offered and threats made. Charlie had somehow to prevent the conviction. For that to happen on top of the Bradbury trial and everything else would just be too much. And, of course, he had a genuine wish to help his brother.

But Assistant Chief Constable Gerald McArthur had also been 'making himself busy'. After Jack Duval had made his statement, Duval had been visited by his friend Benny Wajcenberg in prison, where he had been sent for the passport offences. Soon Wajcenberg, too, was sitting face to face with Gerald McArthur. Frank Prater had also started talking. His own frauds with the air tickets had been admitted, and he was about to come to trial. And during this busy period 'Mac' had been paying repeated visits to Lucien Harris, trying to convince him that he could protect him from the wrath of Charlie Richardson. It was a credit to McArthur's team that Charlie was still blissfully unaware of his particular operation. Had he known, he might possibly have been less reckless in his attempts to interfere with the Mr Smith trial.

After various appearances over a period of several days at Greenwich Magistrates' Court, Eddie and the other men in the affray were committed for trial at the Old Bailey on Tuesday, 28 June 1966. All, that is, except Frank Fraser, who was sent for trial separately, charged with the murder of Dickie Hart, the man who died in the affray. He was finally acquitted of murder, because there was no evidence that he had taken a gun with him to Mr Smith's, and received five years for causing an affray. He was soon to be making other visits to the Old Bailey, however.

Charlie had already been pleased by the way some of the witnesses had performed in the magistrates' hearings. Indeed, many of the witnesses seemed – as in the case involving the fight at the Southport club in August 1964 – remarkably vague in view of the events that had taken place. Charlie had even tried to intimidate some of the members of the management of the club. They had replied that they had to be careful lest they lose their licence. It was just their way of telling him 'no way'.

As Charlie puts it today: 'Somehow Tom Butler got involved in the case, the man who had arrested all the train robbers, and it was a different scene then. It was a right heavy scene. Butler was a fucking maniac in those days and he wanted to be like Sherlock Holmes or whoever it is, Wyatt Earp, all wrapped up together. Catch everybody. All the newspapers were saying that he was the thief-catcher and built him right up into a mythological figure.

'So it was a right heavy scene then and we couldn't give money to get people out so we had to see various witnesses who was in the case. . . . There was a girl who was OK, she went my brother's way. But it still wasn't enough really, because you've got the police pulling all kinds of bloody

309

strokes putting pressure on people, you see. . . .'

So Charlie decided to try and get at the jury, in the hope that he could bribe one of them to find Eddie and his friends not guilty. These were the days when verdicts had to be unanimous, not simply a majority of ten to two as is required today.

On the day that the trial opened, Charlie was there at the Old Bailey, sitting in the public gallery. So too were some of his most loyal henchmen, Johnnie Longman for one. In Charlie's own words again: 'We was in court and we see all the names (of the jurors as they were sworn in) read out and we looked as they come in, and you look at the people as the kind of people you can get into. If a man comes in from the East End you find a man who lives in the next road and you ask what he is like. If they are nice people they go round and fucking see them for you, you understand what I mean. It's all right that way. . . .' After the jury had been sworn in and the case concluded for the day, Charlie was waiting outside the court, all set to follow various jurors home.

Charlie's efforts on the opening day of the case were not the only ones he made to save Eddie. Johnnie Longman and other members of his gang were ordered to approach every single one of the names that Charlie had written down while the jury was being sworn in. Johnnie Longman's girlfriend at this time remembers what was happening:

'Mr Longman picked me up at about 7.30pm in the evening and said that we were going up to Mr Richardson's house. He said he had to pick up a man on the way there. We drove to a pub and Longman spoke to a man in a car there and then came back and said: "He's going to follow us to Charlie's house." '

'Who is he?' she asked.

'Oh, don't worry, he's solid,' Longman replied, 'he's just done ten years for blowing safes.'

All three drove down to Charlie's house in Acland Crescent. 'I waited in the car outside while Longman and the other man went inside. About an hour later Mr Longman came out to the car and I asked to go to the toilet,' the girlfriend later told a court. Once inside the house she

310

listened to what was being said.

Charlie wanted to know if Longman had sorted out one of the witnesses.

'Yes,' Longman replied. 'She was as good as gold. We've paid her the money and seen her off on the train to Manchester.'

Longman made calls to different people.

'Mr Richardson was reading out the names to him from a list which he was holding. Longman was on the phone asking what their names were, what they did for a business and just talking to them. He said one was something to do with the building.'

It was no doubt Longman from whom many of the jurors on that case remember getting a call. Anthony Rea, a writer who was serving on the Smith jury, was sitting at home one night early in the trial when his phone rang. 'The caller was a man. I didn't recognise the voice. The caller began by saying "Tony", upon which I paused because I didn't know the voice but only somebody who would know me well would call me Tony,' he was later to explain in court.

'Tony, I want to speak to you about a property,' the caller said. 'A property development, a property concern in Chelsea.'

'Oh yes,' Mr Rea replied, having got some property in Chelsea. 'Who are you?'

There was no definite reply. 'I am acting for somebody else,' said the caller.

'Why doesn't the person get in touch with me himself?'

'Oh well, he can't because he's having a dinner at the Carlton Tower Hotel.'

'Can you tell me more about it yourself?'

'Could we meet to talk about it?'

'Well, that is rather difficult. I'm very busy.'

The man persisted, but Mr Rea, very wisely, refused to see him. He sensed that something was very suspicious.

With Charlie behaving in such a brazen manner, it was not long before jurors reported to the court the strange calls they were getting. On the fifth day of the trial there was an air of expectancy in court as the proceedings re-opened. The judge, Mervyn Griffith-Jones, disclosed that he had been told of attempts to interfere with the jury. The event was reported in full in the *Daily Telegraph* next morning:

> Two attempts have been made since Thursday to 'nobble' an Old Bailey juror hearing the trial of seven men accused of offences connected with a gang fight at Mr Smith's gambling club, Catford. . . .
>
> Yesterday, the Mr Smith's Club trial was delayed for one and a quarter hours. Six defending QCs and Mr E. J. P. Cussen, Crown Prosecutor, held discussions with the judge and later saw their clients in their cells. . . .
>
> Detective Chief Supt. Thomas Butler, head of the Flying Squad, and Dept. Supt. John Cummins, in charge of the case, conferred in court with Mr Cussen after the barristers had left the judge's room.
>
> When the jury were brought into court the judge said to them: 'It appears that since we adjourned last Thursday one of your members has been twice approached on different occasions by two different persons.'
>
> He said that the circumstances suggested 'an intention to bring to bear improper influence upon you to return a false verdict. . . . ' He continued: 'Unhappily there are often persons who are ill-intentioned or misguided enough to think they can help their friends or relatives by acting in this kind of way.
>
> 'Even if one of the defendants was in any way directly or indirectly responsible for what has been taking place there is no evidence at all to suggest which one it was.'
>
> The juror who was approached had reported the incidents immediately, the judge said.

Charlie was indeed misguided enough to try and bribe the jury; he was also devious enough then to try and throw even greater confusion over the trial.

The particular juror at the centre of the judge's remarks was a man called Charles North. He was among the several jurors who had been approached by Charlie's men. A devious ploy was hatched. Charlie decided that he would throw through the window of Mr North's house a bottle with a note in it. The pre-

312

paration of this ploy had been witnessed by Johnnie Longman's girlfriend. She had been dragged down to Charlie's house yet again and kept waiting in the car while Longman, Charlie and others conferred inside.

'At about 10pm Longman came out to the car and I went in, and when I came out of the toilet I couldn't see how to get out because all the lights were off in the house. I waited outside the lounge door for a few minutes and I heard Charlie Richardson talking. I also heard Longman's voice. After a few minutes I knocked at the door and went to push it open. Mr Longman pushed it back at me so I couldn't get it open and he said, "You can't come in here."

'I wanted to go back and sit in the car. He took me back to the car. I sat there. After a while Mr Richardson and Alf Fraser came out of the house. They seemed in a great hurry and they strode out. They got in a car and took off very fast. After a while Mr Longman came out to the car and he said that we couldn't leave just yet: "I have to wait in case there is a phone call."

'He went back in the house. Then he came out again and got into the car and said he was taking me for a drink. This was at 10.45. He said, "If anybody asks you, you've seen nobody leave this house tonight. Don't dare mention my friends' names to anybody or I'll punch you in the mouth, shoot you up the arse and arrange a convenient accident for you." '

By this time Charlie had arrived outside Mr North's house. It was about 10.50. Mr North's son woke him up. He told him that somebody had just thrown a bottle through their window.

Mr North recalled: 'When I got there I saw a broken milk bottle amongst the broken glass from the window. There was also a piece of paper in it. I picked out the piece of paper and read the words. It said: "Charlie [North] bring them in guilty or else. A lot more where this came from. You're not alone amongst the twelve." '

Charlie Richardson wanted to make it look to the outside world as if it was somebody who hated Eddie and his friends that had been getting at the jury. He also wanted to give the impression that the bottle might have been thrown by the police.

313

Meanwhile, Longman and his girlfriend both left the pub at closing time and drove back to Charlie's house just up the road. Then Charlie's car screeched up and he and Longman went inside the house. A few minutes later Longman came out to see his girlfriend, still waiting in the car.

'Charlie's such a boy,' he proudly told her, 'he just doesn't give a fuck. They've just thrown a bottle through the juror's window with a note in it!'

'Surely', his girlfriend said, 'the police will recognise the handwriting?'

'No,' said Longman, contemptuously, 'Charlie's got ways and means of doing it. . . . Do you know what he wrote in the note? "Find them guilty you cunts." That'll frighten and confuse them. They just won't know what they are doing.'

Charlie came out of the house and ordered Longman to take him to Kensington where Jean La Grange was waiting for him in the mews flat, on the eve of yet another trip to South Africa. He had already spent a glorious month with Jean while his attempts to interfere with the Mr Smith case had been going on. She had come back into Britain in June with Colin Riddoch; she had been virtually his only consolation. She was so bright and frivolous, so passionate, such fun to be with. Charlie had sought her out whenever he could. He was sad, in a way that he had rarely experienced in his life, now that she was due to return to Johannesburg. But she had to go. Charlie hoped that his work for BOSS would help him save the perlite. Jean was going back to see General van den Bergh. . . .

Next day was 15 July 1966. Charlie took Jean to Great Cumberland Place to see a Dr D. G. Ismay who prescribed her some medicine. He ran her down to the airport later that night, telling her how much he loved her, how he wished he too could come with her. She was to travel with Colin Riddoch who was on his way back to join the others who were trying to salvage the perlite. Her tickets had been booked by the Alghanims Travel Agency in Portman Square. She and Riddoch left Heathrow at 10.45pm. They changed at Rome and arrived next day in Johannesburg via Nairobi at five minutes past midday. She was never again to see Charlie as a free man.

314

Charlie went back to his house after seeing Jean off. He walked straight into a blazing row with Jean Goodman. As Charlie and Jean La Grange had lain in each others' arms the night before, Jean Goodman had discovered the affair. She had long suspected something. Charlie had not been sleeping at home for weeks, and she had overheard somebody mention Jean La Grange. As Charlie dozed, Jean Goodman had gone to the Concordia offices in Park Lane. There she had found one of Jean La Grange's suitcases and other evidence of the affair.

After a heated argument with Charlie the next day, she walked out. But Charlie didn't care. He had already divorced Margaret, his first wife, and now the problem of Jean Goodman had sorted itself out. He would soon, he thought, be able to marry the beautiful South African.

Charlie was exhausted. The pressure and strain of the past few months were catching up on him. He was taking various kinds of illegal drugs. These had for a long time been a part of his life. He seemed now to be increasingly dependent on them. It was all that Charlie – despite his freakish energy and drive – could do to try and hold his wretched world together. His health started to fail. He saw a doctor in Harley Street who diagnosed blood pressure, liver problems and exhaustion.

But his worst problem was the one he wasn't even remotely aware of. Gerald McArthur and his team now had Charlie virtually surrounded. But 'Mac' was taking no chances. He knew he had to cross every 'i' and dot every 't'. The slightest weakness in the evidence could be disastrous. A man called Benny Coulston had started making allegations. He said that he had been fearfully attacked by Charlie and his men in January 1965. His claims seemed somewhat confused, and Coulston had his own problems with the police as well. But one thing was certain: on the night of 18 January 1965, he had ended up in hospital with his head split open and with other appalling injuries. He was lucky to be alive.

In some ways, Charlie was fast approaching insanity. Relying on his BOSS connections and the additional help of Major Marks, he was still hoping that he could save the perlite without having to sell out to Stanley Woods. He was plotting crazy schemes in his mind to try and juggle shares between Concordia and his two South African companies so that his total control could not be taken away.

But nobody knew about this, least of all Colin Riddoch, who had gone back to South Africa under the illusion that the draft agreement signed by Charlie and Stanley Woods was all that was needed, and that Charlie's share waivers, which Pretoria were demanding, were being sent out. He and Jean La Grange were met at General Smuts airport by a group of reporters. He soon discovered that the situation gave him little reason for the qualified confidence he had felt on his way out. In fact the position had deteriorated greatly. He wrote to Charlie on 20 July, telling him that things were even worse than he had feared, and that it would be necessary now to move very fast. There had been an approach from 'people in Pretoria' via a firm of solicitors called Dyerson, Douglas Muller and Mayer which did much work for the government. Riddoch explained that Mr Dyerson was a director of the Reserve Bank and of the Steel Corporation and other government industries. Muller was the Minister for External Affairs and brother of the managing director of General Mining. 'A good friend of Ted's [Major Marks] who is a very important man with tremendous contacts came round on Monday evening to warn us of what is afoot.'

Riddoch again strongly warned Charlie of the need to formalise the transfer of his shares and the appointment of Major Marks. But Charlie was still determined to hold out somehow. He did not respond to the urgent requests in the letter. He pretended a few days later, when called by Colin Riddoch, that he had never received his letter. Charlie was in a confused and ugly state of mind. A massive feeling of resentment was building up inside him towards almost everything and everybody. He loathed the desperate defensive measures that he was having to take on all fronts. A sense of hate was amassing within him for 'them' — all those people and officials and policemen who were, for no reason apparent to him, trying to ruin his empire.

However, on 26 July, he received a letter which cheered him up a little. It came from Major Herbert Nicholson, whom Charlie had been avoiding for several months. He couldn't bear the thought of having to explain all the bad publicity from Bradbury and his brother's case. But this didn't seem to bother the Major, who had been so important in the early part of Charlie's grandoise South African plans. The letter made Charlie feel that at least he had some friends left in the Establishment.

The Major told Charlie that he had read many of the newspaper reports of the Bradbury trial. He called Bradbury a 'demented lunatic', saying that nobody with any sense could believe a word of what he said. He sympathised with Charlie for the damage that the bad publicity had caused him, adding that it hadn't done him any good either. He had been visited by the Bedfordshire crime squad in connection with the Anglo-American company from which he had resigned and which had later gone into liquidation. Although Major Nicholson complained to Charlie about the way none of his many telephone calls over the past six months had been returned, his manner was warm and friendly. Indeed, having asked Charlie for some expenses, he then invited him and Jean Goodman down for lunch one Sunday. He also invited them both to the ceremony that was going to be held to honour him with the Freedom of the Borough: 'You would both enjoy it quite a lot as it is something out of the ordinary.' He also told Charlie that he had himself been very busy. There had been the election, and all kinds of glittering occasions . . . he had been presented to the Queen Mother, and had met Prince Philip at the opening of the Graffham Yacht Club. On top of this he had been invited by the Poles themselves to visit Poland as a special guest.

It was an extraordinary letter in the circumstances. Charlie picked up the phone and called the Major. It felt good to talk to him. The genial Bedfordshire alderman was associated with the great days of hope. It was comforting to talk to someone not connected with the present calamities. Charlie asked him to come down to his house four days later. 'Don't worry, one of my men will pick you up from the station,' he told him. When the day came, the Major missed Charlie by about two hours: but he did meet a lot of other people. . . .

On the day he received the letter from the Major, Charlie also got some other very good news – about Eddie's trial over the Smith's affray. Having retired on 26 July, the jury came back after much argument. They found Billy Haward, the leader of the gang which had fought Eddie's, guilty of causing an affray. A guilty verdict was also returned against Henry Botton, one of Haward's men. But Ronnie Jeffrey and Harry Rawlins, two of Eddie's mates, were found not guilty. And, most importantly of all, the jury failed to agree on the cases of Eddie along with Jimmy Moody and the man called Stayton.

Although the news could have been better, Charlie was still pretty pleased. Eddie, after all, had been the leader of the other gang of men. Now he would have to have a retrial, but at least he was safe for the time being. Feeling that perhaps his luck was changing at long last, Charlie set about his efforts to save Eddie with renewed zeal. He hatched one of his most audacious schemes yet. He decided that he would try and discredit Tommy Butler, the head of the Flying Squad. He had long been the object of Charlie's hatred: he had nailed the Great Train Robbers and now was the man behind Eddie's problems. If Charlie could show that he was bent, then, he felt, the retrial of Eddie would have to be dropped.

Charlie went to see Raymond Davis, his London solicitor. He told him that he wanted to meet a certain MP who was also a distinguished lawyer. Charlie said that he had evidence that one of the jurors had been got at by Mr Butler, that he could produce witnesses to prove this. Davis vaguely remembers the occasion. 'I can remember getting in touch with the MP. I do recollect going down to the House of Commons with Charles Richardson. I do recollect that Charlie Richardson said something about the police interfering with the jury. I cannot recall whether anybody else was there. Charlie Richardson did not go into detail.'

Charlie's memory is more vivid. He had already lined up witnesses to the alleged incident in which Tom Butler was supposed to have 'got at' a juror in the Mr Smith trial. By his own admission, Charlie had paid them considerable sums of money. He wanted them to say that Butler had done exactly what Charlie himself had tried to do to jurors earlier

318

on: had offered bribes. He took Eddie's green Bentley and drove to the House of Commons. He managed to persuade the MP to see him in the back of the car, which was parked outside the St Stephen's entrance to the House: 'I explained the ramifications of my brother's trial and the machinations of Thomas Butler,' Charlie explains today. 'He appeared to me to be terribly shocked by it, what I told him, and he said that if I could supply him with proof of my allegations he would take it straight to the Attorney General.'

That is exactly what the MP did, but not quite in the way that Charlie had intended. Charlie had over-reached himself this time. He was striking at the very core of the British legal system. He had pulled his final stroke.

When he got home from this meeting there was an urgent telegram waiting for him. It was from Colin Riddoch, who was beside himself with frustration back in Johannesburg. He urgently needed a signed agreement with Stanley Woods and the share transfer and waivers. Charlie had done nothing about any of this. His vanity would not let him. He had squandered his last chance of keeping the perlite.

Next morning he received two letters from South Africa. One was from Colin Riddoch, sent a few days before the urgent telegram. Charlie learnt that at last some of his precious perlite had actually been expanded. It was only a matter of four bags, but the machine at last had worked. Even better, the product was marvellous. If only some of Charlie's other circumstances had been different. . . .

The second letter was from Jean La Grange, written from 810, Windsor Gardens in Bok Street, Johannesburg. It was a long, passionate love letter written in the small hours of the morning. Jean was pining for her beloved Charlie. 'I have been away from you now for seven days – seven days of hell and I mean it Charles. . . . ' She went on in similar vein for twelve pages, with only occasional interruptions for snatches of news on the perlite. On page nine of her letter she told Charlie how she had met her 'friend in Pretoria'. She also told Charlie how she had met a friend of hers in BOSS and amazed him with revelations about Charlie's work for South Africa. The man had assumed that Charlie was anti-South Africa because of all the bad publicity he had generated. But Jean put him right. She told Charlie that all his messages – to BOSS – would hopefully get through before a decision was taken by the government on the perlite lease.

Later on the same day, 29 July, in the early evening, there was a knock on Charlie's door. It was Albert, his go-between with the corrupt policemen he knew.

'Hello Chas,' he said furtively, sneaking in through the door. 'You better watch it. They're going to turn you over tomorrow morning. They're going to do everywhere. Search the lot.'

Albert for many years had been Charlie's link with the bent cops. Charlie instantly assumed that the planned police raid was connected with his attempt to prove that Tommy Butler had interfered with the jury.

'You tell those poxy cunts that I'm not going to be scared off by Tommy fucking Butler,' he snarled defiantly. 'Tell the cunt that if he don't want to help Eddie then I'll make sure that he finds himself in the bloody dock.'

'No, Chas, this is big, really big. Some of the boys are worried in case they find anything. You got to clear the stuff out.'

At 7 o'clock next morning, Gerald McArthur, two of his senior men and a host of other police were outside Charlie's house. It was 30 July 1966, the day that England was to win the world cup. Detective Sergeant Gwyn Waters crept into the back garden. He slipped expertly through the French windows. All was quiet. He tip-toed to the front door, letting in his 'guv'nor' and the other men.

Mac's moment had come. There had been nine months of intensive and difficult work that, apart from the tip-off the previous evening, had been conducted in remarkable secrecy. He rushed upstairs. Charlie was snoozing in bed. Sergeant Waters shook him roughly.

'We are police officers. We have come to arrest you,' McArthur calmly stated.

'Oh,' said Charlie, 'very well then, let's get up and have a wash.'

Charlie's empire was at an end. He was, as they say in the slang common to both London villains and detectives, 'well overdue'.

320

22. Rough Justice

As Charlie was getting arrested, so too were many other men, all of them members of his gang or people who had somehow been associated with him. Shortly after Charlie was carted away, Arthur Baron pulled up in a car outside Charlie's house, having, as arranged, picked up Major Herbert Nicholson from Euston Station.

The Major strode up the path to the front door and knocked on it confidently. It was to be the first time he had seen Charlie for months. The door was opened by a policeman. The hapless Major was ordered inside. He found the place crawling with police. He did not receive the kind of respect and treatment to which he had become so accustomed. 'Do you realise who I am,' Arthur Baron remembers him demanding of one officer. In the end his identity was established. He, like many of the other respectable associates who had been loosely and unwittingly connected with Charlie's activities, was allowed to go and was never dragged into the subsequent court case.

Elsewhere, Gerald McArthur's massive round-up had been successful. One of the men had been caught with his cases packed and about to go. A couple of other minor characters had also disappeared. But by and large, the bag for the morning had been pretty good. All those arrested were taken to West End Central police station where they all proclaimed their innocence and all demanded bail. There was no way that Gerald McArthur was prepared to allow this. He knew full well the kind of tricks which had been used so often in the past by the Richardsons to get at witnesses and interfere with the course of justice. One of the men's solicitors even rang the Metropolitan Police Commissioner, Sir Joseph Simpson, at his home, to demand that his client be released. It was no good. The sense of grievance which Charlie still maintains today, of his being 'fitted up', took root over the very first weekend of his arrest.

In all, seventeen men were arrested in Gerald McArthur's early morning raids. So too was Jean Goodman, Charlie's common law wife. Even though Charlie had been tipped off the previous night, he had felt that he could brazen it out. He had no idea what was really coming, or just how much work Gerald McArthur had done. But throughout the nine months' investigation, McArthur had also been fed information from Scotland Yard, from the Bradbury trial, and from Tommy Butler and his men on the Mr Smith case. The Yard, indeed, had gleaned a great deal of information from South Africa: not only had Colonel St John Pattle come to London to seek help with his case against Bradbury, but two Yard men, Detective Chief Superintendent Fred Gerrard and his colleague Brian Rees, had gone across to interview Bradbury after his conviction and sentence to death.

Hoping to save himself, Bradbury had been keen to give all the help he could; some of the information he volunteered was undoubtedly exaggerated. Gerald McArthur had in fact had to resist pressure from the Yard to arrest Charlie and everybody else before 30 July. Although he had seen many people who had been beaten up or tortured by Charlie, he wanted to make absolutely sure that he had enough evidence to make his case stick.

During the raids on 30 July, all of Charlie's premises were searched. Drugs were found in his house and in the mews flat he shared with Jean La Grange. Much paperwork was also removed, later to be used in evidence. However, the police did not find the electric box, neither were any guns or weapons found except for a revolver in Roy Hall's flat. It was the weapon he had used to shoot out the windows of the Krays' house in Vallance Road.

The mass arrests received sensational newspaper coverage. So too did the start of the committal proceedings at the magistrates' courts. The charges involved offences linked to violence and fraud. The hearings started at the end of August 1966 and were to run on and off until the following January. At first they were held at Clerkenwell Magistrates' Court while the dock in Bow Street Court was especially enlarged to accommodate the Richardsons. Other building work had also been taking place on their behalf: a specially secure wing was made at Brixton prison where all the gang and the others arrested were held, except for Eddie.

The authorities had to take other extreme measures. Every time the police van brought the men from Brixton to the court, it was escorted by a large number of police cars and motor-cycle outriders, all with sirens blaring. Often this convoy was watched over by a police helicopter as it unzipped its way through the traffic.

The police took no chances either with the witnesses. From this point onwards all the witnesses and their families were given round-the-clock police protection. Over the next year some lasting friendships were to be struck up between some of the witnesses and the policemen looking after them. However, this did have its disadvantages. Many of the witnesses were villains and con-men. It took all their ingenuity to ply their trade in such circumstances.

Charlie, Eddie, Roy Hall and other members of the gang still argue today that all these aspects of their case were highly prejudicial. 'How on earth could we ever get a fair hearing when all this kind of thing was going on?' says Eddie. 'To the ordinary man in the street, we had already been made out to be dangerous villains. We had no chance, the whole world was made to believe that we were guilty already.'

With hindsight, one has to agree with this argument. But in practical terms, Gerald McArthur and the police had little choice. Charlie was a dangerous man. He would try and escape if possible. And he would try to get at the witnesses — as indeed he was to succeed in doing, despite the extraordinary security precautions. What else could the police do?

There were other problems which Eddie alone had at this time. In the Mr Smith's case, Eddie had been given a retrial. Charlie's attempts to bribe the jury may have influenced the result. When the retrial began at the Old Bailey in the third week of September 1966, the various

323

committal proceedings relating to the beatings had already been running for nearly three weeks. They had been widely reported in all the newspapers. It was against this background that Eddie pleaded not guilty to causing an affray at Mr Smith's. It is unthinkable, in view of the very wide newspaper coverage of the torture committal proceedings, that members of the jury in Eddie's retrial were unaware of the other allegations against him. Some prejudice must therefore have been introduced into the jury's mind – a fact which goes against a basic principle of English law, and hardly made for a fair hearing. Even if Eddie had been innocent, he would almost certainly have been found guilty. But as he had indeed played a major role in the fight, his five-year sentence at least amounted to a kind of poetic justice: neither Eddie, nor his men, had brought guns to Mr Smith's. Billy Haward, who was armed, had already been sentenced to eight years.

During his retrial, Eddie bitterly drew attention to the hopelessness of his position. He complained to the judge about the 'tremendous publicity' given to the committal proceedings. His lawyer pointed out as well that Eddie had not carried a gun on the night, nor encouraged his friends to do so, and that he had no previous convictions for violence. Eddie did indeed have cause for complaint. Partly as a result of the circumstances surrounding his retrial, the law on the reporting of magistrate court hearings was later changed. If defendants wished, newspapers could be prevented from publishing evidence given and allegations made during committal proceedings.

As the very committal proceedings which Eddie complained about were getting under way, the newspapers were soon dubbing it 'The Torture Case' or 'The Electric Torture Chair Case'. By September there were fifteen defendants, including Charlie, Eddie, Roy Hall, Jean Goodman, Brian Oseman, Frank Fraser, Tommy Clark, Alfie Berman, Brian Mottram and Jimmy Kensit. The seventeen various charges related to the beatings of Jack Duval, Benny Wajcenberg, Lucien Harris, George Green, Norman Bickers, Jimmy Bloor, Bernard Bridges, Jimmy Taggart, Christopher

Glinski and the man called Benny Coulston. There were also charges relating to frauds and the various long firms that Charlie and his men had been involved in.

Charlie was in a desperately frustrating situation in his special cell in Brixton. He was not allowed to deal with business matters relating to South Africa, and found it difficult to get messages to friends outside to start bribing or threatening witnesses: all his inner team were being held in the same special Brixton unit with him in virtual solitary confinement; when they were exercised, it was alone as a group, without any other contact with prisoners who were about to leave the prison. Eddie was kept at a different prison, Wandsworth.

Charlie could not believe the fuss that was being made about the charges that he faced. The way he saw it, the men he had beaten deserved it because they had taken a liberty. He also knew there was nothing on paper to connect him with the many long firm frauds he was charged with. He was amazed, and genuinely angry, that Jack Duval appeared to be blaming him for many of his own frauds. Charlie, for once, had some reason to complain. But this sense of rightful indignation which Charlie drummed up in his own mind, and which infected the rest of his men, did little to help their cause.

As the magistrates' hearings progressed, many of the defendants became more and more noisy in the dock. While prosecution witnesses gave their evidence, the defendants jeered loudly and fell about laughing. It was almost as if they were watching a cabaret at the Astor Club. Several times, the magistrate ordered the court to be cleared. He had repeatedly to warn the defendants about their interruptions.

As the days wore on, Charlie was able to start getting instructions to his friends outside. Soon Bunny Bridges, one of the most important prosecution witnesses, had been offered £3000 to tone his evidence right down. That is admitted today by both Charlie and Bridges. Money was also offered elsewhere, to Frank Prater's wife for one. In neither case did it do Charlie any good.

It was the risk of this happening that was in part responsible for the very strict security which Charlie and the others complained so much about. And Gerald McArthur soon was aware of what was going on. Charlie's previous power over potential witnesses against him had been the very reason for McArthur's great secrecy. He was determined not to let this ruin his case now. Very soon he had detected what he felt were attempts by friends of Charlie to bribe two potential prosecution witnesses, Christopher Glinski, who had been attacked by Frank Fraser in his office in December 1965, and Benny Coulston, Brixton villain with a record of violence, who had received a terrible beating on 18 January 1965. By January 1967 a number of people had been charged with trying to pay both Coulston and Glinski money to dop their evidence. By March 1967, before the full trial of Charlie and his men, these people had been sentenced to prison sentences of between six months and two years for conspiring to pervert the course of justice. Among them were Eva Brindle (Frank Fraser's sister), Alby Woods (Fraser's close friend who had been involved with the fruit machine business), and Arthur Baron.

All three state that they were not guilty. They say that they were simply trying to assist with the lawful defence of Charlie and the others. There was no question of trying to bribe witnesses. *On the surface*, there do ineed appear to be worrying aspects to their convictions. For example, Coulston's brother, Johnnie, claims that his brother lied in the evidence he gave.

Furthermore, the Richardsons cite these conspiracy cases as just one of the many examples of how they and their associates were railroaded, and how they were not even allowed to prepare their defence for the main case. But Gerald McArthur knew only too well that Charlie had previously engaged in widespread intimidation of witnesses. And it was to be the prosecution case which the jury accepted.

Regardless of the truth of these conspiracy-to-pervert cases, it does seem odd, again with hindsight, that the defendants should have been tried before the main Richardson case. To find people guilty of trying to unlawfully help Charlie and the others before their case was tried, implies guilt. It might have been fairer to try the conspiracy cases after the main trial.

The magistrates' hearings ended on 27 January 1967, when Charlie and the others were committed to be tried at the Old Bailey on all the violence charges and on several charges relating to fraud and the long firms.

At the centre of the case that came before the Old Bailey was Jack Duval. He, or his close associates or friends, were involved in the overwhelming majority of the charges that the gang eventually faced. There were Lucien Harris, Bunny Bridges, Jimmy Taggart, Frank Prater, Benny Wajcenberg, Alfred 'Jimmy' Bloor, all of them associated in some way with Duval. Only three of the ten major prosecution witnesses had not in some way been friendly or connected with Duval. They were Norman Bickers, George Green and Benny Coulston.

The discovery of Jack Duval had been a great break for Assistant Chief Constable Gerald McArthur. When Jimmy Taggart had gone to see him on that fateful day in October 1965 he had told him all he knew. But he was still too frightened to make a full statement. The next man McArthur saw was Christopher Glinski, who, although not a major victim of the Richardsons, knew many of the other people whom Charlie had savaged. The meeting between McArthur and Glinski led quickly to people like Frank Prater, Benny Wajcenberg and, more importantly, to Jack Duval.

By the time Mac met Duval, the intrepid con-man was also being pursued by other police in connection with his numerous passport offences. When, as soon happened, Duval was brought before the court for these, Gerald McArthur gave evidence in mitigation on Duval's behalf. He also gave the judge a report that was not read in open court. What happened then was basically the same that happens today in the Supergrass system: villains who give evidence convicting others look to the courts for more lenient treatment – and very often get it.

Duval made numerous trips from his prison cell to see McArthur in Hertfordshire. He has an excellent memory and told the detective everything he knew. But there is no doubt that Duval distorted matters considerably: he *did* give the essentials of the various beatings he and his associates had suffered; but he certainly didn't reveal the full extent of his involvement with Charlie, and how, for example, he had taken him on with the Common Market Merchants long firm. In fact Duval tried to blame Charlie for many of the various things he himself had done. He told McArthur, and the Old Bailey judge, that he had been forced to work for Charlie, that Charlie had organised the great racket with the Italian stockings. This tendency of Duval to blame others for his own actions is legendary among those who know him. Even Gerald McArthur himself admitted it to the magistrates' hearings: 'Duval certainly included in his statement evidence which shifted some of the responsibility to others,' he said.

Four years after the Richardson trial, Duval, inevitably, was again in serious trouble with others over a large long firm. He tried to tell the police that it had nothing to do with him, that he had been dragged into it by the others. This time the judge, Justice King Hamilton, did not believe him. And he told him in the roundest of terms that he was not again going to get away with his own crimes by blaming others.

But to Gerald McArthur, Duval was a great asset. He had *evidence* which could be used to convict the Richardsons. It didn't matter so much about his own crimes. Gerald McArthur's obsession was to nail Charlie, one of the worst criminals he had ever encountered. Duval quickly named many other people who had suffered from Charlie's treatment, including Bunny Bridges and Lucien Harris. But when McArthur saw these two, neither was happy to give evidence.

Bridges remembers the first visit from McArthur. 'He knew everything. Bradbury must have told them, and Duval. They wanted me to make a statement and I refused. I said I didn't want to be involved, that I had nothing to say. They came back again, and I had to go to the Yard. They came back again and again.' In the end, after endless

328

assurances from the police, Bridges finally agreed to give evidence. Bridges was wanted on some relatively minor charges. He came to understand that these would not be proceeded with if he co-operated.

It was the same with Lucien Harris. Gerald McArthur had to see him three times before he agreed to make a statement. Lucien Harris had witnessed a police inspector being paid off by Charlie at Peckford's. He told McArthur this. It was the latest in a long list of such allegations that he had heard during the course of his operation. 'It was only when McArthur had satisfied me that he really was determined to arrest the Richardsons and that I could be protected that I agreed to make a statement,' he says today.

The majority of the men who could give evidence against Charlie were, at the time they were helping Mac, wanted for various offences themselves. It seems that they all got smaller sentences than they might otherwise have expected, thanks, no doubt, to their co-operation. By the time the Old Bailey trial started on 4 April 1967, Gerald McArthur had inevitably had to cajole, reassure and pressurise the potential witnesses into giving their evidence. There seems little doubt as well that he had offered them the hope of getting lighter sentences for their own offences and that in some minor cases they were let off altogether. In view of the terrifying empire that Charlie had built for himself, it seems a small price to pay. The fact that witnesses had to be treated in this way also indicates the fear that Charlie commanded in the hearts of the men concerned.

The trial itself lasted for ten weeks. It was presided over by Justice Lawton. He was the kind of judge that a policeman bringing up a case would be glad to get: he didn't go in for obvious liberal sentiments. He took a firm control of proceedings from the start, refusing all applications for separate trials on each charge.

By the time the trial came to the Bailey, all the fraud charges had been dropped because the police felt they had more than enough to secure a conviction. By now only nine people were involved: Charlie, Eddie, Roy Hall, Frank Fraser, Tommy Clark, Johnnie Longman, Alfred Berman,

Jimmy Moody and Jean Goodman. They faced a total of thirteen substantive offences, all to do with the violence and extortion. Charlie faced nine charges; Eddie, four; Roy Hall, five; Frank Fraser, two; and the others, one each. Mottram had been allowed to stand down. He had a bad heart condition which the Brixton prison doctor said might kill him at any moment. In fact, he was to live for another fourteen years, sustained by a pacemaker. He had hardly played a major role in the gang anyway – by the time Charlie and everybody else was arrested, Mottram was more friendly with the Duval crowd than with Charlie.

There was a hush over the court when Mr Sebag Shaw QC opened the prosecution. 'The case which the Crown will put before you', he told the jury, 'is that the eight men in the dock are part of a gang of thugs under the leadership of Charles Richardson whose policy and practice over a number of years was to enforce his will and his intentions by violence and intimidation ... the principle object of that policy was to secure for Charles Richardson the absolute domination of a somewhat disreputable business fraternity who were actively engaged in carrying on what I think can rightly be called tin-pot companies, dozens of them, who were busily occupied in buying goods and other things in large quantities and buying large amounts upon credit and in the end not paying for them, or certainly not paying for all of them.

'This case is not about dishonesty or fraud, it is about violence and threats of violence, not, let me say at once, casual acts of violence committed in sudden anger or alarm but vicious and brutal violence systematically inflicted deliberately and cold-bloodedly and with utter and callous ruthlessness. I imagine, members of the jury, when you have heard the evidence, if you accept but half of it, you will come to the conclusion that not one word I have just uttered to you is without ample justification. When the police finally intervened, the policy of the gang had been successful for some years, and Charles Richardson grew in power and influence in that particular fraternity over which he presided, and the policy was so successful that no person

330

who had become a victim of it dared to complain lest worse, if worse were possible, befall him or the members of his family. . . .'

As the trial proceeded, the basic facts about the beatings emerged. But there do seem to be some odd aspects to the evidence. Jack Duval claimed that he had been beaten by Charlie on three different occasions, the first in December 1962. Frank Prater, who is still friendly with Duval today, says Duval didn't even know Charlie then. So, too, do other people such as Tommy Costello. Perhaps it wasn't that important, because in the end Charlie was not convicted of this particular beating.

But some of Duval's evidence was more worrying. He told the court that while on the run from Charlie he had been stabbed in the stomach by a man in Brussels, who was supposed to have said, 'That's a present from Charlie.' Duval even showed his scars. Today, Prater says that this evidence was nonsense. The scars, he says, resulted from the stomach operation he had in Milan to lose some weight. Prater himself had been flown across 'to hold his hand'. The whole thrust of Duval's evidence was that he had been terrified into working for Charlie, and that it had been Charlie who organised the Italian stocking fiddle and the Common Market Merchants long firm. Frank Prater, who helped Duval with the Italian stocking racket, says today this simply wasn't true.

There were other confusing aspects to the evidence. Lucien Harris, who stated that he had been stabbed through the foot during his beating, showed his foot in court. It had a scar on either side. But Harris's doctor then told the court that he could not remember anything having been wrong with Harris's foot. And when Charlie took expert medical evidence, one specialist said he felt that for a knife to have passed through the foot would represent nothing short of a miracle.

It might just have been a fluke, or perhaps the knife didn't pass right through the foot in the way suggested. And perhaps the doctor hadn't made full notes because of the unofficial nature of Harris's visit. There seems little doubt,

331

however, that Harris was stabbed: three days after his beating he was visited by Tommy Costello; his foot was bandaged; he told Costello he had been stabbed by John Bradbury. As well as that, the Customs investigator who was watching the Inter City premises where Harris was working at the time, saw him limping the day after the beating.

The Costello information was not given in court. It was given in an interview for this book. Costello had no axe to grind with Charlie. He only agreed to talk on the grounds that he was 'not going to get anybody into trouble'. When it was put to him that the Harris evidence might be a good example of how the case against Charlie was exaggerated, Costello replied: 'Oh no, Lucien got stabbed in the foot all right, he told me himself a few days afterwards. His foot was in bandages. He said that Bradbury had done it. . . . I know he said Bradbury because every time I saw Bradbury again, I used to think to myself: You're the swine that stabbed poor old Lucien. . . !' In the end the jury concluded that Charlie had stabbed Harris in the foot – and there is no doubt that Harris's evidence that he was stabbed in the foot was true.

Some of the shakiest evidence given came from the man called Benny Coulston. His beating on 18 January 1965 has been left out of the narrative of this book because the evidence surrounding it is too unclear. In the magistrates' hearings he confused Roy Hall for Brian Mottram, when asked to identify them: Brian Mottram was a huge man of well over six feet; Roy Hall was a tiny fellow, totally different in appearance. His brother also says today that Benny lied about the Richardsons.

In the magistrates' courts, Coulston said that Roy Hall had helped torture him. But when it came to the Old Bailey, Coulston suggested only during cross-examination by somebody else's defence counsel that Roy Hall had been involved in his beating. Coulston also said Bradbury was involved. Bradbury, according to his employers in Johannesburg, was in South Africa at the time, working as a lorry driver. What is clear, though, is that Coulston had a terrible beating, and that it was without doubt carried out by friends of the

Richardsons. It is less clear whether any of the Richardson gang named by Coulston was involved and in the way he claimed.

Towards the end of the prosecution case, there was an interruption in the proceedings of a most unusual kind. It was made by Mr Lawson, the lawyer acting for Frank Fraser, during evidence given by Jimmy Taggart, to whom Fraser was charged with causing grievous bodily harm. Mr Lawson stood up, and in a highly embarrassed way slowly got to the point.

'My Lord, I have received instructions that in the latter part of 1964, the beginning of 1965, my client on a railway station spoke to your Lordship at Victoria Station. I do not know whether your Lordship would desire me to recall the details of the discussion?'

Mr Justice Lawton: 'You certainly may, because I have no recollection of ever seeing your client before in his life.'

Mr Lawson: 'He tells me that about the end of 1964, the beginning of 1965, he had arrived at Victoria Station for the purpose of catching a train. He was then, apparently, travelling to Brighton. He saw your Lordship on the railway station, standing, he thinks, between platforms 14 and 15, approached your Lordship and asked whether your Lordship was Sir Frederick Lawton. Your Lordship replied, "Yes." I gather that he then made derogatory, defamatory remarks about your father, and that your Lordship walked away up the platform, I think pursued by my client, who was continuing to make these remarks.'

Mr Justice Lawton: 'Mr Lawson, there is not a word of truth in this, not one word, and I want to say that at the earliest possible moment. I would undoubtedly have recalled such an event, and I have no recollection whatsoever of anything of that kind happening.'

Frank Fraser had told his lawyer that the judge's father had been a prison governor, and was disliked by many prisoners. He tried to argue that he could not be tried fairly because Mr Justice Lawton would be 'prejudiced' against him because of this incident. Charlie had apparently been with Fraser, having taken him to the station, when the alleged incident occurred. But Charlie couldn't bring this up because part of his defence was going to be that he hardly knew Fraser at all.

After the Lawson interruption, the examination of Jimmy Taggart's evidence continued. When that was completed an hour later, Mr Justice Lawton again addressed Mr Lawson: 'There is a matter I want to place on record with regard to your application. You did not do me the courtesy of giving me any warning of the application you were going to make or of the basis upon which you were going to make it, and as a result I had to put my mind directly on to the problem there and then, and I want to say as emphatically as I can that I have no recollection whatsoever of having spoken to your client.

'During the hour or so which has transpired since you spoke to me I have been running through my mind the occasions in my life when strangers have come and spoken to me, and I can just — but only just — recollect one occasion on a London station on a winter's evening when somebody spoke to me and was abusive. I have no recollection of any abuse relating to my father. I feel if there had been any abuse relating to my father I should have remembered it. I have no recollection who was abusive. I thought the man was drunk anyway. I am fairly certain it was not in 1964, and I am certain that I have no recollection whatsoever it was your client, none whatsoever, and I am quite certain if it had been your client I would have remembered ... in the circumstances it would be no ground whatsoever for my not going on with this trial.'

The case continued, and after all the prosecution evidence had been given the defence got off at a brisk pace. Justice Lawton, although he had already been strict with the lines of inquiry pursued by defence counsel in cross examination of prosecution witnesses, was scrupulously polite as Charlie took the stand. He asked him whether he wanted to sit down and if he was comfortable.

Charlie's defence, and that of the others, was a mixture of point blank denials, qualified admissions in a couple of cases, and the erecting of alibis. Charlie's most promising alibi was

334

in the case of the savage beating of Jimmy Taggart on 14 July 1965. He tailored his answers to suit some of the provable facts. He said that he could not have been beating up Taggart at the time stated because he had picked up his brother Eddie from Heathrow airport at 8.45pm, right at the time Taggart was getting beaten.

When Mr Sebag Shaw, prosecuting, came to examine this alibi, he allowed Charlie to develop it. Charlie explained how he had picked Eddie up and then gone to Chislehurst for a drink. Everything that Taggart was alleging was completely untrue. He had left the airport at 9pm and arrived back in Chislehurst about 10pm. When Sebag Shaw had elicited all this detail from Charlie, he stood back and paused.

'If that is true, then Mr Taggart's account of the matter cannot be right,' he stated, looking hard and straight at Charlie.

'Mr Taggart has given perjured evidence.'

Sebag Shaw paused again. He looked at the jury. He picked up a piece of paper and examined it.

'Look at this telegram,' he said, holding it up towards Charlie. 'It bears the date 14 July 1965 from Johannesburg, and that is the telegram you got, isn't it?'

There was a delay while the usher took the telegram and handed it to Charlie. A horrible shiver ran down his spine. It was a telegram from Eddie saying his plane arrived in London at 10.20pm.

'Well,' said Sebag Shaw, 'is that the date?'

'Yes.' It was the only answer Charlie could give.

'You see the time?' asked Shaw. He was going to make Charlie himself give the information that would destroy his bogus alibi.

'10.20,' Charlie answered slowly.

'Not 8.45?' asked Sebag Shaw, just to make absolutely sure.

'I could have sworn it was 8.45.'

Charlie's major alibi had collapsed in the most humiliating way. The facade of his self-righteous indignation was ripped away. Charlie had not realised that the police had taken the telegram when they had searched his premises.

But worse was to come for Charlie in his defence against the Taggart beating. When Alfie Berman came to give his evidence, he confirmed all that had been said by the prosecution. He had turned 'QE', as they say in the trade. For one of the defendants sitting in the dock to confirm all that the prosecution had claimed could hardly have been more damning. Berman by this time had been moved to a much pleasanter prison. A charge that he had faced in connection with the beating of a man who had been messing around with his first wife had also been dropped by the time the case reached the Old Bailey. He was to be released after the torture trial was over.

In the end, the jury brought in guilty verdicts on most of the charges, including the Benny Coulston beating. Charlie was sentenced to twenty-five years; Eddie, to ten – two years for assaulting Jack Duval and then ten to run concurrently, for his part in the attack on Coulston. Roy Hall got ten years; Tommy Clark, eight; and Frank Fraser, who had appeared in court with the leg injury sustained at Mr Smith's, was given ten years.

Jimmy Moody, who had only been alleged to have played a small role in the Coulston attack, was acquitted. Jean Goodman, who was also acquitted, after fifteen days of the trial, had married a decorator from Guildford before the trial was over.

Mr Justice Lawton declared that without doubt Charlie had been the vicious and sadistic leader of one of the most dangerous gangs he had ever heard of. He was less damning with Eddie: 'I am not satisfied that you were at all times and for all purposes a member of this gang.' But he added: 'I am satisfied that from time to time your services were available to your brother when he required them.'

In the case of Roy Hall, the judge said: 'You are in some ways the tragic character in this sordid story. Right from school you came under the domination of Charlie Richardson and but for his evil influence you would not be here.'

It would be hard to argue with Mr Justice Lawton's assessment of the characters, or the relativities of the sentences.

336

When Charlie was sentenced to his eternally long imprisonment, he took it like a man. He looked straight at Justice Lawton. He then turned to the jury, half-bowed, and quickly said thank you very much. He went downstairs, deep under the Old Bailey, and was there given a meal. It was the last thing he felt like but he ate it to show the warders that he was not affected by his sentence. Upstairs, his lawyer was still telling the judge that his client continued to maintain his complete innocence.

The saddest thing about it is that Charlie really felt he was innocent. The Old Bailey trial had dealt solely with the cases of a few of the men he had beaten. To Charlie, they had deserved what they got. They were con-men who had tried to take him on. Their beatings were permitted in the underworld code by which he lived. But even if some of his victims were con-men — some in fact had not taken Charlie on at all — they were not men of violence. Neither had Charlie's violence been spontaneous. It had been premeditated, almost savoured in its anticipation.

There do indeed appear to be aspects of his trial which were unfair or prejudicial, in the narrow legalistic and technical sense. But the extreme measures which the police and other authorities had to take were a necessary reaction to Charlie's own terrifying methods, especially with witnesses. He also corrupted jurors and policemen alike. There may well have been other elements of the arrests and convictions which were unfair. But these pale into insignificance when compared to Charlie's own life of crime. Charlie has little right to get precious about points of law when the treatment he handed out to people was so often savagely inhuman and unfair.

In the end, justice was done. It may have been a kind of rough justice, but it was not as rough as the justice meted out to those who dared to break the laws of Charles Richardson.

Epilogue: the Downing Street Allegation

One of the most extraordinary aspects of the life of Charles William Richardson is a suggestion that he offered to bug the private Downing Street telephone of the then Prime Minister, Harold Wilson, for South African intelligence.

Richardson now admits that he did work for BOSS, as it became known later on. He admits that he pulled off a series of burglaries at important anti-apartheid organisations based in London, and that he helped to organise arms supplies. Richardson also says that he successfully foiled a plot to assassinate Dr Hastings Banda, virtually the only Black African leader who was friendly towards South Africa. But he denies that he organised the tapping of Harold Wilson's telephone.

The allegation about the phone is made by Gordon Winter, the former BOSS agent who knew Charlie in South Africa and who in the 1970s was responsible perhaps more than anyone else for the allegations surrounding Jeremy Thorpe and the former male model, Norman Scott. Winter, whose gun was used to murder Richardson's South African partner, Thomas Waldeck, in 1965, had not included the phone-tap allegation in the final draft of a book he was writing exposing the workings of BOSS, which he showed me in March 1981. He said he had omitted it from his chapter on Richardson because he had no confession from Richardson himself, and he did not want to reveal it, he said, while Charlie was helpless in prison. Nor had he revealed that Richardson had had an affair with Jean La Grange, on whom there was a later chapter. But when I told Winter that Richardson had revealed to me that he carried out jobs for BOSS, he agreed to tell me what he knew, and said that he would still not include the Charlie-BOSS connection in his own book.

He says that in the late 1960s, two or three years after Richardson had been convicted, he met up in London with his former wife, Jean La Grange, with whom Charlie had been having his affair. By this time, Winter himself had been 'deported' from South Africa — the ostensible reason being his vague connection with some of the events surrounding the murder of Thomas Waldeck. But Winter's deportation had only been a cover for him to work as a BOSS agent in London. It worked pretty well — most people assumed that he was an enemy of South Africa because of his deportation and because he also worked for liberal and radical publications like *Drum* magazine and the *Rand Daily Mail*.

When Winter re-met his former wife, she too was working for BOSS in London, he says. She had come to London after Charlie's arrest, having first established from Charlie's secretary that there were to be no charges over the drugs found in the mews flat she had shared with him. She campaigned long and hard for both Charlie and Eddie. After their conviction, she took part in a protest outside jails on their behalf. She became such a nuisance that the police tried to get her deported. But she foiled this through a marriage of convenience with a man many years her senior. The marriage had been organised from prison by Charlie, who knew the man involved. The ceremony took place at a registry office during which the man forgot Jean's name.

Throughout this period after Charlie's arrest and conviction, Jean La Grange stayed with Eddie's wife Maureen at their house in Chislehurst. She stayed there for about three years, according to Maureen Richardson today. Maureen remembers Gordon Winter coming to her house to see Jean. She says: 'I didn't know how to take him. He used to keep everything catalogued — where he had met somebody . . . and he would have all their photographs. . . . He used to say that he had photographs of people and Jean used to tell me about them, but she used to think that it was good. It was very odd . . . they were secret photographs, of everybody that he met. . . . The feeling that I got was that they were collaborating. ... Whenever there was a demonstration outside South Africa House he was always there, taking pictures.'

Winter says that he and Jean started getting on well together after they met again. They went on holiday – staying, among other places, he says, in the Hotel Negressco in Nice where Charlie and Jean had spent their passionate five days – and were soon talking of getting remarried. According to Winter, he became Jean's sub-handler in London. She had penetrated an influential anti-South Africa group extremely well, but was not very successful at writing up her reports. And it was during this period, says Winter, that Jean told him all about Charlie's work for BOSS.

'It would appear,' says Winter from his recollection of conversations with Jean, 'that Charlie had gone cap in hand to General van den Bergh and said: "I have heard from Jean that you have heard about me. I want you to know that . . . I did get a bit naughty once but I am a good boy now and I am only trying to make money here. I want you to know that I am totally pro your country . . . this is the most wonderful country in the world and you keep the blacks in their places. . . ."

'Charles Richardson said that as a show of good faith he would arrange for two friends of his who worked for the GPO to go into a manhole near Downing Street where there were cables that carried the telephones from Harold Wilson's private home at 10 Downing Street and they could intercept.

'Charles said something on the lines: "These two friends of mine are in the GPO and no way could anybody find out. . . . These guys can get there and the wires can be soldered together . . . and they can put in a circuit . . . and make it into a longstanding tape or to be activated whenever they want." '

Winter says he raised the matter himself with 'HJ' van den Bergh. 'I casually threw it across the table when I was talking to HJ many years later when HJ and I were so close I would have died for him. And I said to HJ: "I will never

340

forget that Jean business with the bugging of Harold Wilson's phone. . . ." He changed the subject – but he did not deny it.

'But if I had put that to him and it was totally wrong, he would have said: "That is absolute rubbish! Where did you get that from?" But he knew my ex-wife was an agent. He knew my wife was with Charles, he knew I knew . . . he certainly didn't deny it, he just smiled and he made it quite clear to me that it was on.'

Winter surmised: 'I would say to you that if you are the head of South African intelligence, Harold Wilson is a socialist, he is an enemy, he is also attacking apartheid, I come to you and say that I could bug Harold Wilson's phone, would you say "Yes" or "No"? In intelligence terms, doesn't that mean a thousand tons-worth of gold that we can steal? And if they find out, nobody would know, it is not us – not BOSS. It is Charlie Richardson's maintenance men . . . Charlie . . . he is a crook . . . a rogue . . . and he is wanted in South Africa . . . how dare you suggest that we are involved with that . . . you bring him to us and we will deal with him. It is a marvellous get-out.

'I have no proof that this is true, that Harold Wilson's phone was bugged or even that it was contemplated that Harold Wilson's phone would be bugged. All I am saying to you is that I heard it from Jean, I was her sub-handler, she was my ex-wife, I was very close to her, I processed all her reports . . . we were both going to go back in fact and get married again . . . furthermore she liked Charles, she actually loved Charles and believed in him. . . .'

Winter's assertions are the only evidence for the alleged phone-tapping. But there appear to be some other pointers which suggest that the claims might be true. The first comes from Harold Wilson himself, although he refused repeatedly to discuss the matter for this book. Nine years after Charlie is supposed to have made his offer to van den Bergh, Sir Harold Wilson, as he became after his shock resignation in 1976, made the astonishing claim that he suspected Downing Street had been bugged while he was Prime Minister. Sir Harold said he thought British intelligence itself was responsible. He did not say when, or for how long, he suspected the bugging had been going on. But he indicated that he thought a right-wing faction of British intelligence was against him and passing information on to the South Africans, whom they supported more than the anti-apartheid Prime Minister, who was supposed to be their ultimate chief.

A second pointer which perhaps tends to support the phone-tap suggestion is that Richardson himself seems to be aware of the most intimate secrets of the Harold Wilson Downing Street. At the end of the series of interviews I carried out with Richardson in Benidorm in the summer of 1980, he talked, during a lunchtime pizza, about Downing Street. He claimed to know about an alleged sex-scandal involving a former Labour minister, and about a singer who was having an affair with the wife of another Labour politician.

At the time I completely dismissed the claims. It was only sometime later, when Richardson's work for BOSS had begun to emerge, that I realised there might be some significance in what Richardson had said. I then paid him a visit in Wandsworth prison and put the phone-tapping suggestion to him. He denied it. When he was asked how he then knew of the alleged Downing Street sex-scandals, he said it was because he knew the singer who, he alleged, was having an affair with the politician's wife. But having denied the phone-tapping claim, Richardson then provided me with the name of a man he knew who, he said, had been involved in the much-publicised series of 1970s break-ins at Harold Wilson's various homes. Today, that man is in prison and it has not been feasible to see him.

It is possible that Richardson knows more about these break-ins than simply the name of the man he says was involved. According to a South African journalist who, like many other people in the Republic, has taken a keen interest in the affairs of Charles Richardson since 1966, General van den Bergh came to Britain and visited Charlie in prison. The journalist's understanding is that the head of BOSS wanted Richardson to organise from prison various jobs which

342

BOSS itself did not want to risk doing. To a man of Richardson's standing in the prison world, such a task would, in theory, be quite possible. It has always been easy for him to get messages out of prison, and many a good villain would be only too willing to do Charlie a favour. And, presumably, BOSS would pay handsomely for such work. The journalist who makes this suggestion himself went to see van den Bergh at his farm shortly after his fall from grace a few years ago.

'Incredible the way you got Charlie Richardson to help you,' is what he says he said to him.

'I didn't know you knew about that,' van den Bergh replied, according to the man.

When I put to Charlie the suggestion that he had worked for BOSS from inside prison as well, he was evasive: 'I couldn't, could I, I was inside.' That, of course, would have been the perfect cover and protection for him. During my visit, I also asked Charlie whether he had been offered a new life in South Africa after he had completed his sentence. He looked surprised and then shrugged his shoulders. 'I suppose I was, really.' he said. If such an arrangement really did exist, it indicates the special importance that Charlie had to BOSS: South Africa has a rigid policy of always refusing entry to anybody with a criminal record.

Support for the suggestion that Charlie was indeed offered a new life also comes from a book published in 1974 by John McVicar, the well-known underworld figure who was in a top security prison with Charlie. McVicar recounts how Charlie wanted to take part in an escape plot. Charlie, he says, told him: 'When we get out I'll see you all right for dough and you can come to South Africa if you like.' McVicar also quotes a discussion he had with Roy Hall about Charlie being cut in on the escape attempt. 'He's desperate, John,' Hall is supposed to have said. 'He's got that South African bird and he wants to be out with her. You know what he's like after a bird.'

McVicar's book was written in 1973, long before Charlie had told anybody of his BOSS connections. As far as the world was concerned, Charlie was wanted desperately by the

343

South African police. And yet here he was, talking to somebody to whom he was unlikely to lie, and saying he could come to South Africa with him. On top of this, it is worth remembering that Richardson seems to have had free and easy access to South Africa under an assumed name long after the death of Waldeck, and even after the Bradbury trial, in which it was alleged that he had ordered the murder. And Peter Earle, the *News of the World* reporter, when trying to contact Richardson in April 1966, was told by a relative that he was in a Johannesburg hotel.

The first time, in fact, that Richardson seems to have told anybody of his BOSS work was around the time of van den Bergh's removal. Richardson says that he told a prison governor and that he was visited by a Home Office minister and two men from the security service. With van den Bergh's removal, presumably disappeared Richardson's hopes of the new life he was promised in South Africa.

Charlie had only served a few weeks of his huge, twenty-five-year prison sentence when he was hauled before the Old Bailey again in 1967 to face charges relating to his jury interference on the Mr Smith's affray case. He received another five-year sentence, to run concurrently.

Jean La Grange then helped him prepare an appeal against his major convictions, before the Home Office withdrew permission for her to visit Charlie in prison. But Charlie wasn't even granted leave to appeal. Nor was Eddie, perhaps somewhat unfairly in view of the new alibi evidence he had. The major charge on which Eddie was convicted was the beating of Benny Coulston. The evidence surrounding the terrible plight that befell Coulston on the night of 18 January 1965 was extremely confused. But nothing Eddie could do seemed to have any effect.

When Charlie's application to appeal was refused, he braced himself for the long sentence ahead. He kept writing to Jean la Grange, calling her his wife. But she soon lost interest. She developed friendships with the head of an insurance company and with a well-known personality from the world of entertainment, before geting back for a time with her ex-husband, Gordon Winter.

Charlie's other great South African love, the perlite, also came to nothing. Although Stanley Woods gained a moderate breakthrough in the months after Charlie's arrest, too much damage had been caused for him to save the venture. He decided to cut his losses and pull out. He had lost a fortune. To this day the rights to the perlite have never again been granted. No one since, it seems, has had Charlie's incredible drive and vision. If only Charlie had perhaps been born in different circumstances. . . .

As Charlie's time in prison slowly passed, he had his share of trouble, as did the others. He was involved in a couple of riots, but settled down eventually, coming under the influence of Peter Timms, the liberal but firm governor of Maidstone Prison. There, Charlie developed his Open University studies, doing pretty well. He edited a much-read prison newspaper and generally became a model prisoner in his efforts to get parole – despite being caught with cannabis.

Peter Timms keenly supported Richardson's applications for parole. He helped him to get to Spring Hill Open Prison, feeling certain that it would be the final stepping-stone to Charlie's freedom. But it was not to be. After his escape in May 1980 and his travels round the continent, Richardson eventually came back to London in the autumn of 1980. His earlier caution soon gave way to an amazingly carefree attitude. He walked round the streets of south London, spent whole evenings in pubs, and visited friends at their offices and homes. The police did not seem to be greatly interested, apart from making one raid on a works' premises where they missed Charlie because he was locked in an upstairs office. There seemed to be a general feeling that the fourteen years Richardson had served was quite enough. And, anyway, he had walked out of an open prison; he was not a high-grade convict who had escaped from a maximum security wing. On top of this, Richardson had flown from an Oxfordshire prison, and was thus the responsibility of Thames Valley Police, not the Metropolitan Police in London where he was 'in hiding'.

Charlie did, however, have several accidental encounters with the police. A car he was driving was stopped and driving documents demanded. At a later date he collided with a police car right outside Clerkenwell police station, and still he went undetected. But his luck, as it always did, soon ran out.

In January 1980, Charlie was rushing around trying to raise money for the forthcoming wedding of his eldest son, Charlie-Boy. He had been negotiating with various people to sell to a newspaper pictures of himself dressed up as Father Christmas during an old-age-pensioners' party in a Camberwell pub. He had conducted most of these negotiations from the telephone in an Earls Court porn shop in which a member of his family has an interest. He was by now so careless that he had been standing for hours on end at the phone during every day of the previous week. The pictures of him as Father Christmas were so bad that a professional photographer had had to be brought in to take new shots.

Charlie was in the porn shop on Friday, 18 January 1981, his forty-seventh birthday, when a drugs squad detective walked in. He asked the names of various people, including Charlie. Charlie gave the name of Roy Hall and Hall's address, as he had when previously face-to-face with the police during his escape. But unknown to Charlie, the police were stopping people outside the shop as well. Roy Hall, who had earlier in the day driven Charlie to the shop, was questioned on his way back into the shop, having just had a cup of coffee with a mate. He gave his name and address. Suddenly the police had two Roy Halls, both with the same address and both with wives of the same name.

Charlie and Roy were taken to Kensington police station. They had been questioned for some while by young detectives when an old sergeant came into the interview room. He looked on in amazement. He called the officer doing the questioning outside.

'You know who that is, don't you?'

'No, who?'

'That's Charlie-bloody-Richardson.'

Index

348

351